484- 602-1391

THE COMPLETE LEGAL GUIDE TO

MARRIAGE
DIVORCE
CUSTODY
&
LIVING
TOGETHER

ALSO BY STEVEN MITCHELL SACK

The Salesperson's Legal Guide (co-author)

Don't Get Taken! A Preventive Legal Guide to Protect
Your Home, Family, Money and Job

THE COMPLETE LEGAL GUIDE TO

MARRIAGE
DIVORCE
CUSTODY
&
LIVING
TOGETHER

Steven Mitchell Sack

McGraw-Hill Book Company

New York   St. Louis   Hamburg   Toronto
London   San Francisco   Madrid
Mexico   Panama   Montreal
Paris   São Paulo   Tokyo

The author has used fictitious names and dates throughout the book.
Any similarity to actual persons, places, or events is purely coincidental.

1 2 3 4 5 6 7 8 9 D O C D O C 8 7

ISBN 0-07-054404-2

Library of Congress Cataloging-in-Publication Data

Sack, Steven Mitchell, 1954–
  The complete legal guide to marriage, divorce, custody, & living together.

  1. Domestic relations—United States—Popular works.
I. Title.
KF505.Z9S23   1987   346.7301'5   86-20842
ISBN 0-07-054404-2   347.30615

BOOK DESIGN BY PATRICE FODERO
EDITING SUPERVISOR: MARGERY LUHRS

To romantics and lovers,
who can fight back
by knowing how.

Contents

Acknowledgments

Once again I extend warm thanks to my literary agent, Julia Coopersmith, for her capable vision, guidance, and friendship.

Special thanks are also directed to law clerks Alan Scharf, Spiro Serras, and Jack Panitch for their competent legal research and assistance in the initial drafting of portions of the manuscript.

I would also like to acknowledge the following individuals and sources for permitting me to include helpful text, strategies, tables, and lists in the book:

- West Publishing Company for permission to use several examples of cohabitation agreements
- Matthew Bender & Company for permission to include several examples of prenuptial agreements
- The *Journal of Family Law* (University of Louisville) and Matthew Bender & Company for permission to use various adoption forms
- Michael W. Schaefer, author of *Child Snatching*, for sharing helpful hints on that subject; *Hofstra Law Review*, publisher of the article "The Search for a Solution to Child Snatching," for use of the compendium of felony treatment of child snatching on a state-by-state basis; the *American Bar Association Journal* for the list of state parent locator services; Marjory D. Fields and Elyse Lehman, authors of the *Handbook for Beaten Women*, for the useful text and strategies on wife beating; and the National Center on Women & Family Law for permission to reprint the comprehensive chart of criminal marriage-rape statutes throughout the United States, which was published in *Rape in Marriage*, by Diana E. H. Russell.

- Doris Jonas Freed and Timothy B. Walker for sharing their extensive research and for the use of the tables on divorce laws throughout the United States, together with explanatory text

- Elaine M. Fromm, president of the Organization for the Enforcement of Child Support, Inc., and author of *Child Support Enforcement in Maryland*, for supplying valuable information and strategies on obtaining child support and on countering child-support delinquencies

- Robert Coulson, president of the American Arbitration Association and author of *Business Arbitration* and *Fighting Fair*, for his helpful insights on the arbitration and mediation processes, for permission to use the sample mediator-client agreement, and for supplying the list of regional offices of the American Arbitration Association

In addition, I would like to cite several publications I have frequently consulted in writing this book: *Family Law Quarterly* and *Family Advocate*, disseminated by the American Bar Association Section of Family Law, and a pamphlet entitled *Law & Marriage: Your Legal Guide*, which was prepared by the American Bar Association, Division of Communications.

Gary N. Skoloff is also cited here for his helpful suggestions on the rights of grandparents to visitation, the tax consequences of divorce, and changing a child's surname, topics which he wrote about in articles appearing in the *National Law Journal*, which I read with great interest.

I would also like to thank Doris Jonas Freed and my professor at Boston College Law School, Sanford N. Katz, for their invaluable contributions in the area of Family Law over the years.

In addition, I wish to recognize organizations such as Children's Rights of New York, Inc., Adoptive Parents Committee, Inc., and the Organization for the Enforcement of Child Support, Inc., for their continuing involvement in family matters; I am especially grateful to them for valuable information furnished to me while I was writing this book.

Finally, I would like to extend my personal thanks to my editor, Dan Weaver, for his continued support; to my former editor, Ken Stuart, for his faith and encouragement; to Ursula Smith for her creative copy editing; to Gerald Spielman, Dr. Jacob Plawner, Dr. Robert Zuckerman, David Paymer, Howard Steinberg, Jeffrey Gershon, Stephen Geanacopolous, Kenneth Weisman, and Jay Kerner for their friendship over the years; and to Jonathan Scott Sack and Stacey Sack-Zuckerman, my siblings, for continuing the legal tradition in my family.

I would also like to express my appreciation to my father whose insights and dreams once again helped make an idea a reality.

Author's Note

The information in this book is my attempt to reduce complex and confusing law to practical personal and business strategies. These strategies are meant to serve as helpful guidelines—points to focus upon—when you're confronted with a particular problem situation. They are not intended as legal advice per se, because laws vary considerably throughout the fifty states and the law can be interpreted properly only after your particular facts and needs have been analyzed. Thus, if you have any questions regarding the applicability of any of the information in this book, consult a lawyer, accountant, or other professional.

The Complete Legal Guide to Marriage, Divorce, Custody, and Living Together is sold with the understanding that the publisher is not engaged in rendering legal, accounting, or other professional service. If legal advice or other expert assistance is required, the services of a competent professional should be sought.

Fictitious names have been used throughout this book. Any similarity to actual persons, places, or events is purely coincidental.

How to Use This Book

This book was written to save you money and aggravation.

Like most Americans, you are probably unaware how strongly the law affects your life. But, without this knowledge, there is a good chance you will be exploited, especially in your personal love relationships.

Romantic love may be the same old story, but the tune has certainly changed. Recent sweeping changes have occurred in the once-stable field of family law; the game has changed and the stakes have become quite high. Concepts such as palimony, joint custody, and equitable distribution, which were unknown a few years ago, are today commonly litigated throughout the United States. People are no longer leaving relationships with just a broken heart. Now they are soothing their feelings of rejection by recovering hefty property settlements for their troubles.

What if you, like Liberace, Lee Marvin, Johnny Carson, and Christina Onassis, were named as a defendant in a palimony lawsuit, a divorce action, or a child-custody case? Chances are one day you may be embroiled in a similar proceeding. What advice did these celebrities get from their high-priced lawyers? How would you go about protecting your assets from an ex-lover seeking revenge? What strategies would help you win custody of your child or help you negotiate a separation agreement? How would you preserve your rights in a divorce? What would you be entitled to? How much would it cost you to collect?

I posed these questions recently while teaching a family law course at State University of New York at Stony Brook. Students were fascinated to learn that there are legal consequences for practically all your romantic acts and that the concept of preventive law, when applied to a marriage or divorce situation, worked handily. During the course I demonstrated, for example, how the actual advice I offered my clients enabled:

- A boyfriend to recover an engagement ring after his fiancée canceled the wedding
- A wife and mother to recover support arrears totaling $46,000 from her ex-husband
- A devoted father to regain sole custody of his 6-year-old daughter from his former wife
- A couple to mediate their domestic difficulties and save the marriage rather than resort to time-consuming and expensive divorce litigation
- Divorced wives to obtain shares of their spouses' delicatessen, dental practice, and military pension
- A cohabitant to obtain a share of her lover's insider price when his apartment went co-op

Their enthusiasm for this kind of information was confirmed when my book *Don't Get Taken!* was published. While on tour, I spoke to hundreds of thousands of Americans via television shows, radio programs, and print interviews. People sent me letters thanking me for writing the book. It became clear that most Americans are unaware of how strongly the law affects their lives and that they, unlike many of my business clients, were unable to receive practical, preventive legal strategies at a relatively low cost.

This need, to provide practical legal advice, and to set forth preventive legal strategies for the people who most need them, prompted me to write *The Complete Legal Guide to Marriage, Divorce, Custody, and Living Together.*

In the following pages you will find hundreds of legal strategies related to the romantic acts that affect your life. Whether you are living with someone, getting married, having children, experiencing domestic difficulties, contemplating marriage for a second time, considering adopting children, seeking custody of your children or support from an ex-spouse, interested in obtaining tax and estate planning tips to save money, or are thinking of resolving your disputes via mediation or hiring a lawyer, the information you find here will *give you the edge.*

Armed with this advice, you will become aware of the right steps to take to protect your rights, assets, property, and loved ones, while anticipating and avoiding legal hassles *before* they occur.

To make the book as relevant and useful as possible, I have focused my attention on topics on which Americans are frequently misinformed. I have included numerous questions to ask and points to consider to protect your rights. I have often used tables to analyze an important subject on a state-by-state basis. I have used sample letters and have given the addresses and telephone numbers of important agencies that can help you implement many of my suggestions and guidelines.

In addition, I have provided a brief table of contents at the beginning of each chapter to enable you to locate a particular topic of interest quickly. The glossary at the end of the book will help you understand the meaning of many legal terms and concepts and apply them properly.

This book was not meant to replace a lawyer, but it will help you understand if your problem requires a lawyer's assistance. If you currently have a lawyer, the information given here will help you to make that lawyer work more effectively on your behalf, and it will help you make more intelligent choices and avoid being pressured into making decisions you may not wish to make. I also suggest courses of action to take *before* consulting a lawyer; such advice may prove invaluable to your lawyer once one has been retained. Finally, you will discover that most of my suggestions can be followed without the help of a lawyer.

The book opens with a chapter devoted to a very basic subject: how to know when you need a lawyer, how to find one who will serve you well, and how to work most effectively with your lawyer. The chapters that follow thereafter each deal in turn with the legal aspects of various types of family and love relationships.

In Chapter 2 you will learn the legal ramifications of cohabitant status—including who gets to keep the furniture, bank account, apartment, or co-op when the relationship ends (and the factors a court looks at when deciding who gets what). You will also review actual "living-together" agreements that can minimize future disputes and expensive litigation. And you'll be offered tips on how to avoid paying palimony or supporting your ex-lover for life.

For those deciding to "tie the knot," I discuss in Chapter 3 the legal ramifications of giving engagement rings and gifts. You will also become familiar with the simple moves necessary to putting your estate in order upon marriage, and you will learn the pros and cons of signing prenuptial agreements. Sample agreements are included so you can see the pitfalls of certain clauses.

If you are considering adoption, guidelines given in Chapter 4 will help you avoid rip-offs from dishonest placement agencies and international organizations and from unscrupulous lawyers (and other individuals who sometimes peddle "black-market" babies). You will learn how natural mothers can regain custody of their children after they have been given up for adoption and how to overcome this problem. I also discuss how to receive financial aid for adopting hard-to-place children. All of this will make you knowledgeable about adoption rules and procedures and create an awareness of the types of releases, agreements, and documents that can be used for your protection.

Chapter 5 includes information on how to reduce incidents of child snatching, child abuse, spouse abuse, marital rape, and other forms of domestic violence. These widespread social problems are inflicting horrible physical, emotional, and financial damage on millions of Americans. However, you can fight back by taking proper legal action and I will tell you how.

Chapter 6 deals with divorce and all of its related problems. I describe the types of divorce laws that are currently in force throughout the United States. You will become familiar with the concepts of no-fault divorce, community property, and equitable distribution. Are you thinking about a trial separation? You will learn the consequences of legal separa-

tions and how to incorporate your intentions into a comprehensive agreement. In addition, I provide a complete checklist
of negotiating points for you and your lawyer to consider. To
help in negotiating your divorce package, I discuss the kinds
of settlements people are receiving today. This will help you
determine if you are getting a "raw deal" or are being treated
fairly in your alimony, property, and custody arrangements.

Chapters 7 and 8 describe the major problems of child
custody and support. You will become acquainted with factors
the court looks at when awarding custody to one parent over
another, the difference between joint and sole custody, how to
avoid custody litigation, and how to increase the chances of
winning a contested custody case if you are involved in one.
Of course, grandparents, stepparents, and extended family
members have rights with respect to visitation and custody,
and I talk about these rights as well.

Since I want people to learn how to fight the growing
epidemic of child-support arrears, I provide information in
Chapter 8 about how one goes about obtaining support, when
it legally stops, what amount of support is fair and reasonable,
and the practical steps to take if your ex-spouse fails to pay
child support, steps which go a long way toward helping you
collect what is due, often without spending large sums in lawyer fees.

Chapter 9 discusses alternative methods of resolving domestic conflicts. Mediation and arbitration are two processes
by which you may be able to avoid time-consuming and expensive litigation. I mention the advantages and disadvantages of each and discuss how each is obtained.

The importance of knowing tax law in family matters cannot be overestimated. Chapter 10 will familiarize you with
the tax aspects of alimony, child support, dependency exemptions, child-care expenses, head-of-household status, transfers
of property, attorney fees, IRAs for divorced individuals, and
much more. As this book is written, major tax reforms are
pending, and this chapter offers advice as to the possible effects
of the expected reform. This material will serve as a good
summary so you can discuss these items intelligently with
your lawyer and other advisors. Penalties are frequently im-

posed by the IRS when people overlook the tax consequences in a divorce or other family-related legal matter; this chapter will help you avoid such problems.

Whatever your background, education, age, or experience, the information in this book will help you detect problems before they occur and will make you aware of the legal consequences of your acts. If litigation becomes necessary, your chances of success and the value of your claim will increase substantially because you will recognize potential exploitation and know what to do about it.

I have provided you here with all the practical information my clients receive, but you get it at a fraction of the cost. Keep this guide in an accessible place. Read the applicable sections before making a decision. That is what preventive law is all about. Just as business people keep lawyers on retainer, you too will now have access to ongoing advice. The benefits of applying this information can be significant. The following true story demonstrates what can happen if you don't know your rights.

A client recently came to me for advice. He had been having marital difficulties with his wife, and she had moved out with their 3½-year-old daughter to live with relatives. For a period of three months she refused to let him visit his daughter. She then told him that he would not be able to visit the child again unless he signed a document stating that he would pay $2,000 per month in alimony and child support and that she would be given title and sole rights of occupancy to the marital home in the event of a divorce.

Out of fear and ignorance the man signed this paper in the presence of his wife's attorney. He had not spoken to a lawyer because he didn't know one was required and his wife's attorney never told him to do so!

A friend recommended me and the man came for advice. I told him that the agreement he signed was probably unenforceable and that, as a matter of law, his wife could not deny him the right to visit his child. After a brief but fierce battle, I managed to obtain exclusive custody of the child for the father, as well as exclusive possession of the marital home with all of its contents.

That is the kind of aggravation I want you to avoid.

The taboos of yesteryear are gone, and the law is keeping pace with social change. Now there are legal consequences for your romantic acts. Know the legal ramifications involved in the end of an affair or a marriage. Learn how to fight back and win when you suffer a broken heart.

No one should fall in love expecting the worst. But this book will help you look before you leap into the next love relationship. That is the concept of preventive law and of *The Complete Legal Guide to Marriage, Divorce, Custody, and Living Together*. Remember, if you don't know you are being exploited, you can't fight back!

Steven Mitchell Sack
New York City

1 | Using Your Lawyer Effectively: Domestic Relations and the Law

Introduction

Whether you desire to adopt a child, obtain a divorce, sue your lover in a paternity suit, or gain satisfaction in any of the other areas discussed in this book, you will probably ultimately require the services of a lawyer.

It is hoped that the lawyer you hire will work promptly on your case and will bill you reasonably for services, that you will have your phone calls returned by the end of the next business day, will be accurately informed of your chances of success in the case, and will be apprised at the outset of the amount of money you will be charged for legal services.

Unfortunately, many clients do *not* receive such service. Lawyer-client disputes commonly arise because the lawyer does not clearly discuss fees, inflates the chances of the client's success, fails to return phone calls or perform legal work promptly, and/or fails to inform the client of the status of settlement discussions with opposing lawyers.

This chapter will tell you how to deal properly with your lawyer and avoid being exploited. You will learn what to do before hiring a lawyer, whatever your type of domestic-relations matter. This includes conducting the initial interview, confirming the fee arrangement in writing, and taking the proper steps to get the most from your lawyer while your matter is in progress.

By following the strategies outlined in this chapter, you should greatly increase your chances for a satisfactory relationship with your lawyer.

Deciding If You Need a Lawyer

As a general rule, speak to a lawyer whenever you think you may need one. Certainly, you should expect to hire a lawyer in any matter where you must be represented in court. The following lists give you a good idea of the types of problems which do and do not require the services of a lawyer.

Problems that generally require a lawyer's services:

- Involvement in a complicated divorce proceeding (for example, one that involves the distribution of valuable marital property, pension rights, or a professional practice.)
- Preparation of a separation agreement
- Preparation of a prenuptial or a complex precohabitation agreement
- Involvement in a child-custody or paternity case
- Obtaining, enforcing, or modifying support orders or agreements
- Recovering an engagement ring after your bride-to-be cancels the wedding
- Seeking an annulment to marriage
- Seeking an adoption
- Suing your lover for giving you venereal disease or herpes

Problems that generally do not require a lawyer's services:

- Obtaining a simple (uncontested) divorce
- Obtaining a protection order in family court
- Obtaining an abortion
- Prosecuting sex crimes
- Prosecuting for spouse abuse, marital rape, or child abuse

The best time to hire a lawyer is *before* you contemplate taking action (that is, *before* leaving your lover, *before* moving out of your house or apartment, *before* agreeing to terms in a financial settlement with your spouse, *before* signing a prenuptial agreement, *before* adopting a baby, etc.). The reason is that a lawyer experienced in matrimonial and domestic-relations matters can give you valuable advice for early action to protect your rights and increase your chances of success once litigation begins.

For example, I frequently recommend to my female clients seeking advice on a legal separation or divorce that they learn as much as possible about their husbands' financial status— total income from all sources; value of a closely held business; value of bank accounts, stocks, bonds, real estate, insurance policies, vested pensions, etc.). In an extreme case, I may recommend that the wife withdraw the proceeds from a joint bank account if I believe such action is warranted (if, for example, she might be left destitute while the divorce or separation action is proceeding). Such a tactic could force the husband into playing fair and agreeing to divide the marital assets equitably.

Remember the first rule: The sooner you speak to a lawyer when action is contemplated, the better you can develop your case and protect your rights. (*Note*: When speaking to a lawyer for the first time, always ask if you will be charged for the initial interview or for advice given to you over the telephone. If the answer to either question is yes, you may wish to find another lawyer who will not charge you for these initial discussions.)

Finding a Lawyer

Lawyers should be selected carefully. While the right choice may mean thousands of dollars in your pocket and satisfaction, the wrong choice could cost you untold aggravation. There are several ways to find the right lawyer:

1. *Call a lawyer you know.* The best way to start is to call a lawyer you may already have dealt with. Ask him or her for an opinion concerning your matter and ask whether an interview should be scheduled.

Ask if he or she is qualified to represent you. Bear in mind that many lawyers who represent clients in one area (for example, a personal injury suit) are not qualified to handle other matters (for example, a divorce proceeding), because it is difficult to keep abreast of the latest developments in all fields of law. Most lawyers gain expertise in certain types of cases, which they handle promptly, effectively, and profitably. When they are presented with a matter outside their realm of experience, they should refer the case to a specialist. Lawyers who accept matters outside their daily practice have a greater tendency to postpone work and take a greater chance of making mistakes.

Ask the lawyer what proportion of his or her time is spent in the area of law related to your particular matter. If the answer is less than 30 percent, you may wish to consult with another lawyer. Request the names of other lawyers who handle your type of problem at a reasonable rate. Such referrals are often the source of excellent legal assistance.

2. Ask around for recommendations. If you've never dealt with a lawyer before, ask friends and relatives if they can recommend someone. Lawyers often receive clients by word of mouth. However, be sure to ascertain that the lawyer recommended is experienced in handling your particular problem. Be especially wary of referrals from adoption-agency personnel, court clerks, welfare-agency aides, and process servers because their motives may be self-serving.

3. Call your local bar association. Another way of finding a lawyer is to contact your local bar association and ask for the names of lawyers who handle your type of problem. These associations are listed in the phone book; some maintain rosters of lawyers who agree not to charge more than $15 to $25 for the first half-hour of consultation.

People who handle incoming calls for local bar associations are generally unbiased when giving the names of lawyers. However, both experienced and neophyte lawyers list their names with such associations. Be sure to tell the person handling your inquiry that you want an experienced practitioner if that is important to you.

4. Be wary of lawyer advertising. Although some good lawyers advertise, many top lawyers don't. They get their cases from other clients and other lawyers. *Be aware of this.*

A few lawyers have misled the public with their advertising. One common practice is to run an ad which states that a particular matter costs only some small amount. When the potential client meets the lawyer, he or she learns that the advertised fee is for the court costs and filing fees *only*, and that the lawyer's fees are extra.

In addition, beware of ads proclaiming that the lawyer is a "specialist." Most state bar associations have not adopted specialist certification programs. The "specialist" may only be the lawyer's personal proclamation, nothing more.

Conducting the Initial Interview

The initial interview serves several important purposes. It helps you obtain a sound evaluation of your legal problem and helps you decide if you should hire this particular lawyer. The initial interview is also the time to discuss important working details such as the fee arrangement.

Bring all pertinent written information with you to the initial interview. For example, if you are considering a divorce and seeking a property settlement, it is best to gather, if available, the following types of items—both yours and your spouse's:

1. Paycheck vouchers
2. Income tax returns
3. Statements of nontaxable income
4. Closely held business or professional-practice records showing assets, liabilities, income, and expenses
5. Bank books and monthly statements
6. Certificates of deposit
7. A list of stocks and bonds, with names of brokers
8. Deeds to real estate
9. Title certificates to all automobiles
10. A list of all outstanding obligations and liabilities
11. Statements of net worth used to obtain bank loans or for any other purpose (for example, to establish values for casualty insurance)

12. Life insurance policies, along with any indication of loans against them

13. Retirement plans

14. A marital history, including dates and other detailed information on assets acquired by both parties prior to and during the marriage (including gifts) and contributions to the family's net worth (including the wife's role as homemaker or as participant in the family business)

15. Any other information useful in establishing the income and net worth of the parties

16. A listing of current living expenses (see example given in Chapter 8)

Tell the lawyer everything related to your matter. Feel free to communicate relevant information without inhibition because your discussion is privileged and confidential. All of this will save time, make your lawyer's work easier, and give you a better chance at achieving desired results.

Once the lawyer receives all the pertinent facts, he or she will then:

1. Decide whether your case has a fair probability of success, after considering the facts and the law in the state where the action is brought

2. Give you an estimate of how long your matter will take to resolve

3. Make an estimate of the approximate legal fees and disbursements

4. Tell you what legal papers will be filed, when, and what their purposes are

5. Discuss the defenses your spouse is likely to raise and how you will deal with them

If the lawyer sees weaknesses in your case and believes that litigation will be unduly expensive, he or she may advise you to compromise and settle without resorting to litigation. In any case, the chosen course of action should be instituted without delay so you will be able to achieve the desired results. This will ensure that the requisite time period within which to start the action will not have expired (in accordance with the Statute of Limitations).

If, as in an adoption, a lawsuit is not involved, the lawyer should advise you what legal work needs to be done, how long it will take, and how much it will cost.

The lawyer should give you an unbiased evaluation as quickly as possible. Some lawyers neglect to give honest appraisals. Clients are then misled and spend large sums of money on losing causes. Be wary if your lawyer makes statements such as, "You have nothing to worry about." Optimistic statements like this usually result in more harm than good. Prudent lawyers tell clients that "airtight" cases do not exist and that the possibility that unforeseen circumstances may develop is always present.

One of the best ways to protect yourself is to request an "opinion letter" from the lawyer.

The following is an example of an opinion letter requested by a wife whose spouse wants to obtain a divorce because he has fallen in love with another woman:

Sample Opinion Letter

STEVEN MITCHELL SACK

ATTORNEY AT LAW

450 SEVENTH AVENUE, SUITE 1011

NEW YORK, N.Y. 10123

———

(212) 695-2535

(Date)

Barbara Jones
1000 Main Street
Centerville, N.Y. 12345

Re: Opinion Letter regarding Jones v. Jones

Dear Ms. Jones,

After our initial meeting, I reviewed our notes and the documents you furnished me. As I understand the situation, you and your husband were married on September 10, 1979, in Atlanta, Georgia. At that time you were a respiratory therapist and your husband was about to enter medical school.

All during medical school, you worked full-time to support the marriage, earning approximately $300 a week (net). After your husband graduated, you continued to work while he was employed as a resident in a local hospital. Since finances were a problem, you agreed to forego having children until your husband was able to earn sufficient money to enable you to devote your full time to childbearing.

You have advised me that your husband has recently informed you that he is in love with one of his former patients and wishes to obtain a divorce.

You have asked me to advise you about your rights, the chances of success, the amount of money you may recover, the costs involved, and my ability to represent you in this matter.

Financial Considerations

Basically, you have informed me that the entire extent of the Jones's marital assets consists of the following:

1.	Apartment furniture	$ 7,500
2.	Joint checking account	1,500
3.	Money-market account (joint)	15,000
4.	Stocks	600
5.	Automobile given to you as a gift by your parents	6,000

Under the laws of this state, you are entitled to an equitable share of all the marital assets (that is, property and/or liquid assets acquired during the marriage). Since your 1981 automobile was given to you as a gift by your parents, it is not included in calculating your marital assets. Thus our settlement discussions would include the $24,600 you presently have in the furniture, joint checking, money-market accounts, and stocks.

However, the courts have ruled that your husband's professional degree is also considered a marital asset, capable of being calculated at present net worth and a portion distributed to you. I handled a recent case in which opposing counsel and I agreed that the husband's medical degree was presently worth $200,000, and the wife received a lump-sum settlement of $100,000 for it. Based upon the fact that your husband intends to be a brain surgeon, I would expect that his degree is worth substantially more than $200,000, perhaps as much as $400,000. So you can see that you are entitled to a far greater settlement than the $24,600 your marriage has presently produced and that your husband has informed you he is willing to give you.

Possible Course of Action

You have advised me that you feel abused and cannot understand why your husband has fallen in love with another woman. Although I can sympathize with you, my principal motivation is to see that you receive a fair and adequate settlement for your troubles. In this state your husband must prove fault to obtain a divorce, and from the facts you have furnished me, it appears that he may have trouble doing this. Thus my inclination is to fight the divorce for you and/or negotiate the best financial settlement which includes a lump-sum payment for his medical degree.

My Services

I am familiar with your type of problem, having represented many clients in matrimonial matters, and am qualified to represent you. My fee would be based on my normal hourly charge of $125 for myself and $75 for associates, and I require an initial retainer of $1,000 to open a file.

If you have any questions, please call me.

Very truly yours,

Steven Mitchell Sack

An opinion letter will spell out the pros and cons of a matter and help you as a prospective client to evaluate whether or not you should proceed to spend money to accomplish your objectives. Even if you are charged for it, an opinion letter can minimize future misunderstandings between you and your lawyer; it is usually worth the fee.

A properly drafted opinion letter should provide you with all the essential facts necessary to evaluate a problem. Don't forget to ask for one if you feel it is appropriate.

Making the Choice

It is important to leave the interview feeling that the lawyer is open and responsive to your needs, that he or she is genuinely interested in helping you, that your inquiries will be promptly returned, and that your case will be prepared and handled properly. Although it is difficult to predict how well the lawyer will perform, there are certain clues to look for at the first interview. The following points are worth considering:

- Does the lawyer present an outward appearance of neatness and good grooming?

- Are you received at the appointed interview hour or kept waiting? Some lawyers believe that if a client is kept waiting it will appear that the lawyer is busy and, therefore, good. However, keeping you waiting is really merely a sign that the lawyer is inconsiderate.

- Does the lawyer leave the room frequently during the interview or permit telephone calls to intrude? You deserve his or her complete attention.

- Does the lawyer demonstrate boredom or lack of interest by yawning or finger-tapping?

- Is the lawyer a clock-watcher?

- Does the lawyer try to impress you by narrating in detail other matrimonial or palimony cases he or she has handled and the size of awards obtained? Good lawyers do not have to boast to get clients.

- Does the lawyer discuss the fee arrangement with you up front? Some lawyers have a tendency to wait until all work is done before submitting large bills. The failure to discuss fee arrangements at the initial interview may be a sign that the lawyer operates this way.

Do not be fooled by appearances; plush offices, fancy cars, and expensive clothes might simply mean that exorbitant fees are charged for routine legal services. And don't be impressed by the school from which the lawyer graduated. Most law schools do not give their graduates *practical training*. In fact, many less prestigious law schools offer superior nuts-and-bolts training, and that is what you are paying for.

The lawyer's reputation in the field of domestic relations is another factor to consider. The major factor in determining whether you should hire a particular lawyer should be the amount of experience and expertise he or she has in handling domestic-relations problems similar to yours. Use a lawyer who devotes at least 30 percent of his or her practice to domestic-relations problems. *Avoid inexperienced lawyers if possible*. Novices charge less, but they often require more time to handle a problem. If you are being charged on an hourly basis, you may pay the same amount of money and not obtain the expertise of a pro.

If you are seeking a divorce, you should make it your business to inquire about the approach the lawyer will take. For example, is the lawyer willing to first try to resolve the matter amicably? This can be done via the conference method— both spouses and their attorneys meet to try and systematically resolve issues concerning (1) the marriage, (2) the children, and (3) the finances. The conference method, if successful, can help prevent hostilities and psychological trauma that might arise in the period leading up to and during a courtroom trial. It may also help reduce feelings of financial vulnerability and alleviate fears the spouses may experience as separated parents. The conference approach can also afford sufficient time to effect a realistic visitation plan. (The courtroom is usually an inappropriate atmosphere to do this.) Moreover, a properly drafted agreement resulting from the conference approach will undoubtedly be more comprehensive and tailored to the personal needs of the family than the terms of a judgment after a courtroom trial.

Finally, the conference method can save substantial legal fees and other expenses that would be incurred if the case were litigated in the courts. While he or she may have to seek prompt court action in cases where ongoing physical violence represents an immediate threat to you or where your spouse is siphoning off assets to your detriment, your lawyer should otherwise be willing to attempt to resolve your case via the conference approach, unless that is not your desire.

Be sure that the lawyer of your choice will be working on your matter. People often go to prestigious firms, expecting their problem to be handled by a full partner. They pay large fees and sometimes wind up being represented in court by a junior associate. This is a common practice among some firms, so be aware of it. To avoid this, state in the retainer agreement that your matter is to be handled by the lawyer of your choice.

A *final word*: When you choose a lawyer, you are choosing someone to guide you and protect your interests. Make your choice carefully. Select someone you think is honest. Hire a lawyer to whom you can relate. Ask the lawyer about his or her outside activities and professional associations. Inquire if you can speak to previous clients; references will help you learn more about the lawyer. If you do not feel comfortable about the first lawyer you interview, shop around and schedule appointments with others. As always, it is better to be safe than sorry.

Confirming Your Arrangement

After you have decided to retain a lawyer, you must discuss a variety of points to eliminate potential misunderstandings.

The Fee Arrangement

Most lawyers generally charge a nominal fee for the first visit to the office. Fees should be charged only when actual time is spent working on a matter. Charges are based on the amount of time and work involved, the difficulty of the problem, the dollar amount of the case, the lawyer's expertise and reputation in handling that type of case, and the urgency of the problem. For example, response to a summons and complaint served upon you in an action for divorce which the lawyer must handle the day after he or she is contacted should command a higher fee than the same amount of work done over several weeks. Operating expenses and office overhead are elements which might also affect the fee arrangement.

Frequently, a lawyer cannot tell you exactly how much will be charged because he or she is unable to predetermine the amount of work that is involved. In such a case, ask the lawyer to estimate what the minimum and maximum limits of the fee will be. If the figure seems high, do not hesitate to question it. If necessary, say that you intend to speak to other lawyers about fees.

The fee arrangement is composed of several elements which must be clearly understood. For example, *costs* are expenses that the lawyer incurs while working on your case. These include photocopying, telephone, and mailing expenses, fees paid to the court for filing documents, and numerous other expenses. Be certain that the fee arrangement specifically mentions *in writing* which of these costs you must pay.

There are several different forms of fee arrangements: the flat fee, the flat fee plus time, the hourly rate, and the contingency fee.

1. *The flat fee.* In a flat fee arrangement, you pay the lawyer a specified sum to get the job done. Most attorneys offer a number of services which are performed on a flat-fee basis— an uncontested divorce action, an adoption, the preparation of a simple separation agreement, and other standard services.

2. *The flat fee plus time.* Here a sum for a specified number of hours is charged. Once the lawyer works more hours than specified, you are charged on an hourly basis. The following retainer agreement illustrates this:

Sample Retainer Agreement

STEVEN MITCHELL SACK

ATTORNEY AT LAW

450 SEVENTH AVENUE, SUITE 1011
NEW YORK, N.Y. 10123

—

(212) 695-2535

(Date)

Barbara Jones
1000 Main Street
Centerville, N.Y. 12345

Re: Retainer Agreement regarding Jones v. Jones

Dear Ms. Jones:

This letter confirms that you have retained me as your attorney to negotiate a settlement agreement with your husband, if that is reasonably possible, or, if not, to represent you in a divorce action. You agree to pay me promptly an initial retainer of $2,500, which is my minimum fee in this matter. If I devote more than twenty hours to this case, based upon my time records commencing from the initial conference, you shall pay an additional fee counted at the rate of $125 per hour.

If you should decide to discontinue my services in this matter at any time, you shall be liable for my time computed at the rate of $125 per hour, except that the minimum fee shall in any event be $2,500.

These fees do not include any work in appellate courts, any other actions or proceedings, or out-of-pocket disbursements. Out-of-pocket disbursements include, but are not limited to, costs of filing papers, court fees, process servers, witness fees, court reporters, long-distance telephone calls, travel, parking, and photocopies normally made by me or requested by you, which disbursements shall be paid for or reimbursed to me upon my request.

You are aware of the hazards of litigation and that, despite my efforts on your behalf, there is no assurance or guarantee of the outcome of this matter.

Kindly indicate your understanding and acceptance of the above by signing this letter below where indicated. I look forward to serving you.

Sincerely yours,

Steven Mitchell Sack

I have read and understand the above letter, have received a copy, and accept all its terms:

_____

Barbara Jones

3. *The hourly rate.* Many lawyers set their fees on an hourly basis. This hourly fee can range from $75 to $200 or more. Under this arrangement, you will be charged on a fixed hourly rate for all work done. If you are billed by the hour, ask if phone calls between you and your lawyer are included. If they are, tell him or her that you should be charged only for calls exceeding a certain number of hours per month. You can justify this by arguing that you shouldn't be charged when the lawyer calls you to clarify a point, obtain additional information, or discuss news regarding the progress of your case. You will save money in legal bills by insisting on this.

4. *The contingency fee.* Here your lawyer receives a specified percentage of any money recovered via court action or settlement. Many people favor contingency-fee arrangements in certain kinds of cases (for example, personal injury) since they are not required to pay legal fees unless they are

successful. In matrimonial actions, however, an agreement providing for purely contingent fees is looked upon unfavorably by courts and disciplinary boards because it is viewed as encouraging divorces. If your lawyer proposes contingent fees in this area, think twice before accepting the arrangement.

Additional Points about Fees

There are distinct advantages and disadvantages to using different fee arrangements. For example, when you pay a flat fee you know how much you will be charged, but you do not know how much care and attention will be spent on your matter. The hourly rate might be cheaper than a flat fee for routine work, but some dishonest lawyers "pad" time sheets to increase their fees. This is why, no matter what type of fee arrangement is agreed upon, it is essential to hire a lawyer who is honest and who has your best interests in mind at all times.

Always insist that your fee arrangement be spelled out in writing. All provisions should be explained to you so that they are clearly understood; be sure to save a copy for your records.

The lawyer may also ask you to pay a retainer at the interview. The retainer guarantees the availability of the lawyer to represent you. It is an advance paid to demonstrate your desire to resolve your problem via legal recourse. *Ask for a receipt if you pay in cash.* Inquire whether the retainer is to become part of the entire fee and whether it is refundable. In addition, ask if you can pay the retainer and other fees by credit card. Some states allow this. If so, be sure that interest will not be imputed if you are late in paying fees. Some lawyers are beginning to charge interest on late payments, so be aware of this.

Request that all fees be billed periodically. Insist that billing statements be supported by detailed and complete time records which include the number of hours (or partial hours) worked, a report of the people contacted, and a list of the services rendered. Some lawyers may be reluctant to do this, but by receiving these documents and statements on a regular basis, you will be able to question inconsistencies and errors before they get out of hand. You will also be aware of the amount of the bill as it accrues and can pay for it over time if you choose.

Ask your lawyer to send copies of all incoming and outgoing correspondence so you will be able to follow the progress of your case. If your lawyer is reluctant to do this, tell him or her that you will come in once every month to make photocopies of your file. You may be amazed to see how fast you have your way.

Ask your lawyer whether your legal fees are tax-deductible. Request that the fee arrangement be structured to maximize your tax deductions and ask for a written statement which justifies the bill on the basis of time spent or some other allocation. This will help you support your claim. Keep the statement in a safe place until tax time and show it to your tax preparer. Accountants and other professionals often clip copies of the statement directly to the return so that the IRS won't question the deduction.

Legal fees are deductible provided they are ordinary and necessary business expenses. This means that you can deduct cost of legal fees paid or incurred for the "production, ction, maintenance, or conservation of income" or of property used in producing income. Deductions are also allowed for legal fees paid to collect, determine, or refund any tax which is owed.

The following are deductible legal fees:

- Attorney fees paid to obtain *taxable* alimony payments incident to a separation or divorce
- Attorney fees paid to obtain tax advice incident to a separation or divorce

Attorney fees paid to obtain the divorce itself, however, are *not* deductible. Hence, you should ask your lawyer to itemize fees according to (1) the separation or divorce itself, (2) the securing of alimony, and (3) advising on taxes. In addition, part of the legal fee allocated to a property settlement may be added to the basis of the property obtained in that settlement. This is important because by increasing the basis of such property, you may be able to decrease the amount of taxes owed when the property is sold.

Other Items to Clarify

Before you hire the lawyer, the following points should also be discussed:

1. *Will the lawyer be available to you?* Complaints often arise because of poor communication. At the initial interview, ask the lawyer what his or her normal office hours are. It is important that the lawyer be available since you are paying for service. Request that your phone calls be returned within twenty-four hours. Insist that a secretary or an associate return your phone calls if the lawyer will be unavailable for extended periods of time. (Make it clear that you will not be calling unnecessarily.)

2. *Will the lawyer work on your matter immediately?* Some lawyers fail to work promptly on legal matters, despite good intentions. The legal system is often a slow process. Don't stall it further by hiring a procrastinating lawyer. Insist that the lawyer begin working on your matter as quickly as possible. Ask him or her to estimate when the matter will be resolved. *Include this in the retainer agreement for your protection.*

3. *Are there hidden conflicts of interests?* A lawyer owes loyalty and confidentiality to a client. One of the rules of professional ethics (which lawyers are bound to follow) states, "A lawyer should avoid even the appearance of impropriety." This means that a lawyer must decline to represent a client when his or her professional judgment is likely to be affected by other business, financial, or personal interests. (If a lawyer is disqualified, his or her associates and partners are also disqualified.) For example, when a lawyer represents both a husband and a wife in a divorce, there is an inherent conflict that limits any ability to zealously promote the best interests of each. Always ask the lawyer up front of there is any potential conflict of interest.

4. *How will your funds be handled?* Lawyers are obligated to keep client funds in separate accounts. This includes unearned retainer fees. The rules of professional conduct state that lawyers cannot "commingle" client funds with their own. For example, bank accounts for client funds must be

clearly marked as "client trust accounts" or "escrow accounts."

A lawyer must notify you immediately when funds are received on your behalf. You must also receive an accurate accounting of these funds. This consists of a complete explanation of the amount of money held by the lawyer, its origin, and the reason for any deductions. *Insist on nothing less.*

Additional Point: Tell the lawyer to place your funds in an interest-bearing escrow account. Later on, when your funds are remitted, be sure that the interest is included in the amount returned to you. Some lawyers neglect to return the interest portion to clients. You may be entitled to the interest, so don't forget to ask for it.

Problems Encountered after Hiring the Lawyer

After a lawyer has been hired and begins to work, the following questions may arise:

Should You Settle Your Case?

Most people are unsure about settling cases. Some are intimidated by their lawyers and accept small settlements. Although every case is different and some people seek the personal satisfaction of going to court, the following points should be borne in mind if you are involved in a lawsuit and are considering settling the matter before it goes to trial.

Most matrimonial actions take several years (usually two to three) to be tried. By accepting a fair settlement early on, you have use of the money and the proceeds can be invested to earn more money. You will eliminate large legal fees, court costs, and the possibility of eventually losing the case in a trial.

However, if you have a good case, it may pay to wait before discussing and accepting a settlement. Some divorce lawyers believe that larger settlements are obtained by waiting until a case reaches the courthouse steps. This is because the opposing party may not negotiate in earnest until just before a case is tried. Time may be on the side of the opposing party.

It often benefits him or her to wait and see how strong the case is—whether it is properly prepared, whether strong witnesses are ready to testify, whether the evidence will prove the claim, etc.

The decision to accept a settlement should always be made jointly with your lawyer. He or she knows the merits, pitfalls, and true value of the case better than you do. However, do not let the lawyer pressure you into accepting a smaller settlement than you think you deserve. Some lawyers will accept smaller settlements because they are lazy. Do not let this happen.

Instruct your lawyer to provide you with a detailed explanation of the pros and cons of settling your case. Inform the lawyer that you prefer to control your own affairs—including the decision on settling your claim. Do not let your lawyer push you around. If you disagree, say so. Your lawyer cannot settle or compromise the case without your approval. If that happens, you can sue for malpractice. Remember, lawyers are paid to act on your behalf, never vice versa.

Should You Change Lawyers?

You have the right to change lawyers at any time if there is a valid reason. Valid reasons include improper or unethical conduct, a conflict of interest, and malpractice. (You cannot change lawyers merely to stall for time.) If you are dissatisfied with your lawyer's conduct or the way the matter is progressing, get another lawyer's opinion. It is best to obtain the opinion of a professional as to whether your lawyer is acting improperly. Do this *before* taking any other action; *never fire your lawyer until you have hired a replacement*, or you will be unrepresented.

If you fire your lawyer, you may still be required to pay for the work already rendered. You may even have to go to court to settle the issue of legal fees. However, this should never impede you from taking action if it is warranted.

If you have evidence that your lawyer misused your funds for personal gain or committed fraud, you should file a complaint with the grievance committee of your state or local bar association. Don't be afraid to do this. All complaints are confidential, and you cannot be sued for filing a complaint if it is later determined that the lawyer did nothing wrong.

Another alternative is to commence a malpractice suit against your lawyer. Legal malpractice arises when a lawyer fails to use "such skill or prudence as lawyers of ordinary skill commonly possess and experience in the performance of the tasks they undertake." This doesn't mean that you can sue if your lawyer gets beaten by a better lawyer. You can only sue if a lawyer fails to render work or assistance of *minimal competence*, and you are damaged as a result. You can also sue for malpractice when there is a breach of ethics (like failure to remit funds belonging to you), in addition to suing for breach of contract and/or civil fraud.

Attorneys specializing in matrimonial law are being exposed to an increasing number of malpractice suits. In one California case, a lawyer failed to advise his client (the wife) that her husband's pension benefits were divisible under community-property laws. His client was awarded $400 per month in alimony and child support. After she discovered that she was entitled to half of her husband's military pension, she went into court seeking a modification of the award. The court denied her request. She then commenced a malpractice action against her lawyer, alleging that he was negligent in failing to inform her that her husband's pension was divisible community property. The jury agreed and awarded her $100,000.

The following are some examples of lawyer malpractice:

- Failing to advise you about your rights to a pension, professional degree or license, and other marital assets (for example, social-security benefits) subject to distribution

- Failing to promptly protect judgments by placing liens on property to secure money owed to clients

- Procrastinating on a matter

- Failing to notify you of a trial or hearing date or failing to appear at such hearings

- Charging improper fees and threatening collection tactics to recover a fee not warranted

- Failing to file a claim within the requisite time period (that is, in accordance with the Statute of Limitations)
- Failing to inform both husband and wife that a conflict-of-interest situation exists, if one does

Again: Speak to another lawyer before deciding whether you have a valid claim. It is essential that you have another attorney's opinion and advice as to what steps should be taken to protect your rights.

Should You Appeal Your Case?

The vast majority of lawsuits never go to trial; they are either discontinued or settled. However, every case that is tried has a loser, and the losing party must decide whether or not to appeal the unfavorable decision. *Talk to your lawyer immediately if you receive an unfavorable verdict.* There is a limited period of time to file a notice that you intend to appeal, and you must do this without delay to preserve your rights.

The appeals process works in the following way: An appeals judge reads the transcript of the trial, together with legal documents called "briefs," to determine if the trial judge or jury erred in the decision.

Less than 30 percent of all civil cases are reversed on appeal. To evaluate the chances of a successful appeal, you must carefully reconstruct the reasons why you lost the case. You must also decide whether to hire your present lawyer or to hire a specialist in appeals matters. Although your lawyer is quite familiar with your case, there is much to be said for hiring a lawyer who makes a living writing briefs and arguing appeals (which is an art).

Be certain you know how much the appeal will cost. Always sign a retainer agreement (similar to the following), which clearly spells out lawyer fees, costs, and disbursements.

Sample Appeal Retainer Agreement

STEVEN MITCHELL SACK
ATTORNEY AT LAW

450 SEVENTH AVENUE, SUITE 1011

NEW YORK, N.Y. 10123

—

(212) 695-2535

(Date)

Barbara Jones
1000 Main Street
Centerville, N.Y. 12345

Re: Retainer Agreement regarding Appeal

Dear Ms. Jones:

This letter confirms that you have retained me as your attorney to represent you in the prosecution of an appeal of a custody decree granted by Justice Johnson on January 27, 1985, in the state family court, and entered on January 28, 1985, in the office of the clerk.

You have agreed to promptly pay a fee of $3,500 for my legal services in addition to disbursements. Disbursements include but are not limited to the cost for the transcript of the trial (which the court reporter has estimated at about $950), the cost of the printer to print the record on appeal, the cost of the briefs we submit, the cost of serving the appeals papers, and other costs. The actual disbursements may vary from the estimates, which are only approximate.

You are aware of the hazards of litigation and that despite my efforts on your behalf there is no assurance or guarantee that the court will grant permanent custody of your children to you rather than your spouse.

Kindly indicate your understanding and acceptance of the above by signing this letter below where indicated. I look forward to serving you.

Very truly yours,

Steven Mitchell Sack

I have read and understand the above letter, have received a copy, and accept all its terms:

_____

Barbara Jones

No matter who serves you, obviously you are in a better position when you win your case the first time, since appeals are uphill battles. Remember, appeals are generally costly, time-consuming, and frequently do not produce anticipated results.

Summary: How to Use Your Lawyer Effectively

1. If you contemplate legal action, speak to a lawyer to determine if you have a case and if you need legal services.

2. If necessary schedule an interview; inquire if you will be charged for it.

3. Bring relevant documents to the interview.

4. Ask for an opinion letter when appropriate.

5. Do not be overly impressed by plush surroundings.

6. Be sure the lawyer of your choice will be handling your matter.

7. Look for honesty and integrity in a lawyer.

8. Hire an experienced practitioner who devotes at least 30 percent of his or her working time to your type of problem.

9. Insist on signing a retainer agreement to reduce misunderstandings.

10. Have the agreement read and explained to you before signing, and save a copy for your files.

11. If the lawyer cannot tell you exactly how much you will be charged, get minimum and maximum estimates. Include this in the agreement.

12. Be certain you understand how additional costs are calculated, and who will pay for them.

13. If an hourly rate is agreed upon, try to negotiate an agreement that you will not be charged for telephone calls to your lawyer.

14. If you pay the fee in cash, get a receipt. Inquire if you can pay your bill by credit card.

15. Structure the fee arrangement to maximize your tax deduction.

16. Insist on receiving copies of incoming and outgoing correspondence, and monthly, detailed time records.

17. Be sure the lawyer will be available, will commence work immediately on your matter, and has no potential conflicts of interest.

18. Insist that all funds received on your behalf be deposited in interest-bearing escrow accounts. Don't forget to ask for the interest later on.

19. Never allow your lawyer to pressure you into settling a case.

20. Always consult another lawyer before deciding to fire your present one, to file a complaint with the grievance committee, or to commence a malpractice suit.

21. Do not expect miracles.

2 | Living Together: Cohabitation and the Law

Introduction

The number of unmarried couples living together these days has increased dramatically because of a relaxation of social mores, the assumption of different lifestyles, and other factors. According to a Census Bureau report published in 1979, more than 2.2 million people were living together as couples at that time. More recent figures indicate that that figure doubled over the next six years. This is an amazing statistic considering the fact that living with a person of the opposite sex, that is, living "out of wedlock," was once considered a crime in virtually every state.

The vast majority of unwed cohabitants are unaware of the legal and financial consequences of their status. Serious problems frequently arise upon the death of one partner or when the couple decides to split. These disputes typically concern the cohabitants' residence (their apartment, co-op, or house) and property (their savings, personal property purchased with joint funds, even businesses).

Problems also arise from such statements as "I'll support you for life even though we are not married" or "You'll own half of the apartment after it goes co-op," which are sometimes viewed as legally binding promises. In addition, a variety of entanglements may ensue over the birth of a child to parties living out of wedlock.

Many of the legal problems of the unmarried first emerged publicly as a result of the *Marvin v. Marvin* case in 1976. In that case, the California Supreme Court, in outlining the property rights of nonmarital cohabitants, determined that Michelle Triola, the lover and companion of film actor Lee Marvin, was entitled to go to trial to prove she had an agreement to divide and distribute the proceeds and property accumulated during their relationship.

Michelle and Lee Marvin lived together for seven years. During that time Triola alleged that there was an oral contract made between herself and Marvin. The agreement was that in return for giving up her career as a singer and assuming the domestic duties of the house, she would be provided for for life and would share all accumulated property. Then one day Lee Marvin's lawyers served Triola with a notice to vacate the house. Eighteen months later, when Marvin stopped sending support payments, Triola sued for a division of property and support.

The term coined by the press for the lawsuit was "palimony." Like a suit for alimony, it is brought to recover a money settlement; the difference is that it is awarded to an unmarried partner if he or she can prove there was a contract to share property and earnings. In the Marvin-Triola case, the judge found no evidence of a contract, either express or implied, between the parties. He also pointed out that they had kept their earnings separate and owned nothing in both their names. Michelle Triola was awarded $104,000 for rehabilitative purposes so she could learn a new employable skill, but this was stricken on appeal.

Although Triola lost, the case was instrumental in causing state legislators to change laws that had not kept up with the times. In addition, the supreme court of California, as in many other states, recognized that "the fact that a man and woman live together without marriage, and engage in a sexual relationship, does not in itself invalidate agreements between them relating to their earnings, property or expenses." The Marvin court also found that "the courts may inquire into the conduct of the parties to determine whether that conduct demonstrates an implied contract."

This is an important concept for cohabitants to know. People may decide to live together rather than marry because they believe there are no strings attached. However, as seen from the Marvin case and hundreds of others throughout the United States, a cohabitant can now sue for palimony and win, even without having a written cohabitation agreement.

Since *Marvin v. Marvin*, many well-known personalities have been sued for palimony. These include rock star Peter Frampton, tennis player Billie Jean King, and pianist Liberace. King was sued in May 1981 by a former lover, Marilyn Barnett. Barnett claimed that during their seven-year relationship, King promised to provide for her for life and to eventually deed her a Malibu beach house then worth $200,000. She sued for half of King's 1973–1979 income and title to the Malibu house. Despite the existence of joint credit cards, bank checks, and love letters, the judge ruled that there was no express or implied contract between the parties and thus denied Barnett's claim for palimony.

In still a different type of palimony suit, Scott Thorson sued Liberace for $113 million. He claimed that he had acted as Liberace's bodyguard, lover, and confidant for a period of six years and that Liberace had promised to support him for life as well as to adopt him. The suit was brought after Thorson claimed to have been thrown out in 1982. Thorson's lawyer claimed that his client's palimony case was stronger than previous palimony claims because a personal valid-services contract existed between the parties. However, Thorson lost the case because he could not convince a judge that Liberace had promised him anything.

Finally, in what was reported as the largest settlement in a palimony suit in 1981, a man settled with a former lover by paying her $245,000 in cash and assets. The woman had saved his love letters, which stated that he would support her for life. The existence of these letters prompted the huge settlement.

This chapter will discuss the area of cohabitation in great detail. It will help clarify the confusion that presently exists and offer practical strategies for protecting yourself when you enter or leave a living-together arrangement. Sample checklists and cohabitation contracts are included to illustrate the kinds of agreements that can be used. By applying some of the guidelines outlined in the chapter, you can acquire greater flexibility in validating your relationship in a legal manner while preserving your freedom to consider arrangements other than marriage.

General Points to Remember

Unlike marriage (which is favored in the eyes of the law), courts do not generally allow for the distribution of property acquired during cohabitation. The law treats marriage as a partnership or joint venture between the parties; it does not accord such treatment to a nonmarried relationship that exists in the absence of a contract.

A nonmarital partner has a legal right to his or her property acquired during the cohabitation. Personal assets purchased by one of the cohabitants belong to the individual with title or to the one who can prove ownership. For example, the person whose name is on the automobile registration and certificate of title owns the auto and is liable for paying the insurance.

Unlike a married partner, an unwed cohabitant is *not* automatically entitled by law to a share of a deceased spouse's estate. If an individual wishes to leave property to an unmarried cohabitant, it must be done by will. If there is no will (that is, if the person dies intestate), the surviving unwed cohabitant will probably get nothing.

In addition, in the absence of a contract, nonmarital cohabitants are not entitled to future support or to a property settlement when the relationship ends. Compensation, such as alimony, is only awarded when the court has evidence of a legal marriage.

What does this mean? It means that partners who live together do so *at their own risk*. If you are not married, you get nothing when you split up except the property that is in your own name or that which is specifically designated by contract.

Most states do not have specific laws regarding cohabitation. This means that the ramifications of such a relationship remain subject solely to judicial decision. When the couple decides to split or is not in agreement, a court will interpret the rights and responsibilities of the parties.

When an unmarried couple goes to court, a judge will attempt to render an award that is fair, reasonable, and equitable. Factors used in rendering a decision will include:

1. The presence or absence of a valid agreement (preferably written) between the parties
2. The duration and nature of the relationship
3. The presence or absence of children

Most judges will enforce the terms of an express contract between nonmarital partners, provided the contract is not explicitly founded on the furnishing of sexual services. Sexual services are not valid consideration for a contract since most states, as a matter of public policy, have criminal statutes making prostitution illegal.

For example, if a woman was promised that she would share in the proceeds of her lover's book if she slept with him on a continuous basis, the court would not enforce the woman's claim, even if she proved that such a promise was made. However, if the woman was promised a half share in the proceeds of her lover's book in return for her care of the author's sick mother, such an agreement might be upheld, provided it could be proved.

Thus, while the marriage certificate may be "just a piece of paper," it gives married couples superior rights over unmarried cohabitants. The advantages include inheritance rights, lower insurance rates, and injury and death benefits for the surviving spouse, including worker's compensation, social security, pension, and military benefits.

However, cohabitants can make agreements (sometimes called "cohabitation contracts") which will be enforced and will give them similar rights, providing the agreements are not based upon sexual services and no policy precludes the courts from upholding such contracts. The following sections will discuss how you can use these agreements to your advantage.

The Primary Strategy: Get an Express Agreement in Writing

The fact that a man and woman (or two members of the same sex) live together and engage in a sexual relationship without benefit of marriage does not invalidate agreements between them relating to their earnings, property, or expenses. Typically, such agreements fail because they cannot be proved, are ambiguous or uncertain, or are founded solely upon the furnishing of sexual services by one of the parties.

Cohabitants may enter into express contracts, written or oral, regarding the terms and legal consequences of at least some aspects of their relationship. For example, there may be a sharing-of-earnings agreement as alleged in the Marvin case, a written or oral trust, a partnership agreement, or a joint business venture agreement. There may also be a commitment to support one party for life or for some other period of time.

If the agreement is shown by the *direct words* of the parties, either spoken or written, then it is said to be an "express agreement." However, although an express contract between the parties does not necessarily have to be in writing, it is much easier to prove if a signed written document reflecting the partners' intentions can be produced.

Some unwed cohabitants have proved that there was an understanding between them without an express contract. Judges have also made decisions on the basis of equity (fairness) when warranted by the facts of the case. Usually, the court inquires into the conduct of the parties, the subject matter of the purported agreement, and the surrounding circumstances to determine whether there was an agreement of partnership, joint venture, or some other tacit understanding between them. Such an understanding is referred to as an "implied agreement."

However, if you don't put your agreement in writing, you may have trouble proving what the understanding was. The reason is that a handshake—that is, an oral agreement—only confirms that an agreement was made; it does not prove what that agreement was. The same oral words agreed upon often have different meanings to the parties who uttered them. When spoken words are reduced to writing, potential misunderstandings are minimized, and it is easier to prove the terms of your agreement.

When a written agreement is signed, the law presumes the parties incorporated their intentions into the contract. The instrument "speaks for itself," and courts will not hear testimony about understandings or discussions before the agreement was signed unless the information is necessary to interpret ambiguous terms.

In addition, all agreements concerning the transfer or disposition of property worth more than $500 must be in writing to satisfy a legal principle referred to as "the Statute of Frauds." This means that without such a document, any agreement regarding valuable property could be unenforceable *despite your intentions.*

In a recent New York case, for example, a woman was unable to recover anything from her dead lover's estate for labor and services performed by her in the operation of a bar and grill owned by the decedent or for her services as an ostensible wife. The woman claimed she had been promised orally that she would be compensated for the fair and reasonable value of the services, that the decedent would marry her, and that she would be amply provided for in his will.

You know the story. The marriage did not take place. The man died and left no provision for the woman's compensation and care in the will. The New York Court of Appeals ruled that the alleged oral agreement was unenforceable under the Statute of Frauds.

Thus it is wise to execute a written cohabitation contract whenever you enter a prolonged cohabitation relationship. Such a contract gives both parties legal control over the distribution of their finances and property. It also protects the parties if the relationship breaks up. For example, in the event the couple must go to court to litigate a dispute, the focus of the court will be on the contract rather than on the couple's personal relationship. In this way, the couple's privacy will be maintained. The contract can also contain a provision which refers all disputes to binding arbitration. This will further protect the couple's privacy because arbitration is conducted behind closed doors without spectators.

Examples of Cohabitation Contracts

Cohabitation contracts can cover many issues. For example, they can include:

- Disposition of estates and jointly accumulated property upon termination of the living-together arrangement
- Agreements to furnish reasonable support and maintenance for a specified period of time after the parties separate or upon the death of one of the cohabitants
- Title and interest to specified real estate, citing who is responsible for the mortgage, taxes, insurance, etc.

- Agreements to keep property separate
- Agreements that all money transferred by one party to the other or on behalf of the other shall be treated as a loan to be repaid over a certain time and at a certain rate
- Agreements with respect to business ventures, arrangements, or enterprises commenced or operated by the parties
- Agreements to comingle joint bank accounts or to maintain separate accounts
- Agreements to specifically waive any claims for palimony or support from the other in the event of a termination of the living-together arrangement
- Agreements with respect to apartment leases and who gets the apartment in the event it goes co-op
- Statements that the parties agree not to hold themselves out as man and wife
- Agreements with respect to an acknowledgment of paternity, together with an agreed-upon obligation of custody, support, and care for the child

These are examples of the kinds of topics typically covered in cohabitation contracts. Usually, the first item discussed concerns property. The cohabitants can decide either to keep all previously owned property separate or to share the property equally. Property acquired during the relationship can be shared equally or in some predetermined ratio (for instance, 35 percent to the male, 65 percent to the female) or held separately by the purchaser. There are many options.

Another issue often dealt with concerns how the couple intend to share their income. For example, many couples stipulate whether their income is to be pooled or kept separate. This is important where one person provides the main source of income, while the other party undertakes the task of being primarily responsible for housekeeping and domestic affairs.

The couple should also decide whether any palimony payments will be paid when or if the relationship ends. Child support, custody, and visitation rights for children born during the cohabitation should also be incorporated into the contract when appropriate. (*Note*: Each state has its own laws pertaining to what is considered "in the best interest of the child." This means that provisions for child support in a cohabitation contract may be overruled if they conflict with state law.)

In addition, some cohabitants may have children from previous marriages. Terms for support, if the child is living with the cohabitants, should be detailed in the contract. Also, the couple may wish to define the extent of the obligation—that is, if support will be continued after the relationship ends. Remember, however, that each state has its own laws governing child support.

Finally, the parties should decide how they will maintain bank accounts, credit cards, etc., and who will pay for the rent, mortgage, etc. When all of these items are included in a properly drafted agreement, future misunderstandings and problems can be minimized.

The following agreements are examples of the kinds of items contained in cohabitation contracts.*

Short Letter Agreement (One Working Party)

Dated: ...., 19..

Dear ....:

You and I have been living together since ...., 19 .., and we intend to continue to do so.

In consideration of your [domestic, personal and extraordinary business services and giving up your career as ...., assisting me in my career, and otherwise taking care of our household], I agree that you will be entitled to share equally in any and all property, real or personal, that I may acquire during the period of our living together through earnings and accumulations acquired other than by

---

*These two sample agreements are taken from *West Legal Forms*, Vol. 7, West Publishing Company, St. Paul, Minnesota. They are provided here for illustrative purposes only. Although an agreement need not be prepared by a lawyer to be valid, a lawyer's help is recommended for many reasons.

bequest. Such property will include all our household goods, but not [here specify].

You will receive your share of the property, in money or its equivalent, when and if we cease living together, or upon my death if we are living together at that time.

You will have, by reason of our living together, no claim against me or my estate other than as specified above, but you will, of course, be entitled to receive anything additional that I may choose to leave you in my will.

In the event that we, in future time, do get married, the terms and conditions specified herein will apply only with respect to the period of time of this cohabitation and will thereafter terminate, although the property rights acquired during this period shall not.

As you know, I care deeply for you and believe that our relationship is of a deep and abiding nature. The purpose of this letter is to protect you as much as myself, and to avoid any possible dispute later on. You may wish to consult an attorney about the terms and conditions of this letter before agreeing to them. This letter was drafted by my attorney [name, address and telephone number].

In order to indicate your agreement to the foregoing, please sign and date this letter where indicated below.

Dated: _____   Sincerely,

                        _____

                        [*Signature of Working Party*]

                        Agreed to and confirmed:

                        _____

                        [*Signature of Cohabitant*]

General Form; Property and Support Agreement; Both
Parties Working; Ownership of Household Goods; Lease of
Apartment; Household Expenses; Joint Bank Accounts;
Capital Outlays; Personal Expenses; Income Taxes; Division
of Property; Disclaimer of Property and Estate Rights;
Acknowledgement of the Parties; Arbitration; Entire
Understanding

Property and Support Agreement

AB and *CD* are presently living together in apartment No.
. . . . in . . . . , City of . . . . ,
State of . . . . It is their intention to continue to
do so until either decides to terminate said living arrangement.

The parties do not intend, by this agreement or the living
arrangement contemplated herein, to create a form of marriage recognized by this or any other state as a "common law"
marriage.

To avoid any misunderstanding or dispute as to property
rights or otherwise, in the case of a future separation they
agree as follows:

1. *AB* owns the real and personal property listed on
Schedule A, attached hereto and incorporated in this agreement by reference.

2. *CD* owns the real and personal property listed on Schedule
B, attached hereto and incorporated in this agreement by reference.

3. The parties agree that all property shown on Schedules A
and B is, and shall remain, the separate property of the person
owning it as of the date of this agreement, and that neither
acquires any right or interest in the property of the other by
virtue of this agreement. Neither party may acquire any interest in the property of the other as set forth on Schedules A
and B except by a written instrument, executed after the date
of this agreement by the owner of the property.

4. The parties acknowledge that they presently own, as tenants in common, all the furniture, furnishings, books, records,

works of art, household goods, and appliances presently in the apartment with the exception of [here specify], which is and shall remain *AB*'s sole property, and [here specify], which is and shall remain *CD*'s sole property.

5. The lease dated ...., 19.., pertaining to the occupancy of the apartment is presently in *AB*'s name. As between them, the parties shall share equally the obligations under this lease and any renewal thereof, as well as under any new lease that *AB* may enter into for their mutual benefit.

6. The parties have heretofore established a joint bank account (herein called the Joint Account) at the .... Branch of the .... Bank, located in ...., City of ...., State of .... They have, from time to time, made [equal] contributions to the Joint Account, and all household expenses of any kind (i.e., for rent, food, utilities, insurance, books, newspapers, magazine subscriptions, cleaning, laundry, etc.) have been paid from the Joint Account. They propose to continue this practice.

7. If the parties agree to make any capital outlays for the household (i.e., for the purchase of works of art, a television set, a stereo, etc.), or for their common use (i.e., the purchase of an automobile, a boat, etc.), the funds required for this purpose shall be paid from the Joint Account. All property so acquired shall be owned and held by the parties as tenants in common, each party holding an undivided one-half interest therein. Any expenditure for their common benefit (i.e., for theater tickets, vacations, gifts, entertainment of friends, etc.) shall likewise be made from the Joint Account. Whenever the funds in the Joint Account are insufficient for any of these purposes, the parties shall, to the extent necessary, replenish the Joint Account by making [equal] contributions thereto.

8. Any automobiles, trailers, boats or other items of personal property in the possession of either party, with the registration and certificate of ownership in the name of [state name] shall be the property of the person whose name is shown as the registered owner on the certificate of ownership. If title is

taken in both names, the interests of each shall be an undivided one-half interest as tenants in common.

9. Neither party shall draw upon the Joint Account for any purpose other than as hereinabove set forth, and each party shall keep the other informed of any withdrawals.

10. Hereafter, any real property acquired by the parties jointly, shall be owned by each as the interest is shown on the deed or document of title. Unless otherwise specified on such title document, the parties shall be as tenants in common, each party holding an undivided one-half interest.

11. All real and personal property subsequently acquired by the parties, except by the purchase from the Joint Account, shall be the separate property of the party acquiring the property. Each party shall, from his or her separate funds, defray his or her respective personal expenses, for clothing, medical or dental care or otherwise. Any tangible items received as a result of the payment of these expenses shall be the separate property of the acquiring party.

12. Each party shall file his or her separate income tax return, and shall pay his or her individual income taxes from his or her personal funds.

13. Each party acknowledges that, except as herein specified, he or she shall have no right, title or interest in (a) the other's income, (b) the other's individual bank accounts now or hereafter maintained, and/or (c) any other assets or property now owned or hereafter acquired by the other. Neither party has any right to support from the other, except as provided by this agreement.

14. Each party hereby waives any and all rights in the other's estate, but nothing contained herein shall in any way affect or impair any testamentary provision that either party may voluntarily make by will for the other's benefit.

15. *AB* is presently employed as a ...., with the firm of .... in the City of ...., State of .... In addition to his salary of

$................ per annum, he has certain benefits incident
to his employment including ....

16. *CD* is presently self-employed as a ...., in
the City of ...., State of .... She
has had earnings in each of the past three years in excess of
$................

17. In the event the parties separate, or in the event this
agreement is terminated in any other manner, both parties
waive any right to recover attorney's fees, court costs, or support in any action to enforce this agreement.

18. The consideration for this agreement consists of the
mutual promises of the parties as expressed herein. The furnishing of sexual services forms no part of the consideration
for this contract.

19. Both parties agree that this contract contains their entire agreement and that there are no representations, either
oral or written, made by either party or relied on by either
party, except those contained in this agreement. This agreement may not be altered or amended except by a written agreement subsequently executed and signed by both parties, and
which specifically makes reference to this contract.

20. This agreement shall terminate upon the marriage of the
parties to each other, or of either party to any third person.
Upon the termination of the agreement, any property held
jointly or separately by the parties at that time shall continue
to be held as a separate property interest of each for the purposes of the property laws of the State of ....

21. The parties acknowledge that they have consulted independent legal counsel during the negotiation and drafting of
this agreement, in its entirety, and that they rely solely on the
meaning, construction, and legal effect of this agreement as
given to each individually by that independent legal counsel.

22. This agreement shall be construed under the laws of the
State of ....

Dated: _____   _____

                                   [*Signature of AB*]

Dated: _____   _____

                                   [*Signature of CD*]

Approved as to form and content

_____   _____

Attorney for *AB*   [*Attorney for CD*]

Sample Document

AGREEMENT FOR PURCHASE OF HOUSE
PROVIDING FOR PROPORTIONATE OWNERSHIP*

_____ and _____ agree that they hereby enter a joint business venture, to wit, the purchase of a house located at _____, and that the parties hereto shall acquire an interest in proportion to their financial contribution to the same.

It is agreed that the property shall be deeded to both parties, as individuals or as partners, and all deeds and instruments shall be in both names as individuals or as partners.

It is further agreed that each party shall be liable for the debts and obligations' arising from the purchase, maintenance, repair, insurance, taxation, inspection, and sale of said residence only in proportion to each party's financial interest in the property.

It is further agreed that each party will make payments by check or money order and will maintain an accurate record of his or her financial contributions to the purchase, maintenance, repair, insurance, taxation, and sale of the house.

It is further agreed that each party shall contribute such services, work, and energies towards the maintenance and repair of the premises as is proportional to his or her financial interest therein.

---

*This sample agreement is taken from *West Legal Forms*, Vol. 7, West Publishing Company, St. Paul, Minnesota. It is provided here for illustrative purposes only. Although an agreement need not be prepared by a lawyer to be valid, a lawyer's help is recommended for many reasons.

It is further agreed that either party may, with thirty days notice to the other party, withdraw from the herein joint venture and the other party agrees to buy out the withdrawing partner's interest within ninety days, or else list the property for sale at a fair market value within ninety days of notice, and the proceeds and costs of sale shall be apportioned between the partners in relation to their respective financial interest in same.

Each party shall act in good faith to preserve the value of the property and keep the same in good condition and repair.

Should either party breach this agreement, said party agrees to pay such reasonable attorney's fees and costs as the other shall require in order to enforce the provisions thereof.

Dated: ———

—————————————————————
[Name and signature of party]

—————————————————————
[Name and signature of party]

Sample Document

TERMINATION OF LIVING-TOGETHER ARRANGEMENTS*

It is hereby agreed that ——— and ———, who have been living together, shall separate and go their own ways, and as of this time have no intention of resuming their former living together arrangement.

It is agreed that the property and furnishings owned by either party shall be taken with each party, respectively, as follows:

*This sample agreement is taken from *West Legal Forms*, Vol. 7, West Publishing Company, St. Paul, Minnesota. It is provided here for illustrative purposes only. Although an agreement need not be prepared by a lawyer to be valid, a lawyer's help is recommended for many reasons.

[Name] _____	[Name]_____
[List of items belonging to this person:]	[List of items belonging to this person:]
1.	1.
2.	2.
3.	3.
4.	4.
5.	5.
6.	6.
7.	7.
8.	8.
9.	9.
10.	10.
11.	11.
12.	12.
13.	13.
14.	14.
15.	15.
16.	16.
17.	17.
18.	18.
19.	19.
20.	20.

(Continue list as necessary)

It is further agreed that the following items have been purchased with both parties contributing money towards purchase, and these items have been divided in order to make a fair and equal division of the value of the jointly purchased items:

	Item	*Est. Value*	*Person Who Gets to Take It*
1.			
2.			
3.			
4.			
5.			
6.			
7.			
8.			
9.			
10.			

11.
12.
13.
14.
15.
It is further agreed that the joint bills and obligations shall be disposed of in the following manner:

Creditor	Amount of Obligation	Person Who Pays This
1.		
2.		
3.		
4.		
5.		
6.		
7.		
8.		
9.		
10.		
11.		
12.		

It is further agreed that both parties are leaving the shared premises, or, in the alternative, that _____ is leaving and _____ is staying, and the one staying shall assume all responsibility for said premises henceforward, except for those common debts listed above of this separation agreement. The party who is leaving agrees not to reenter the premises without the remaining party's permission, nor to remove anything therefrom.

It is further agreed that neither party shall have a claim to the other's business, pension or retirement fund, insurance proceeds or refundable policies, or any other property not described in this agreement.

It is further agreed that neither party shall have a claim to compensation from the other for services rendered during the time that they lived together, nor for "spousal support," nor for any other property, assets, or money not described in this agreement.

It is further agreed that should litigation or the services of an attorney be necessary in order to enforce this agreement, the default ing or losing party shall pay to the prevailing party such attorneys fees and costs as may be fixed by the court.

Dated: _____

_____

[Name and signature of party]

_____

[Name and signature of party]

Although your agreement need not be prepared by a lawyer to be valid, a lawyer's help is recommended for many reasons. When an agreement is drafted and reviewed by experienced counsel, it reduces the risk that language in the agreement will be viewed as ambiguous and unenforceable. In addition, you will reduce the risk of having the agreement declared invalid because one of the parties signed it under coercion, duress, or mistake. This is an important point that should never be overlooked.

Thus the trick is to draft an agreement which clearly reflects the needs and intentions of the parties. Pains should be taken to demonstrate that there is adequate consideration (that is, a bargained-for exchange of benefits to the parties) and that sexual services are not a factor for entering into the agreement. The contract should also state that if any clause is deemed invalid by a court, the agreement will still be upheld, despite the questionable provision.

Finally, the agreement must be signed by two competent parties to be valid. It is a good idea to have both signatures witnessed if possible. Include the date and initial all changes. If the contract refers to a schedule or additional terms contained in another document, attach the document to the contract so it won't be misplaced. Obtain a signed copy of the agreement for your files; keep it in a safe place where you store other valuable documents.

Additional Strategies to Be Considered

1. *Prepare a will to accurately reflect your desires.* All possessions, including property, go to the next of kin in the absence of a will. Most cohabitants are unaware that, according to intestate succession laws in all fifty states, no relationship exists between them. Therefore, a will is vital for cohabitants who wish to enable partners to receive their possessions in the event of death. Speak to a lawyer for further information if this is applicable in your case.

2. *Protect yourself whenever you move into an apartment or co-op with a lover or friend.* When unwed cohabitants decide to split, disputes typically arise over their residence (that is, the apartment, co-op, or house where the parties lived together). Substantial sums of money are often involved when one of the parties is required to vacate the premises. The lack of desirable apartments in major U.S. cities, the rapid growth of the co-operative housing market, and the escalation of property values are economic factors which sometimes increase the amount at stake. This, of course, is in addition to the inconvenience one of the parties must suffer by moving out.

The following discussion will set forth rights to possession of an apartment, co-op, or house when a live-in couple decides to part. It will outline the proper steps to take to protect your rights when you decide to move into a residence with a lover and will show you how to reduce the chances that you will be forced to leave without your consent. In addition, you will learn the best ways to ensure your right to a portion of your lover's "insider" price when his or her apartment goes co-op.

Consider these points if you move into an apartment with a lover:

Try to get your name on the lease. The person who signs the lease is the lawful tenant. Significant responsibilities and benefits result from this. The signer has the right of occupancy and is the person who is first offered the right to renew the lease. Conversely, he or she is the person the owner sues for nonpayment of rent.

An unnamed occupant does not have the same rights. Even if you have lived with someone in the same place for five years and have contributed all the rent, your lover has first claim on the apartment, especially if he or she signed the lease alone, occupied the apartment before you, and though taking your money to pay the rent each month, used his or her own personal check.

Thus the trick is to *get your name on the lease as a cotenant to protect your rights.* (*Note*: If you are planning to stay for only a short while or are sure the apartment will not be converted into a co-op, you may be better off not including yourself in the lease since you won't then be legally obligated to pay the rent.)

It may also be necessary to amend the lease to avoid exposing both you and your cohabitant to eviction proceedings. Many residential leases expressly limit occupancy to the named tenant and his or her immediate family. Unless written permission is obtained (many standard leases throughout the country state that such consent cannot be *unreasonably* withheld), you may be forced to vacate the premises by your lover's lessor. Review the lease and take all necessary steps to avoid this problem.

Sign a residence agreement with your cohabitant. Partners who plan ahead incorporate their intentions into a simple agreement—as unromantic as it seems. By doing so they protect themselves in many ways. As explained previously in this chapter, an agreement spelling out the rights, duties, and obligations of the parties will reduce misunderstandings during the relationship. In addition, it should minimize problems in the event the couple decides to split.

The following is an example of a residence agreement; it is given here for illustrative purposes only.

Sample Document

RESIDENCE AGREEMENT FOR COHABITANTS

It is agreed between (Party A) and (Party B), who are sharing an apartment located at _____, that the lease of this apartment shall be a joint lease, even though the name of only one of the two parties may be on the actual lease. Said apartment shall be under the equal and joint control and direction of both parties.

(Party A) will move into (Party B's) apartment on (Date) and thereafter contribute $_____ per month on the first day of each succeeding month. This represents one-half of the monthly rent. (Party B) will continue to pay the owner as agreed to in the lease.

(Party A) will pay one-half of the electric, gas, water, and garbage to (Party B) on the first day of each month. (Party B) will pay the bills. Telephone bills will be apportioned between the parties according to their respective use thereof, except that the fixed monthly service and installment charges shall be paid equally by the parties.

In the event (Party A) decides to move out (Party B) will receive reasonable written notice, in no event less than two weeks. (Party A) agrees to pay (Party B) the pro rata share of the rent from the first day of the month up to the day he (or she) vacates the premises.

It is agreed that (Party B) has first choice to remain in the apartment and (Party A) must leave upon written request. In the event (Party B) decides that (Party A) must move out, (Party A) will abide by said request. (Party B) will give (Party A) reasonable written notice, in no event less than two weeks.

All personal items brought into the apartment shall remain the property of the respective party owning title. Personal property acquired with joint funds or obtained by gift from third parties shall be divided in the following manner (specify particular property or manner): . . . .

In the event (Party A) lives in said apartment with (Party B) for more than two years from the date hereof, and (Party B) receives a preliminary prospectus to convert the building to co-operative ownership after said date, the parties agree that (Party A) shall have the right at his (or her) election to contribute fifty percent (50%) of the subscription agreement price to purchase an equal share and ownership in said co-op.

Should one party fail to comply with any of the terms of this agreement, causing the other party to employ the services of an attorney, the party failing to comply agrees to pay to the other such reasonable attorney fees and costs as may be fixed by the court.

In witness thereof we affix our signatures this _____ day of _____ in the year _____.

_____

[*Name and signature of party*]

_____

[*Name and signature of party*]

_____

[*Name of witness*]

It is not necessary for a lawyer to prepare the document. However, if you draft the document yourself, be sure that all clauses are clear and unambiguous.

It is wise to sign a simple agreement such as this with your cohabitant, especially if you cannot obtain your name on the lease. The agreement can serve as valuable evidence indicating the intentions of both parties. It may also prove that you were an equal tenant with equal rights. In addition, such a written agreement is *essential* if you wish to maintain a claim for a portion of your lover's "insider" price when the apartment goes co-op. The following case demonstrates why.

A woman lived with her lover for six years and contributed a substantial amount to the monthly rent until their relationship deteriorated. When the building was converted to co-op ownership, the woman sued her lover for $25,000 and judgment for possession of the apartment. The woman lost her case. The judge ruled that since no proof of a partnership or joint venture existed between the parties, the woman needed written proof to support her claim. Sufficient evidence would have been either her name on the lease or a written agreement between them crystalizing their rights and interests in the proposed co-op. This was to satisfy the Statute of Frauds, which requires that agreements concerning interests in land must be in writing to be enforceable. Since there was no written agreement between them, the woman was out of luck.

Document your intentions with other evidence. If you are unable to obtain your name on the lease or to sign a written cohabitation contract, there are still ways in which you may be able to prove your claim. This is through other evidence that reflects the conduct of the parties. For example, it is best for you to pay the lessor directly from time to time on behalf of your lover. Assuming the check is accepted by the owner and clears the bank, this would indicate some sort of arrangement with your cohabitant that could be used to your advantage. The same is true for utility bills: You should at times pay some of these bills directly rather than giving the money to your partner to pay with his or her own personal check.

In this way you may demonstrate by conduct that you and your partners had an *implied contract* that you were to share in the proceeds when the apartment went co-op since you were responsible for making actual rent and maintenance payments for both parties' benefit. Don't forget this point and don't forget to save all your receipts and checks for your records.

Avoid signing a release or any other document indicating your relinquishment of any claims. In addition, don't forget to respond in kind if you receive a letter that states your partner's version of the story (if it differs from your own). The failure to respond to any accusing document may cause you to waive your rights.

3. *Get a receipt when you contribute money for the purchase of property or assets used by both cohabitants.* In *Marvin v. Marvin*, the California court ruled that property acquired by Lee Marvin during his cohabitation with Triola might be apportioned between them even in the absence of an express agreement. An implied-in-fact agreement might be found to exist if the conduct of the parties evidenced the appropriate intent to pool and share earnings and property during a relationship.

One way of demonstrating an implied-in-fact arrangement is by obtaining a receipt that indicates that your funds were used to purchase cohabitation property. For example, if you gave your live-in partner $2,000 to buy $4,000 worth of living-room furniture, and your partner paid for the furniture with a personal check in the amount of $4,000, it is best to get a receipt from him or her that acknowledges payment of $2,000 toward the furniture purchase. This would strengthen a claim that you owned half of the furniture.

Better still, you should try to get a brief letter or other written record acknowledging that you contributed half of the funds and that you own half of the furniture. If this is not practical, the least you can do is write your check for $2,000 with a notation on the face of it such as "50% contribution toward the purchase of jointly owned furniture."

Remember, the goal is to obtain evidence establishing your contribution and ownership in property purchased with your funds. This is why you should try to obtain receipts wherever possible.

4. *Learn how the law in your state treats common-law marriage.* Thirteen states still recognize common-law marriage. This means that a couple will be considered to be lawfully married if they hold themselves out to be husband and wife, regardless of whether they obtain a marriage license, have blood tests, or participate in a civil ceremony.

Many cohabitants hold themselves out to the public as husband and wife and acknowledge the family relationship. For example, if you accept mail under the names "Mr. and Mrs. Jones," file joint tax returns, and tell people you are married, then you may be legally married in a common-law state.

If you cohabitate with another, be sure you know the law in your particular state. If you live in a state that authorizes common-law marriage and you wish to preserve your single identities, there is good reason to sign a formal cohabitation contract evidencing your intentions. This way you can produce the contract as proof of cohabitation rather than marriage if the case goes to court. Conversely, if you reside in a state that recognizes common-law marriage and you wish to be considered married, do not sign a cohabitation contract.

5. *Avoid making promises you don't intend to keep.* This is apparent in view of the large number of palimony cases brought each year. The legal ramifications of a nonmarital cohabitant's rights continue to grow and expand. As more people become aware of their rights, they are consciously asserting them at every turn. Thus, never make a

promise regarding the amount of support or property you wish to give a cohabitant unless you intend to keep it. Where possible, avoid documenting any promise in a letter or written instrument.

6. Speak to an experienced lawyer if you believe you have been victimized. Judges are applying a variety of legal theories in awarding judgments. One theory is called *quantum meruit* (also known as "unjust enrichment"). Under this theory, money is awarded to nonmarital partners such as women who provide homemaking services with the expectation of remuneration. For example, if the woman takes all household duties out of the man's hands, leaving him free to do nothing but make money, then the court could award her part of his assets when the couple splits under this theory. The amount of money awarded would be the reasonable value for the hostess and/or homemaking services rendered, less the reasonable value of support received while the couple remained together, depending on the circumstances.

Alternatively, the court may award a judgment by declaring the existence of an implied business partnership or joint venture. If a member of a couple can prove that he or she helped the other partner with a business, then that member may be granted a recovery under this theory. In 1972, for example, the Washington Supreme Court found the existence of a business partnership between an unmarried couple who had been living together for sixteen years. A woman and her children helped run a cattle ranch owned by her lover; the court ruled that she was entitled to a fair amount of his estate on the basis of business-partnership theory (which totally excluded their sexual relationship).

In another recent case, a Wisconsin woman was granted a court order enjoining her ex-lover from selling the house they had lived in for four years, even though the house was in the man's name and he had paid for the bulk of it. A judge accepted the woman's contention that their arrangement constituted a joint business venture by virtue of their joint bank accounts, credit cards, and other jointly purchased assets. This was so even though the judge commented that the precise nature of their business relationship was never defined and that the woman had not contributed an equal financial share. Some states, including Washington, have gone a step further. They consider whether a long-term, stable, nonmarital family relationship exists. In making this decision they look at such factors as the duration of the relationship, whether the cohabitation was continuous, and whether resources and services were pooled for joint projects. If a long relationship is seen to exist, the court adopts the view that each member in some way contributed to the acquisition of the property, and money is sometimes awarded under this theory.

If you believe you were denied promised benefits or support from a lover and business partner, speak to an experienced lawyer immediately to protect your rights. You may learn that you are entitled to a greater share of assets and property accumulated during the cohabitation than you imagined.

7. *Check the law in your state.* Laws concerning live-in lovers vary considerably on a state-by-state basis. For example, some states enforce both express and implied agreements. Others only recognize agreements that are in writing. Still other states will not enforce any type of agreement between live-in couples. For maximum protection, be sure you know how your state treats cohabitation status.

8. *Be aware that concurrent marital status can decrease your claims.* Many states refuse to enforce promises made by one lover to the other while one or both of the parties are still legally married. In recent case decisions in New York and Tennessee, for example, the court stated that adultery would not be given a "seal of approval" as a result of cohabitation status.

3 | Thinking of Marriage: Commitment and the Law

Introduction

The decision to marry is probably the most significant act of a person's life. Tremendous legal, financial, and moral consequences flow from such a decision. This chapter is written for all of you who are contemplating marriage, to advise you how to protect your rights in a variety of important areas relative to the marriage function. For example, you will learn:

- How is marriage obtained?
- What legal problems arise if you change your mind before the marriage is consummated?
- How does the law treat the return of engagement rings and gifts when marriage plans have been broken off?
- What are the pros and cons of prenuptial agreements and what clauses do they frequently contain?
- What tax and estate-planning steps should be taken before marriage to protect your investments and assets?
- What legal duties and obligations are owed by each spouse to the other?

This information will help clarify much of the confusion and ignorance that many people have about marriage, prenuptial agreements, and other problems that sometimes emerge when couples decide to "tie the knot."

What Is Marriage?

Marriage has been defined as an agreement between a man and a woman who love one another to spend the rest of their lives together as husband and wife. Marriage is a private bond between two individuals that requires freedom from state intervention. However, certain aspects of marriage are regulated by governmental processes. For instance, all fifty states have created certain procedural prerequisites to a valid marriage and have established certain rights and duties incident to marriage. Each state is sovereign over its own laws affecting marriage; thus these rights, duties, and obligations often vary between states. In addition, some states are more attuned to changing the law in order to keep pace with changing moralities and lifestyles than are others.

More and more states are coming to regard marriage as a contract—a negotiable understanding between equals—involving very limited state intervention. Accordingly, there is an increasing tendency on the part of the courts to allow marriage partners to decide for themselves what rights and obligations each owes to the other. This will now be explored in greater detail.

Different Types of Marriage Arrangements

1. *Common-law marriage.* A common-law marriage is much like a traditional marriage without the religious and civil ceremony. A common-law marriage exists if a couple live together as husband and wife and hold themselves out to others as such (for instance, they are listed on the post-office box as "Mr. and Mrs.," they introduce themselves as married, etc.).

Most states have revoked their recognition of the common-law marriage because of the misunderstandings and fraud which have resulted from that status. Be aware that even if you think you are, you may not be properly "married" under common law in your state.

2. *The traditional marriage.* Typically, two people of opposite sex who are not currently married are eligible to marry (although each state imposes its own requirements as to age, health, and other factors).

It is generally necessary for one or both of the proposed partners to apply for a marriage license from an appropriate state or county agency. Also, in most states both parties must submit to blood tests.

The most common method for getting married is the ceremonial marriage. A ceremonial marriage consists of the presentation by the couple of the marriage license to an authorized state official. This can be a judge or a clerk, or a member of the clergy. The authorized official will then conduct a civil or religious ceremony according to state laws. Other than the promise to marry, the content of the ceremony is within the discretion of the couple.

The Consequences of Marriage

Once a couple is married, the marital obligations that are legally enforceable are very few (although there may be many *moral* obligations between a husband and wife).

1. *Name change.* One of the most common consequences of marriage is that the wife assumes the surname of her new husband. However, with the onset of the women's movement, this is becoming less common. In most states, a woman who wants to use her husband's surname and her own in combination—for example, Doris Grant-Jones—need only start and continue to use the chosen name. This is called a "common-law" name change.

2. *Financial support.* Each spouse owes the other the legal duty of financial support. This means that if a spouse is in need of financial support and the other spouse is able to provide such support, he or she is obliged to do so. The extent of this support has never been judicially established, although it appears to be legally accepted that a spouse may not allow the other to become a public charge, provided he or she has the financial means to prevent this. (*Note*: The Supreme Court has ruled that laws regarding marriage must be sex-neutral. This means, for example, that the duty of one spouse to provide financial support for the other applies equally to wives as to husbands.)

One of the biggest changes in the institution of marriage has occurred in the treatment of money and property. In a predominance of states, each spouse retains control over the property he or she brings into the marriage. Each spouse has the right to buy, sell, and borrow money or claim profits from his or her "separate property." However, a spouse may voluntarily relinquish control over such separate property by holding it jointly with the other spouse.

Generally, neither spouse is responsible for the premarital debts of the other. For example, the property a wife brings into marriage cannot be encumbered for the debts the husband incurred prior to their marriage. Similarly, a husband is liable for his wife's premarital debts only up to the amount of property she conveyed to him at the time of their marriage.

If you incur a debt, your spouse is not automatically obliged to pay it. Any debt incurred in your own name is your sole responsibility and can be collected against your property only. (*Note*: If you have been paying your spouse's bills and no longer wish to do so, you must notify all appropriate credit-card companies and merchants before you abrogate responsibility.)

Traditionally, a woman relinquished her personal credit when she married. However, this tradition has changed. The Equal Credit Opportunity Act prohibits discrimination based on sex when a person applies for credit. This means that a creditor is not allowed to ask about a person's marital status in an individual credit application. (However, a creditor can ask for information about your spouse if you are relying on a spouse's income to support your credit application.)

In most states, the working spouse's pension and any money set aside for retirement is treated as common property of the marriage. A surviving spouse will be provided with the deceased spouse's pension in certain circumstances. Many company-sponsored pension plans allow a surviving spouse to receive up to one-half of the reduced benefits a spouse received while alive.

A surviving spouse may receive social-security benefits based upon his or her spouse's earnings if said surviving spouse is 62 years of age or older and was married to the decedent for more than one year. These benefits will be one-half of the spouse's benefits and may be reduced by other benefits accruing.

3. *Other personal aspects.* Although it is usual for a married couple to live together, it is not required. However, it *is* expected that spouses will remain sexually loyal to each other—in many states, adultery is still illegal (although this criminal offense is rarely prosecuted).

The law makes a few general statements regarding sexual relations between husbands and wives. Generally, one spouse may not deny the other sex without good cause; the failure to do so may allow the other spouse to obtain a divorce on the grounds of "constructive abandonment." However, a husband may not rape his wife to obtain sex. Many states have written into their criminal laws that marriage is not a defense to rape. Other states still adhere to the theory that a husband continues to have the right to have sex with his wife as long as they are married. (See Chapter 5.)

In addition, a woman's right to have children or not is solely her own choice. Women do not need their spouse's consent to use birth control, and a woman has the sole right to decide whether to abort a pregnancy. The Supreme Court has ruled that during the first three months of pregnancy, the baby's father and/or the woman's husband does not have any say in whether the expectant mother can obtain an abortion—the decision is the mother's alone. In the second trimester of pregnancy, the Court allows the states to regulate the procedures of abortion because of the inherent dangers during that period of gestation. After the sixth month and during the third trimester, a woman no longer has a legal right to abort, no matter her own or her husband's wishes.

Prenuptial Considerations

Ownership of Engagement Gifts

Each year, more than 2 million people get engaged and married in the United States. During the betrothal period, individuals often exchange gifts. This section will clarify who is the legal owner of the engagement ring and gifts when the engagement is broken and the marriage does not occur.

Ownership rights to engagement gifts are governed in most states by case decisions (that is, common law); few states have passed laws governing this area. What this means is that each case is decided by a judge based on its own particular facts and circumstances.

Different types of gifts are often exchanged by betrothed parties. These include personal gifts, holiday gifts, birthday gifts, and gifts in contemplation of marriage. Third parties, of course, also give engagement presents to the couple. As you will see, the reason for the gift, the actual item given, and the date on which it is received all play a significant role in determining proper legal ownership.

Generally, a gift is a voluntary transfer of property to another that is made gratuitously and without consideration. The person receiving the gift (referred to as the "donee") then receives title to that property. However, some gifts are not absolute (that is, they do not convey complete title) but are given with the intent that the marriage take effect before legal title is transferred.

Thus if you decide, for example, that you cannot go through with a planned marriage, you are legally obliged in most states to return any gifts you received that were "conditional on performance of the marriage." For a woman, this includes the engagement ring, any other gifts given on the assumption she was going to marry, wedding presents, and shower gifts.

To recover an engagement present, then, ordinarily requires proof that the gift was made in contemplation of marriage and the decision not to marry was not caused by the person seeking recovery. In most instances, it is difficult to prove that a gift was only given in contemplation of marriage. Because of this, the law generally makes an exception with respect to engagement rings. Courts view engagement rings in the nature of a pledge for the contract of marriage. The ring is usually considered a *conditional* gift because of its symbolic significance, whch sets it apart from other betrothal gifts.

In the event of an engagement broken after the ring has been given, the right of ownership is generally as follows:

1. **Mutual consent.** If both parties mutually consent to breaking the engagement, the donor (the person giving the gift) will normally acquire the right to regain the ring.

2. **Donee break.** If the donee breaks the engagement without legal justification, she is required, upon demand, to return the ring.

3. **Donor break.** If the donor breaks the engagement without legal justification, the donee will normally be entitled to keep the ring.

Other gifts given before and during the engagement period (frequently referred to as "gifts of pursuit") are more difficult to recover in a lawsuit, especially when they are received on the donee's birthday, an anniversary, a holiday, or some special occasion. This is because when you give someone a gift on a special occasion, you are weakening any defense that the gift was *conditional. Remember this.*

The following hypothetical cases illustrate these general principles:

> Jack gives Cindy an expensive necklace while they are engaged. The necklace is received on Cindy's birthday; Jack says nothing about having given her the gift in contemplation of their upcoming marriage. Two weeks later, Cindy breaks the engagement. In this case, Cindy is entitled to keep the necklace because it will probably be viewed as a birthday present.
>
> However, suppose Jack gives the necklace to Cindy on an "ordinary" day and tells her it is hers to wear now and that it will be hers after the wedding. This may be viewed as a conditional gift belonging to Jack after the breakup.
>
> Now suppose again that Jack gives Cindy the necklace on her birthday, telling her basically the same thing: that it is hers to wear now and that it will be hers after the wedding. Here, Jack will have a more difficult case recovering the necklace, despite his words, because it may be viewed as a birthday gift, especially if no other witnesses were present who overheard his conditional statement.

Each engagement has its own unique and varying events which may or may not change the outcome of legal ownership of gifts. However, if you are giving a gift in contemplation of marriage, be sure to do the following:

1. Stress that the gift is conditional upon consummating the marriage.
2. Announce these intentions in front of witnesses if possible.

3. Demand the prompt return of the item once the engagement is broken.

4. Avoid giving the gift on a special day if possible.

5. Recognize that you may have difficulty recovering the gift, even the engagement ring, if you are the one who breaks the engagement or provokes the breakup.

There are several additional points you may wish to remember. If the recipient of your gifts never intended to marry you even when receiving your conditional gifts, you may be able to recover these items on the grounds of fraud. In addition, if you are engaged to a minor (that is, a person under 18 years of age), you may be unable to recover the gift under any circumstances.

Finally, you are probably legally obligated to return all shower and wedding gifts to third parties after the engagement is called off, particularly if you are responsible for that decision.

Prenuptial Agreements

The number of couples signing prenuptial agreements (also called "antenuptial agreements") has risen greatly in the past few years. Although such contracts were used by the rich for generations, they are now being signed by middle-class wage earners, people with family businesses, and people alarmed by skyrocketing divorce rates and changing lifestyles. But the use of prenuptial agreements is most popular with people entering second marriages. Many older couples who have accumulated money and property desire to leave it to children and grandchildren upon death, rather than to a future spouse. Others have businesses or professional practices they wish to protect. Still others, traumatized by a "messy" divorce the first time around, seek to define their rights and responsibilities toward the other partner on paper.

While the use of these agreements before marriage is hardly romantic, it does allow parties to express their intentions for dividing property, altering inheritance rights, limiting spousal support, and gaining an equitable share in a business when the marriage ends. Experts suggest that this reduces costly and messy litigation because potential problems are anticipated and discussed by a couple before they occur.

Another advantage is that couples often include personal preferences in these agreements. For example, topics such as who will do the dishes, how frequently the parties will have sex, and how the children will be educated can be included along with the more traditional topics. This is valid, provided the topics are not illegal or contrary to public policy.

In this section, you will learn why more couples are electing to sign prenuptial agreements and how those agreements are enforced. Sample agreements are included to demonstrate the types of clauses frequently contained in such forms.

Why Would You Have a Prenuptial Agreement?

The decision to sign a prenuptial agreement with a future spouse should be well reasoned and carefully considered. Great financial and legal ramifications flow from the execution of a valid prenuptial agreement. Thus both parties should understand the effect such a document may have on their future.

Advantages of a Prenuptial Agreement:

- It usually avoids costly and messy divorce litigation.
- It invites candor and openness between the parties before marriage.
- It protects assets and property acquired by a spouse before marriage.
- It reflects the parties' intentions as to the disposition of marital and nonmarital (separate) property acquired during the marriage.

Disadvantages of a Prenuptial Agreement:

- It minimizes the illusion of love.
- It strips a spouse of potentially valuable marital rights

(for example, a share of inheritance, a pension, etc.).

- From a practical perspective it may be hard to enforce.
- It may not be legally valid.
- It has caused potential marriages to break up over the emotional issue of trust.

What Can Be Included in Prenuptial Agreements?

Almost anything can be inserted in the prenuptial contract. Matters including support, maintenance, and education of children, the providing of a home, the release of rights in each other's estate and assets, and all manner of property arrangements may be agreed upon in contemplation of marriage.

The following is a checklist of topics which are frequently included:

1. *Inheritance rights.* Parties can agree to waive, modify, or enlarge inheritance rights that the law ordinarily gives to a surviving spouse. For example, a prenuptial agreement can specify that vested pension funds or proceeds from a family business pass to the children of a prior marriage rather than to a surviving spouse.

2. *Insurance benefits.* Likewise, a surviving spouse may agree to be removed as a beneficiary under a life insurance policy.

3. *Manner and amount of assets distributed from family-controlled businesses and professional partnerships.* It is particularly common for couples marrying the second time around as well as for successful, career-minded men and women to make provisions for the distribution of assets.

4. *Modification and/or elimination of spousal support.* *Note:* Some states, including California, Colorado, and Illinois, prohibit prenuptial agreements that eliminate spousal support (that is, alimony) upon divorce. Be sure to check the law in your state on this point.

5. *Release of rights in each other's assets and estate.*

6. *Distribution of property, including real estate, upon divorce.*

7. *Provisions with respect to caring for children and the expenses of maintaining a home* (for example, who will pay what bills, etc.). Note, however, that courts will not agree to enforce provisions regarding support, education, and care of children if such provisions are not in the best interests of the children. This means the court is free to fashion its own policy with respect to the children, regardless of the couple's preference as stated in the prenuptial agreement.

8. *Adoption of children.*

9. *Commitments to divide household and child-care chores.*

10. *Mediation of potential disputes.*

The following examples of prenuptial agreements* illustrate the inclusion of such clauses. Due to the complexity of such agreements, it is recommended that you contact a lawyer for further information if applicable.

General Form; Wife To Receive Specified Sum Upon Husband's Death; Mutual Waivers of Rights in Property and Estate

THIS AGREEMENT made between [George Brown], residing at ...., City of ...., State of ...., herein called [Mr. Brown] and [Mary Smith], residing at ...., City of ...., State of ...., herein called [Miss Smith],

WITNESSETH

The parties are about to marry. In anticipation thereof, they desire to fix and determine by ante-nuptial agreement the

---

*These sample agreements are taken from Alexander Lindey, *Separation Agreements and Antenuptial Contracts*, Matthew Bender & Co., New York, 1984.

rights and claims that will accrue to each of them in the estate and property of the other by reason of the marriage, and to accept the provisions of this agreement in lieu of and in full discharge, settlement, and satisfaction of all such rights and claims.

Now, THEREFORE, in consideration of the premises and of the marriage, and in further consideration of the mutual promises and undertakings hereinafter set forth, the parties agree:

1. [Miss Smith] shall receive and accept from [Mr. Brown's] estate after his death, subject to the conditions set forth in clause 3 hereof, the sum of [$100,000] free of any and all inheritance and estate taxes, in place and stead of, and in full and final settlement and satisfaction of, any and all rights and claims which she might otherwise have had in [Mr. Brown's] estate and property under any statute or statutes now or hereafter in force in this or any other jurisdiction, whether by way of her right of election to take against [Mr. Brown's] will, her share of the estate in intestacy, or otherwise.

2. Subject to the conditions specified in clause 3 below, the aforesaid sum of [$100,000] shall be paid, without interest, to [Miss Smith] by [Mr. Brown's] estate as follows:

(a) [$35,000] thereof within [thirty] days after the probate of [Mr. Brown's] will, but in no event later than [sixty] days after [Mr. Brown's] death;

(b) [$35,000] thereof within [six] months after [Mr. Brown's] death; and

(c) [$30,000] thereof within [twelve] months after [Mr. Brown's] death.

3. It is of the essence of this agreement that [Miss Smith] shall be entitled to receive, and shall receive, the aforesaid sum of [$100,000] if and only if (a) she survives [Mr. Brown], (b) the parties were living together as man and wife at the time of [Mr. Brown's] death, and (c) they were living together as such

continuously from the time of marriage to the date of [Mr. Brown's] death. If [Miss Smith] does not survive [Mr. Brown], or if the parties were not living together as man and wife at the time of [Mr. Brown's] death, or if they did not live together as such continuously from the time of marriage until the date of [Mr. Brown's] death, [Miss Smith] shall not be entitled to receive any sum whatsoever from [Mr. Brown's] estate; and in such event, her waiver and release of any and all rights and claims she may have had in [Mr. Brown's] estate, as more particularly set forth in clause 4 hereof, shall be of full force and effect and shall be conclusive and binding on her.

4. [Miss Smith] hereby waives and releases any and all rights and claims of every kind, nature and description that she may acquire as [Mr. Brown's] surviving spouse in his estate upon his death, including (but not by way of limitation) any and all rights in intestacy, and any and all rights of election to take against [Mr. Brown's] last will and testament under [here insert the title and section of the applicable statute], any law amendatory thereof or supplementary or similar thereto, and the same or similar law of any other jurisdiction. This provision is intended to and shall serve as a waiver and release of [Miss Smith's] right of election in accordance with the requirements of [here insert the title and section of the applicable statute].

5. [Miss Smith] acknowledges that she has certain property of her own. [Mr. Brown] hereby waives and releases any and all rights and claims of every kind, nature and description that he may acquire as [Miss Smith's] surviving spouse in her estate upon her death, including (but not by way of limitation) any and all rights in intestacy, and any and all rights of election to take against [Miss Smith's] last will and testament under [here insert the title and section of the applicable statute], any law amendatory thereof or supplementary or similar thereto, and the same or similar law of any other jurisdiction. This provision is intended to and shall serve as a waiver and release of [Mr. Brown's] right of election in accordance with any statutory requirement.

6. Each party shall during his or her lifetime keep and retain sole ownership, control and enjoyment of all property, real and personal, now owned or hereafter acquired by him or her, free and clear of any claim by the other.

7. The consideration for this agreement is the mutual promises and waivers herein contained and the marriage about to be solemnized. If the marriage does not take place, this agreement shall be in all respects and for all purposes null and void.

8. Each party shall, upon the other's request, take any and all steps and execute, acknowledge and deliver to the other party any and all further instruments necessary or expedient to effectuate the purpose and intent of this agreement.

9. [Miss Smith] hereby acknowledges that [Mr. Brown] has fully acquainted her with his means and resources; that he has informed her in detail that his net worth is in excess of [$500,000] and that he has a substantial income; that she has ascertained and weighed all the facts, conditions and circumstances likely to influence her judgment herein; that all matters embodied herein as well as all questions pertinent hereto have been fully and satisfactorily explained to her; that she has given due consideration to such matters and questions; that she clearly understands and consents to all the provisions hereof; that she has had the benefit of the advice of counsel of her own selection; and that she is entering into this agreement freely, voluntarily and with full knowledge.

10. This agreement contains the entire understanding of the parties. There are no representations, warranties, promises, covenants or undertakings, oral or otherwise, other than those expressly set forth herein.

11. This agreement shall enure to the benefit of and shall be binding upon the heirs, executors and administrators of the parties.

IN WITNESS WHEREOF, the parties hereto have hereunto set their hands and seals this .... day of ...., 19...

Witnessed by: ....(L.S.)
                                         [George Brown]

....(L.S.)
   [As to George Brown]   [Mary Smith]

....
   [As to Mary Smith]

[ACKNOWLEDGMENTS]

Conveyance Prior to Marriage; Payment of Money and Insurance Provision After Marriage; Mutual Waivers of Property and Estate Rights

THIS AGREEMENT made between [John Doe], residing at ......,........., City of ...., State of ...., and [Mary Roe], residing at ...., City of ...., State of ....,

WITNESSETH

The parties are about to contract marriage with each other. In anticipation thereof, they desire to fix and determine by contract the rights that will accrue to each in the property and estate of the other by reason of the marriage, and to accept the provisions of this agreement in lieu and in full discharge and satisfaction of all such rights.

Now, THEREFORE, in consideration of the foregoing, and of the promises and undertakings hereinafter set forth, the parties agree:

1. By deed executed, acknowledged and delivered simultaneously herewith, [John Doe] has granted and conveyed to [Mary Roe] the real property known and designated as ...., in the City of ...., State of ...., and more particularly described in the aforesaid deed.

2. Within [one] month after marriage is solemnized between the parties, [John Doe] shall:

(a) Pay to [Mary Roe] the sum of [$10,000];

(b) Effect insurance on his life in a sum not less than [$25,000], with [Mary Roe] as the beneficiary thereof; and

(c) Provide by last will and testament that if [Mary Roe] survives him as his widow, she shall receive the sum of not less than [$25,000] from his estate.

3. So long as [Mary Roe] remains his wife, [John Doe] shall not change the designation of beneficiary on the insurance above referred to. He shall keep the same in full force and effect during his lifetime, and shall duly pay all premiums and assessments in connection therewith.

4. In consideration of the foregoing provisions made and to be made by [John Doe] for her benefit, [Mary Roe] hereby waives, discharges and releases any right, title or interest whatsoever that she may acquire in the property or estate of [John Doe] at any time hereafter by reason of the marriage.

5. Similarly, [John Doe] hereby waives, discharges and releases any right, title or interest whatsoever that he may acquire in the property or estate of [Mary Roe] at any time hereafter by reason of the marriage.

6. Each party waives, discharges and releases any and all claims and rights that he or she may acquire by reason of the marriage:

(a) To share in the estate of the other party upon the latter's death, whether by way of dower, thirds, curtesy, widow's allowance, statutory allowance, or distribution in intestacy; and

(b) To elect to take against any last will and testament or codicil of the other party under [here insert the title and section of the applicable statute], any law amendatory thereof or supplementary or similar thereto, and the same or similar law of any other jurisdiction; and

(c) To act as executor or administrator of the other party's estate.

This provision shall serve as a mutual waiver of the right of election in accordance with any statutory requirement.

Nothing herein contained shall be deemed to constitute a waiver by either party of any bequest or legacy that may be left to him or her by any will or codicil of the other. However, the parties acknowledge that no representations or promises of any kind whatsoever have been made by either of them to the other with respect to any such bequest or legacy.

7. If [John Doe] fails duly to perform any of the terms of this agreement on his part to be performed, the waivers of [Mary Roe] under clauses 4 and 6 hereof shall be of no force and effect.

8. Except as herein provided, each party shall keep and retain sole ownership, control and enjoyment of all property, real and personal, now owned or hereafter acquired by him or her in any manner whatsoever.

9. Each party shall, upon the request of the other, execute, acknowledge and deliver any and all instruments appropriate or necessary to carry into effect the provisions of this agreement.

10. The consideration for this agreement is the mutual promises herein contained and the marriage about to be solemnized. If the marriage does not take place, this agreement shall in all respects be null and void, but [Mary Roe] shall not be obligated to re-convey to [John Doe] the property which he has conveyed to her simultaneously herewith.

IN WITNESS WHEREOF the parties have hereunto set their hands and seals this .... day of ...., 19..

Witnessed by: ....(L.S.)
                                        [John Doe]
....(L.S.)
[James Brown]   [Mary Roe]
as to [John Doe]

....
[Lucy Brown]
as to [Mary Roe]

How Do You Increase the Chances the Agreement Will Be Upheld?

Most prenuptial agreements are enforced by the courts when they are reasonable and when both parties honestly and fully disclosed their assets and net worth to each other *before* the agreement was signed. Years ago, judges in many states would refuse to enforce such agreements under the theory that such agreements encouraged divorce by providing inducements to end the marriage and allowing one spouse (typically the husband) to avoid the obligation to support the other after the divorce.

Today, however, courts in at least fourteen states are upholding prenuptial agreements that were fair and reasonable when made and are not unconscionable at the time of enforcement. However, an agreement is not worth the paper it is printed on if it cannot be enforced. Thus, if you wish to execute a valid prenuptial agreement, follow these strategies to increase the chances it will be deemed valid in your state:

1. *Be sure the agreement is in writing and is clearly drafted.* In most states prenuptial agreements will not be valid unless they are in writing.

2. *Use separate lawyers to draft and review the agreement.* It is very difficult to claim that the contract is not enforceable because it was signed under fraud, duress, or mistake when the party is represented by his or her own counsel. That is why each party should hire a separate lawyer to review the contract. Ethical problems also ensue when one lawyer is called upon to represent both parties (because it is difficult to adequately represent the competing interests of both). In fact, most authorities believe that a prenuptial agreement not negotiated by two lawyers is not likely to hold up in court.

3. *Exchange complete information concerning all your assets and net worth.* Under ordinary circumstances, parties in an antenuptial agreement do not deal at arm's length; they stand in a relationship of mutual confidence that calls for the exercise of good faith and sincerity in all matters based upon the agreement.

However, since the agreement must be fair and reasonable, a court will not enforce it if it gives one person a much better deal than the other. For example, where the future wife elects to waive her statuatory rights to her husband's estate, the court will carefully scrutinize whether the husband disclosed all material facts relating to the amount, character, and value of his property, so that the wife had sufficient knowledge on which to base her decision when signing such an agreement.

Thus it is best to include a description of all property and assets owned by each party in the agreement. (This description is usually attached as an addendum to the agreement.) This may eliminate the claim that one party lacked knowledge as to what composed the other's estate. Remember, the failure to spell out all of your assets and property may be a valid reason to overturn the agreement if its legitimacy is in dispute.

4. *Attach a signed acknowledgment for additional protection.* Courts carefully scrutinize prenuptial agreements before approving them, especially when the contract provides for the elimination of alimony upon divorce. One standard defense used to attack such agreements is that the contract is not valid because the wife will become a public charge, incapable of supporting herself.

This can be avoided by obtaining a signed acknowledgment similar to the following and including it in the agreement. Such a document may state, for example, that the wife is capable of supporting herself and that she was not forced into abandoning her career to enter the marriage.

Disclosure Clause to Be Incorporated in Ante-Nuptial Agreement*

[Helen Young] acknowledges that:

(a) She is fully acquainted with the business and resources of [Robert Elder];

*This form is taken from Alexander Lindey, *Separation Agreements and Antenuptial Contracts,* Matthew Bender & Co., New York, 1984.

(b) She understands that he is a person of substantial wealth;

(c) He has answered all the questions she has asked about his income and assets;

(d) She understands that by entering into this agreement she will receive, as his widow, substantially less than the amount she would otherwise be entitled to receive if he died intestate or if she elected to take against his last will and testament pursuant to statute;

(e) She has at all times received the advice of counsel of her own choosing;

(f) She has carefully weighed all the facts and circumstances, and desires to marry [Robert Elder] regardless of any financial arrangements made for her benefit; and

(g) She is entering into this agreement freely, voluntarily and with full knowledge.

5. *Include a provision for modifications in the event of changed circumstances.* One problem with antenuptial agreements is that a judge may decide that the agreement is not presently fair (although it was fair when signed) because of changed circumstances. Including a clause which permits a spouse to stop support in certain instances (for example, when the other dies, remarries, or wins a million dollars) or to accelerate or increase payments (for example, if the spouse sells his or her business for a large profit) may minimize this problem. *Discuss this with your lawyer if it seems applicable in your case.*

6. *Be aware that clauses pertaining to lifestyles may not be legally enforceable.* As a practical matter, many courts will not enforce provisions pertaining to "lifestyle" decisions (for instance, who will cook). Thus such provisions may carry only moral, rather than legal, weight. However, a discussion of such issues encourages candor and communication.

7. *Try to limit the agreement to a certain number of years if possible.* In a recent case in Indiana, a woman signed a prenuptial agreement that stated she would receive a lump sum of $5,000 in the event of a divorce. The parties were married for twelve years. At the time of the divorce, her husband was worth $3 million. The judge rejected the agreement on the grounds that it was "grossly unfair." However, if the agreement had stated that, for example, the wife would receive $5,000 if the couple was divorced within five years of their marriage, the husband would have stood a greater chance of having the agreement approved.

Final Tips on This Subject

Be aware that signing a prenuptial agreement carries a certain degree of risk. You won't actually know if the agreement is enforceable unless it is tested in court. Remember, prenuptial agreements are governed by state law and are subject to judicial modification and legal attack. Do not rely on the agreement as an absolutely foolproof method to protect your assets upon divorce; you may face an unpleasant surprise.

Remember, too, that in practice, prenuptial agreements are carefully scrutinized when the couple is divorced or when one of the spouses dies.

It is a good idea to check the agreement periodically to see if both spouses are living up to its terms. If you are both acting in a manner different from that specified in the agreement, it is a good idea to have a lawyer change the contract to reflect your present intentions. This will help reduce the chance that the agreement will be stricken upon divorce or death.

Finally, the strategies I have discussed here should never be applied unless and until you contact an experienced attorney. Prenuptial agreements are tricky instruments; preparing and signing them without consulting a lawyer may prove to be a tragic mistake.

Financial and Tax-Planning Tips to Consider before Marriage

Few individuals entering marriage for the first time usually give much thought to financial planning except where one or both parties has a considerable estate. However, every couple, regardless of their financial situation, and especially those entering a second marriage, should consider certain tax and financial implications. As you will see, you can coordinate your assets and estate and save money in a variety of ways. (See Chapter 10 for further tips on tax matters.)

1. **Wills.** Most individuals getting married do not have a will; upon their death, the laws of intestacy will govern the distribution of their estate. Usually, the laws of intestacy are consistent with a person's intent for distribution prior to his or her marriage—that is, that the closest relative, usually a surviving mother or father, will inherit all the decedent's assets. However, that intent is likely to change after marriage, and the manner of distribution under state law will no longer be consistent with such intent.

For example, a deceased spouse may have intended that the surviving spouse inherit all of his or her property. However, without a will, the surviving spouse may be entitled only to a one-half or one-third share, depending on the law of the particular state of the decedent's domicile. There must be a will to reflect the changed intent. Also, the use of a will can minimize federal and state estate taxes so the surviving spouse will inherit more assets.

In situations where one or both parties have made a prior will, a new will becomes necessary upon marriage, although some state laws provide that a subsequent marriage operates to revoke a will executed prior to the marriage. If you have any doubts about this, consult a lawyer for further information.

2. **Life insurance.** Upon marriage it is important that a couple reexamine their life insurance policies to establish the adequacy of existing coverage and to confirm the benefi-

ciaries. Such an examination may cause you to change or add contingent beneficiaries, as well as to reevaluate the amount of coverage.

3. *Employee benefits.* It is also wise to review the beneficiary designations under existing employee-benefit plans—pension, profit-sharing, stock bonus, thrift, and stock-option plans, and prior IRA and Keogh plans. It may be necessary to change the beneficiary currently covered under such plans. *Note*: If one or both of the parties are covered by a qualified corporate or Keogh retirement plan, the postmarital financial deduction may preclude voluntary employee contributions to such plans (and the resulting tax shelter of earnings on such contributions). Speak to a financial advisor about this if it is applicable in your case.

4. *Property ownership.* When a couple decides to marry and one or both own a piece of property as an individual, the couple must determine whether that property will be held individually or whether it will be held in some form of co-ownership after the marriage. Frequently, married couples transfer or own property as "tenants in the entirety" or "joint tenants."

You should also recognize that property acquired solely by one spouse before the marriage will probably be treated as separate property and will not be subject to distribution upon divorce. Thus questions such as the maintenance of separate or joint checking, savings, and stock-brokerage accounts should be considered and understood.

Final note: When property is changed from sole ownership to some form of co-ownership, estate and gift tax considerations may be involved. Speak to your lawyer, accountant, or financial advisor for more information if it seems necessary.

4 | Enlarging the Family: Adoption and the Law

- Introduction
- Adopting a Child
- Adopting an Adult
- Agency Adoptions
- Private Adoptions
- The Legal Implications of Adoption
- Specialized Adoptions
  Mixed Adoptions
  International Adoptions
  Special-Needs Adoptions
- For Further Information . . .

Introduction

Adoption is the process whereby one or more persons enter into a legal parental relationship with another. The practice dates back to the beginning of civilization; the adoption process was regulated by the ancient Greeks, Egyptians, and Romans. Back then, the main purpose of adoption was to permit the family name to continue into subsequent generations when it was biologically impossible (perhaps because of infertility).

Early U.S. adoption laws were based on Roman law since English common law, from which most American law is derived, had no provisions governing adoption. However, while Roman adoption laws focused on the interests of the adoptive parents to perpetuate the family name, early U.S. laws were characterized by their focus on the needs of the adoptee (usually a child).

Adoption was originally considered a private matter in this country. In the mid-1800s, many American cities had large numbers of orphans living in squalid conditions, roaming the streets, and committing crimes. These children were often set to work for low wages since there was no prohibition against child labor. When Massachusetts enacted the first American adoption statute in 1851, the problem of orphaned and unwanted children became recognized by legislators.

Current American adoption laws and procedures have undergone great changes to accommodate the needs of *all* the parties involved—that is, the adopting parents, the natural parents, the child or other adopted person, private investigators, lawyers, and judges. However, the process of adoption has retained many of the earlier characteristics. These include:

- Consent of the natural parent(s), guardians, or older children to the adoption

- A home study by an adoption agency to review the suitability of the prospective adopting family

- Supervision of the adopting family for a trial period to determine competency

- Review of the petition for adoption and issuance of the final adoption decree by an appropriate court
- Sealing an adoptee's birth records to maintain secrecy about the identity of his or her natural parents

Each of these factors has been intensely debated in and out of the courtroom. As more and more couples vie for fewer available babies, adoption laws remain in a state of flux. One particular volatile issue concerns the growing practice of independent adoptions arranged by lawyers or "baby brokers" (as opposed to adoptions conducted through public and private agencies), some of whom have been accused of charging prohibitive fees, even selling babies.

Other issues of major concern include:

- The right of the natural father, particularly an unmarried father, to give or withhold consent in an adoption
- Attempts by adoptees to discover the identities of their natural parents
- Attempts by natural parents to revoke consent and reclaim their children
- Attempts by adopting parents to abrogate their parental duties
- Changing criteria as to the fitness of the potential adopting parent(s)—marital status, race, religion, etc.
- The problem of "special-needs" children—that is, minority and handicapped children, who often go unwanted
- The role of lawyers and other professionals in the adoption process and the question of fees

The adoption process can be complicated, but it doesn't have to be aggravating. Experts estimate that more than 100,000 adoptions occur in the United States each year. Obviously the more you know about your rights and obligations, the greater the likelihood that adoption will be a successful and rewarding experience.

This chapter will provide you with information on how to obtain an adoption *properly*. The following strategies can minimize many of the legal and administrative problems that often frustrate the adoption effort. If you are seeking to adopt a child, you will learn, for example, how to protect yourself from a natural parent who may one day seek to reclaim the child. You will also learn how to reduce the risk of dealing with an unscrupulous lawyer or baby broker.

The rights of unmarried fathers, homosexuals, grandparents, and adoptees seeking to unseal their records will also be discussed.

Adopting a Child

1. *Learn about the process of adoption.* In order to adopt a child, you must be intimately familiar with how the law works in your state. This can be accomplished by talking to other adoptive parents who can provide information about procedural requirements as well as personal insights about their own experiences. Many adoptive parents belong to self-help and outreach groups. Information about these groups can be obtained through a local religious organization or by con- · tacting:

OURS, Inc.
20140 Pine Ridge Drive
Anoka, MN 55303

2. *Contact an adoption agency.* Once you have decided to adopt a child, you should contact an adoption agency. There are basically two types of adoption agencies: (1) public agencies run by state and local governments and (2) private agencies administered by religious, charitable, and other community organizations. Information about both public and private agencies is available through your local department of social services or the welfare department in your state.

The following is a list of the welfare departments in the fifty states, District of Columbia, and Puerto Rico:

Alabama

State Department of Pensions
and Security
64 North Union
Montgomery, AL 36104

Alaska

State Department of Health
and Welfare
Pouch H
Juneau, AK 99801

Arizona

Department of Public Welfare
State Office Building
Phoenix, AZ 85007

Arkansas

State Department of Public
Welfare
Welfare and Employment Secu-
rity Building
State Capitol Mall, Box 1437
Little Rock, AR 72201

California

State Department of Social
Welfare
2415 First Avenue
Sacramento, CA 95818

Colorado

State Department of Public
Welfare
1600 Sherman Street
Denver, CO 80203

Connecticut

State Welfare Department
State Office Building
Hartford, CT 06115

Delaware

Department of Public Welfare
Wilmington, DE 19899

District of Columbia

Department of Public Welfare
499 Pennsylvania Avenue,
N.W.
Washington, DC 20001

Florida

State Department of Public
Welfare
Jacksonville, FL 32203

Georgia

State Department of Family
and Children Services
State Office Building
Capitol Square
Atlanta, GA 30334

Hawaii

Department of Social Services
Honolulu, HI 96809

Idaho

Idaho Department of Public Assistance
Boise, ID 83701

Illinois

Illinois Department of Public
Aid
400 South Spring Street
Springfield, IL 62706

Indiana

State Department of Public
Welfare
100 North Senate Avenue
Indianapolis, IN 46204

Iowa

State Department of Social
Welfare
State Office Building
Des Moines, IA 50319

Kansas
State Department of Social
Welfare
State Office Building
Topeka, KS 66612

Kentucky
Department of Economic Security
Capitol Annex Office Building
Frankfort, KY 40601

Louisiana
Louisiana Department of Public
Welfare
Baton Rouge, LA 70804

Maine
Department of Health and Welfare
State House
Augusta, ME 04330

Maryland
State Department of Public
Welfare
1315 St. Paul Street
Baltimore, MD 21202

Massachusetts
Massachusetts Department of
Public Welfare
600 Washington Street
Boston, MA 02111

Michigan
Department of Social Services
Lewis Cass Building
Lansing, MI 48913

Minnesota
Department of Public Welfare
Centennial Office Building
St. Paul, MN 55101

Mississippi
Department of Public Welfare
Jackson, MS 39216

Missouri
State Department of Public
Health and Welfare
Jefferson City, MO 65101

Montana
State Department of Public
Welfare
Helena, MT 59620

Nebraska
Department of Public Welfare
Lincoln, NE 68509

Nevada
State Department of Health,
Welfare and Rehabilitation
State Welfare Division
210 South Fall Street
Carson City, NV 89701

New Hampshire
Department of Health and Welfare
State House Annex
Concord, NH 03301

New Jersey
State Department of Institutions and Agencies
Trenton, NJ 08625

New Mexico
Department of Public Welfare
Santa Fe, NM 87501

New York
New York State Department of
Social Services
112 State Street
Albany, NY 12201

North Carolina
State Department of Public
   Welfare
Raleigh, NC 27602

North Dakota
Public Welfare Board
Capitol Building
Bismarck, ND 58501

Ohio
State Department of Public
   Welfare
408 East Town Street
Columbus, OH 43215

Oklahoma
State Department of Public
   Welfare
Oklahoma City, OK 73105

Oregon
State Welfare Commission
422 Public Service Building
Salem, OR 97310

Pennsylvania
Department of Public Welfare
Harrisburg, PA 17120

Puerto Rico
Department of Health
Ponce de Leon Avenue
Santurce, PR 00908

Rhode Island
State Department of Social
   Welfare
1 Washington Avenue
Providence, RI 02905

South Carolina
State Department of Public
   Welfare
Columbia, SC 29202

South Dakota
Department of Public Welfare
Pierre, SD 57501

Tennessee
State Department of Public
   Welfare
410 State Office Building
Nashville, TN 37219

Texas
State Department of Public
   Welfare
John H. Reagan Building
Austin, TX 78701

Utah
Department of Health and
   Welfare
223 State Capitol Building
Salt Lake City, UT 84114

Vermont
Department of Social Welfare
Montpelier, VT 05602

Virginia
State Department of Welfare
   and Institutions
429 South Belvidere Street
Richmond, VA 23220

Washington
State Department of Public
   Assistance
Olympia, WA 98501

West Virginia
Department of Welfare
State Office Building No. 3
1800 Washington Street
Charleston, WV 25305

Wisconsin
State Department of Public
Welfare
State Office Building
Madison, WI 53702

Wyoming
State Department of Public
Welfare
State Office Building
Cheyenne, WY 82001

Have a clear understanding of what you want from the prospective adoption *before* dealing with an agency. Be open with agency representatives about the kind of child you are seeking and the kind of adopting parent you want to be. Be sure to get answers to questions about eligibility standards and other legal requirements. Such questions should include:

- How long must I wait before I receive a child?
- What process will I go through in order to become an adopting parent?
- Can I lose the child?
- How much will it cost in placement fees and expenses?
- What legal steps are required in order to make the adoption final?

The adoption agency you visit can provide you with much information and assistance. However, contact a lawyer with experience in handling adoptions if you want a realistic evaluation about your chances and options. You may wish to do this before going to an agency—particularly if adoption laws in your state are in a state of flux. Your lawyer can advise you about pending changes in the law and assist you in preparing the various petitions, affidavits, and other documents that are required to be filed in court to consummate the adoption. Your local bar association or legal referral service can assist you in locating an attorney with expertise in these matters. (*Note:* For further details on how to hire and work effectively with a lawyer, consult Chapter 1.)

3. *Know the Eligibility Requirements.* Any adult can generally become an adopting parent, but many states impose additional age requirements. Some judges are reluctant to grant adoptions to grandparents for reasons of age. However, such decisions are undergoing tremendous scrutiny by appeals courts, particularly where circumstances dictate that it is in the best interests of the child to remain with his or her grandparents rather than live with a stranger.

Table 4-1 is a current state-by-state listing of age requirements for prospective adopting parents. Legislation is changing rapidly in this area, however, so be sure to consult a lawyer or agency officer for further details on eligibility requirements in your state.

Residency requirements as well as age requirements can affect your eligibility as an adoptive parent. You will probably not encounter residency-requirement problems if you wish to adopt a child living in your state. If the child lives in another state, you must either bring the child to your state or institute adoption proceedings in the state where the child resides. The decision will depend upon the circumstances of your case and applicable state law.

While it may be cheaper to commence adoption proceedings in your own state and easier for the court to evaluate your qualifications for the adoption, other problems may arise. For example, if the child resides in a temporary foster home in another state, you would have to obtain consent from the person or organization having legal custody of the child before bringing him or her into your state. In addition, most states require you to obtain permission from the state welfare department before "importing" the child for adoption.

If there are problems bringing the child into your state for the adoption, your only option may be to proceed in the state where the child resides. Be aware, however, that many states have residency requirements for adopting parents. This means that you would have to reside in that state for a minimum length of time before being allowed to adopt the child.

Table 4-2 indicates those states which currently impose residency requirements for adopting parents and those which do not. *Note:* Many of these statutes are being challenged on the basis of their constitutionality. Be sure to consult with a lawyer or appropriate agency official before taking action.

Table 4-1
Age Requirements for Adoptive Parent

State	Basic Requirement	Additional Age Requirement
Alabama	Any proper adult	
Alaska	Any person	
Arizona	Any adult	Must be 10 years older than adoptee
Arkansas	Any person of lawful age	
California	Any adult	Must be 10 years older than adoptee
Colorado	Any person	Must be 21 or older
Connecticut	Any person	Must be 18 or older
Delaware	Any resident	Must be 21 or older (unless married)
District of Columbia	Any person	
Florida	Any adult	
Georgia	Any married adult resident	Must be 25 or older if unmarried and must be 10 years older than adoptee
Hawaii	Any proper adult person	
Idaho	Any adult	Must be 15 years older than adoptee (unless married to biological parent of adoptee)
Illinois	Any person of lawful age	With court permission and under special circumstances, minors may adopt
Indiana	Any resident	
Iowa	Any person of lawful age	Married minors may adopt
Kansas	Any adult	
Kentucky	Any adult resident	
Louisiana	Any person	
Maine	Any person	
Maryland	Any person	Must be 21 or older
Massachusetts	Any person of lawful age	
Michigan	Any person	

Table 4-1 (*Continued*)

State	Basic Requirement	Additional Age Requirement
Minnesota	Any resident	
Mississippi	Any adult	
Missouri	Any person	
Montana	Any married couple, jointly, or unmarried parent of illegitimate child	Must be 21 or older, if single or legally separated, and must be 10 years older than adoptee (if adoptee is an adult)
Nebraska	Any adult	
Nevada	Any married couple or adult	Must be 10 years older than adoptee
New Hampshire	Any person	Must be an adult if adoptee is an adult
New Jersey	Any adult citizen	Must be 10 years older than adoptee (15, if adoptee is adult)
New Mexico	Any resident or nonresident relative	Must be 20 years older than adoptee if adoptee is an adult
New York	Any adult	Minor may adopt child of spouse
North Carolina	Any married couple or adult	
North Dakota	Any adult	Must be 10 years older than adoptee
Ohio	Any person	
Oklahoma	Any married couple, jointly, or married parent of illegitimate child	Must be 21 or older if single or legally separated
Oregon	Any person	
Pennsylvania	Any adult	
Puerto Rico	Any person	Must be 21 or older, and must be 16 years older than adoptee
Rhode Island	Any person	Must be older than adoptee

(*continued*)

Table 4-1 (*Continued*)

State	Basic Requirement	Additional Age Requirement
South Carolina	Any married couple, jointly; stepparent; single person of lawful age; legally separated person of lawful age; unmarried parent of illegitimate child	Must be an adult in order to adopt another adult
South Dakota	Any adult	Must be 10 years older than adoptee
Tennessee	Any U.S. citizen	Must be 21 or older
Texas	Any adult	
Utah	Any adult	Must be 10 years older than adoptee
Vermont	Any person of lawful age	
Virginia	Any person	
Washington	Any person	
West Virginia	Any person	Must be 15 years older than adoptee (unless adoptee is a stepchild)
Wisconsin	Any resident married couple or adult	
Wyoming	Any resident married couple, or stepparent	Must be 21 or older

Adopting an Adult

Usually, a married couple or single person will establish a parental relationship with a minor. However, adoption is *not* limited to children. A majority of states provide for the adoption of adults as well as minors. There are only seven states currently prohibiting this: Alabama, Arizona, Hawaii, Michigan, Nebraska, North Carolina, and Ohio.

The practice of adult adoption involves some interesting

Table 4-2
Residency Requirement for Adoptive Parent

Residency Requirement	No Residency Requirement
Arizona	Alabama
California	Alaska
Delaware	Arkansas
District of Columbia	Colorado
Florida	Connecticut
Georgia	Hawaii
Idaho	Iowa
Illinois	Kansas
Indiana	Louisiana
Kentucky	Maine
Michigan	Maryland
Minnesota	Massachusetts
Mississippi	Missouri
Montana	New Jersey
Nebraska	New York
Nevada	Ohio
New Hampshire	Oregon
New Mexico	Pennsylvania
North Carolina	South Carolina
North Dakota	South Dakota
Oklahoma	Vermont
Puerto Rico	Washington
Rhode Island	
Tennessee	
Texas	
Utah	
Virginia	
West Virginia	
Wisconsin	
Wyoming	

variations from the typical child adoption. In 1927 one Kentucky man was allowed to adopt his mistress. A recent New York case in which a 32-year-old man sought to adopt his 43-year-old male lover attracted national media attention. At the trial, the lovers told the court that they wished to "formalize themselves as a family unit for purposes of publicly acknowledging their emotional bond." The men also said they sought the adoption because their East Side New York City apartment building was going co-op and the landlord had been evicting tenants with minor lease violations. (The lease contained a clause restricting occupancy to immediate family members.) The New York Court of Appeals ruled in their favor. The court stated that adoption of an adult by an adult in New York is permissible when the parties' primary intent is neither insincere nor fraudulent. Here, the New York court determined that the couple had profound feelings of love and responsibility for each other.

Whether such an arrangement is permissible in your state depends upon the wording of the adoption statute and the manner in which the statute has been interpreted by the courts. Speak to an attorney for further details.

Agency Adoptions

Adoption agencies require you to undergo a "home study" to determine whether you meet predetermined standards of suitability. Assuming you qualify, you will then be shown files containing information on available children. Once you select a child, he or she may be placed in your home under your care and the agency's supervision. You will then be ready to commence adoption proceedings with the aid of a lawyer.

1. *File an adoption petition.* The adoption proceeding is instituted by filing a petition with the appropriate court. Adoption proceedings are conducted in either probate, superior, chancery, family, district, or county court, depending on where you live.

The petition must contain certain facts in order to be accepted for filing by the court. These include information about the natural parents, the adopting parents, the adoption agency, and the adoptee (the person being adopted).

The following is a sample of the adoption petition used in New York. Note that the form and content of the petition will vary from state to state and will depend on the facts of the case.

Sample Petition to Adopt

In the Matter of the Adoption by [Name of parents] of a minor having the first name of _____ whose last name is contained in the schedule annexed to the Petition herein.

To the Surrogate of the County of _____:

The petition of [Name of parents] respectfully shows:

1. That your petitioners are of full age, married and living together as husband and wife, citizens of the United States of America and reside at [Address].

2. That [Name of adoptee] has resided with and has been in the care and custody of your petitioners since [Date], and until the filing of this petition; that said infant was placed with your petitioners by [Name of agency], an authorized adoption agency, so that [Name of adoptee] would reside and might have a good home and become the adopted child of the petitioners.

3. That _____, the mother of said infant is dead and that _____, her late husband and the father of the said infant, has married again and lives with his wife and two other children at _____ Street, City of _____, County of _____, State of New York.

4. That your petitioners are informed and verily believe that the said father of said infant is without sufficient pecuniary means to pay for the support and provide a proper home for said infant; that your petitioners have become greatly attached to said infant since the said infant has resided with your petitioners. That about one year ago the little girl of petitioners, named _____, died and little _____, the infant herein, has come into their hearts and home to take the place of their deceased child, _____, and petitioners are desirous of adopting and treating said infant, _____, as their own child and are able and willing to provide for her proper support and education during her minority and to provide a proper home for her.

5. That the said _____ has had a position for above five years past with the _____ company; that petitioners have an income of about

$_____ per year; that they can and will provide a good home for said infant; that petitioners, father and said infant are of the _____ faith.

6. That the said infant was born in _____ on or about the _____ day of _____, 19__, that she has no income or property, now or in expectancy, and has no guardian of her person or property; that there is no other person other than those hereinbefore mentioned in this proceeding who are interested in this proceeding or in said infant, and that no previous application has been made for this order now and hereby sought.

7. That no previous application has been made for the adoption of said minor.

8. That, on information and belief, there will be annexed to this petition a schedule verified by a duly constituted official of an authorized adoption agency as required by Domestic Relations Law §112, Subd. 3.

WHEREFORE, your petitioners pray that the Surrogate of the County of _____ will entertain the proceeding for the adoption of said child by your petitioners as prescribed by state law, and after said proceedings, that an order may be granted, filed and recorded in accordance with such law, allowing and confirming said adoption and directing that the said child, _____, shall henceforth be regarded and treated in all respects as your petitioners' own lawful child with the name of _____ and with all the rights and privileges conferred by law; and your petitioners pray for such other relief as to this court may seen just and proper in the premises.

Dated: _____, the _____ day of _____, 19__

_____
Petitioner

The court will also require a verification in addition to the petition. A verification is a statement signed by you under oath which confirms your identity and the facts contained in the petition. In many states you will also be required to present a copy of the adoption agreement that has been executed with the adoption agency.

A typical adoption agreement may look like this:

Sample Adoption Agreement
[Caption]

AGREEMENT, made this _____ day of _____, 19__ by and between _____ and _____, his wife, parties of the first part, hereinafter called the adoptive parents, and the _____, a charitable corporation duly organized under the laws of the State of New York, and having its principal office at _____ Street in the City of _____, County of _____, and State of New York, party of the second part;

WITNESSETH

WHEREAS, the undersigned institution was informed by the department of public welfare of the City of _____ that [First name], a minor child, was born on _____, 19__, at _____, and was abandoned by its father prior to its birth; and that its mother being unable to take care of it, it was committed to the department of public welfare of the City of _____ on _____, 19__; and

WHEREAS, the said _____, on or about the _____ day of _____,19__, was placed with said _____, a charitable corporation and an authorized agency, by said department of public welfare for the City of _____, for placement with adoptive parents for adoption, and said institution thus came into lawful custody of said _____; and

WHEREAS, said child was by said institution placed with said _____ and _____ on _____, 19__; and

WHEREAS, said department of public welfare of the City of _____ has informed said institution that the mother of said child was of the _____ religious faith; and

WHEREAS, said child is by reason of the religious faith of her mother, of the _____ religious faith, and the said _____ and _____ are also of said faith; and

WHEREAS, said _____ and _____ desire to adopt said child pursuant to the provisions of the Domestic Relations Law, and agree to treat said child as their own lawful child, and to extend to such child all the benefits, privileges and rights contemplated by such statute; and

WHEREAS, said party of the second part approves of and consents to the said contemplated adoption of said child;

NOW, in consideration of the premises, the said parties hereby mutually covenant, agree and consent as follows:

FIRST. They, the said adoptive parents, hereby covenant and agree to adopt and treat the said _____ as their own lawful child and rear it in the _____ religious faith, and further agree that the adoptive parents and said child shall sustain toward each other the legal relation of parents and child, and that they shall severally have all the rights and be subject to all the duties of such legal relation.

SECOND. That the party of the second part hereby consents to said adoption.

THIRD. The parties hereto agree that the name of said child shall be changed to and said child shall hereafter be known by the name of _____.

IN WITNESS WHEREOF, _____ and _____, his wife, the parties of the first part, have severally set their hands and seals, and the _____, the party of the second part, has caused this instrument to be signed and sealed in its corporate name by _____, duly authorized in writing by its directors to sign the corporate name thereof, and its seal was thereunto affixed by like order and authority, the day and the year first above written.

In the presence of _____   [*Signatures*]

[*Verifications and acknowledgements*]   [*Indorsement*]

2. *Obtain all necessary consents.* One of the most important phases of an adoption involves obtaining the consent of the various parties connected with the adoption. Those parties are:

- The natural parent(s), unless parental rights have been terminated because of abuse, neglect, incompetence, or some other reason
- The child, if old enough under state law, or the adult adoptee
- The child's guardian or next of kin or the adoption

agency having legal custody of the child, if there are no natural parents

Specific requirements as to content and form of the consent vary from state to state. However, it is crucial that you or your lawyer knows or fully investigates these requirements in your state. Since you obviously do not want to receive a surprise in the form of a notice from the adoption agency that the child's natural mother (or parents) has revoked consent for the prospective adoption, you must take proper steps for your own protection. *The failure to obtain the proper consents (in the proper manner) can hinder your efforts to consummate the adoption.*

Be sure the agency verifies that all laws were complied with in transferring the child from its natural parents to the adoption agency. In addition, seek assurances that there was no fraud, duress, or undue influence behind the execution of the instrument of surrender negotiated between the natural parent(s) and the agency.

The right of natural parents to revoke consent of an adoption varies from state to state. In some states, the natural parent has an absolute right to revoke consent prior to a final adoption decree by the court. In other states, a parent's surrender of a child is deemed irrevocable unless there was fraud or duress. Most states employ a "discretionary rule" which puts the parent's right of revocation at the court's discretion. Under such a rule, the court looks at the particular facts and circumstances of each case to decide whether approval of the natural parent's revocation of consent would be in the *best interests of the child.* This is because the child's welfare, rather than the rights of the natural parent(s) to care for the child, is the primary consideration of the court. In some cases, even if the natural parent *is* found to be fit to care for the child, the court will not take the child away from prospective adopting parents who have been caring for the child for a sufficiently long period (for example, two years or more).

Thus, if your state has adopted the discretionary rule, you may not automatically lose custody of a child you wish to adopt simply because a natural parent wants to revoke consent. A judge may be cognizant of the fact that the natural parent's unfitness, unwillingness, or inability to care for the child was the reason the child was placed for adoption in the first place; the natural parent has the burden of demonstrating that a revocation of consent is warranted.

In one recent case, for example, a family-court judge refused to undo the adoption of a 9-year-old boy by his grandparents on the complaint of his natural mother that she was defrauded of custody of her son. The mother told the court that she had agreed to the adoption by her parents because her estranged husband had threatened that he would take their son and remove him to another state. The judge observed that the child was happily adjusted with his grandparents (with whom he had been living for three years). Furthermore, the court ruled that the natural mother had voluntarily agreed to give up the child several years before. Thus, she did not meet the burden of proving that fraud, coercion, or duress existed at the time the adoption was consummated. The judge read the sealed transcripts of the original adoption proceeding. He noted that careful steps had been taken by the preceding judge to make sure there was no sham concerning the adoption. This had included appointing a law guardian for the natural parents so that "any attempt by the petitioner (natural mother) to claim she did not understand the nature of the proceeding or the permanency of the result that would follow" would not succeed.

Consider the rights of the unwed natural father. The Supreme Court has recently ruled that unwed fathers have the right to withhold their consent to the adoption of their illegitimate children. Under prior law in many jurisdictions only the consent of the natural mother was required for the adoption. However, numerous court decisions now mandate that the natural father receive notice of an impending adoption so that he can come forward and have his say.

This is important and should not be overlooked. If the natural father has been given notice of the impending proceeding, but fails to come forward, the natural mother's consent alone will suffice.

To protect yourself in this area, inquire whether the natural father was given notice of the impending adoption. Request that the adoption agency show you copies of a certified letter, telegram, or other document sent to the father's last known address.

While an adoption agency must use every means to obtain the consent of the natural father, failure to locate and serve him with such notice will not cause the adoption to be revoked, provided the agency acted in *good faith* (for example, known friends and relatives of the father were interviewed, and conscientious attempts were made to contact him at his last known address).

3. *Be prepared to submit to a court-ordered investigation.* Every state requires an official investigation of the adopting parents before approving a final order of adoption. This is required even if an adoption agency has conducted its own home study.

Typically, the court will order such investigation after receiving the petition for adoption, agreement for adoption, and various consents. The purpose of the investigation is to verify the truth and accuracy of the allegations contained in the petition. In addition, the court is interested in discovering:

- The physical and mental health of the adopting parents and adopted child
- The marital and family history of the adopting parents and the adopted child
- The income and property owned by the adopting parents (to establish the financial ability of the adopting parents to care for the child)
- Whether either adopting parent has ever been abusive to or neglectful of the child
- Other pertinent information concerning any social, religious, economic, or emotional problems of the adopting parents

A written report which details the findings of the investigation is then submitted to the court. Recommendations regarding the fitness of the adopting parents are also given. The court then conducts a hearing; the judge evaluates the investigative report and confers with the adopting parents (and child, if he or she is old enough). Judges sometimes hear testimony from witnesses confirming favorable reports or substantiating why the adoption should *not* be allowed to take place.

4. *Obtain an order of adoption.* If the report is favorable and the court is satisfied with the suitability of the adopting parents, an adoption order is then issued. Depending on the state, the order can be final or it can be temporary, subject to a future review. Table 4-3 indicates which states issue final decrees and which issue temporary decrees subject to final court approval.

With the temporary decree, the court can exercise the option of annulling the adoption if the arrangement doesn't work out. However, once a *final* order is issued, the adoption cannot be undone, except under unusually serious circumstances (for example, a breakdown in the adoptive parents' ability to care for the child).

The order of adoption looks somewhat like the form given here (again, the form may vary in your state):

Sample Order of Adoption*

[Caption]

The petition of _____ and _____, husband and wife (and of _____, the [person] [minor] proposed to be adopted, who is over eighteen years of age, verified the _____ day of _____, 19__, having been duly presented to this Court, together with an agreement on the part of the proposed foster parents to treat _____, the proposed foster child as their own lawful child, and the consents required by Section 111 of the Domestic Relations Law [except the consent of _____ (which is not required by reason of _____) [which is dispensed with by this Court)], [and the affidavit required by Section 115(6) of the Domestic Relations Law]; and

Notice of this proposed adoption having been duly given to the persons and in the manner directed by Order of this Court dated

*This sample form is taken from *Bender's Forms for Civil Practice,* Matthew Bender & Co., New York.

Table 4-3
Decrees Issued by Respective State Courts

Giving Final Decrees*	Giving Temporary Decrees†
Alaska	Alabama
California	Arizona
Delaware	Arkansas
Florida	Colorado
Georgia	Connecticut
Hawaii	District of Columbia
Idaho	Illinois
Indiana	Louisiana
Iowa	Maryland
Kansas	Michigan
Kentucky	Mississippi
Maine	Montana
Massachusetts	New Hampshire
Minnesota	North Carolina
Missouri	Ohio
Nebraska	Oklahoma
Nevada	Puerto Rico
New Jersey‡	South Carolina
New Mexico	Tennessee
New York	Virginia
North Dakota	Washington
Oregon	Wyoming
Pennsylvania	
Rhode Island	
South Dakota	
Texas	
Utah	
Vermont	
West Virginia	
Wisconsin	

*Some states may have a trial-period requirement in conjunction with the granting of the final decree.
†In some states, granting of the temporary decree is followed by an additional trial-period requirement.
‡The decree is final only with an agency-arranged adoption.

_____, 19___; and the aforesaid petitioners and the said proposed foster child and all the persons whose consents are required as aforesaid having personally appeared before his Court for examination (except _____whose appearance is dispensed with for good cause shown, to wit, _____); and

The aforesaid petition having been verified, agreement and consents having been acknowledged, and the proof having been given by the respective persons before this Court except the _____which was duly (verified) (acknowledged) (proved) and certified in accordance with the requirements of the Domestic Relations Law; and

An investigation into the allegations set forth in the said petition and to ascertain such other facts relating to the said proposed foster child and the proposed foster parents as would give an adequate basis for determining the propriety of approving the adoption having been made by _____ specifically designated by this Court by Order dated _____, 19___, to make such investigation, and the said _____ having made such investigation and having filed and submitted a written report thereof, dated _____, 19___; and

This Court being satisfied that the moral and temporal interests of the proposed foster child will be promoted by the adoption and that there is no reasonable objection to the proposed change of the name of the proposed foster child;

Now, and upon all the papers and proceedings herein; it is

ORDERED, ADJUDGED AND DECREED, that the adoption of _____ by _____ and _____, his wife, be and the same hereby is allowed and approved; and it is further

ORDERED, ADJUDGED AND DECREED, that the said foster child shall henceforth be regarded and treated in all respects as the lawful child of the said foster parents; and it is further

ORDERED, ADJUDGED AND DECREED, that the name of the said foster child be and the same hereby is changed to _____ and that the said foster child hereafter be known by that name; and it is further

ORDERED, ADJUDGED AND DECREED, that this Order be filed and recorded in the office of the _____ of the County of _____ in a book which shall be kept under seal in accordance with the provisions of the Domestic Relations Law and that the written report of investigation, together with all other papers pertaining to the adoption, shall be kept by the undersigned as a permanent record of this Court and such papers shall be sealed and withheld from inspection and no person shall be allowed access thereto except upon an order of a Judge of this Court or a Justice of the Supreme Court granted upon due notice to the foster parents on good cause shown; and it is further

ORDERED, ADJUDGED AND DECREED, that upon the filing and recording of this Order as aforesaid the _____ of the County of _____ be and he is hereby authorized and directed to prepare, certify and deliver to the petitioners herein or to _____, Esq., the attorney(s) for said petitioners, upon payment of the usual fee therefor _____ copy(ies) of this Order of Adoption.

Enter,

_____

[*Signature of judge*]

Private Adoptions

Many states allow people to adopt without the assistance of an adoption agency. (*Note:* Only Delaware, Georgia, Massachusetts, and the District of Columbia prohibit private adoption.) Be aware, however, that abuses are common. In addition, private adoptions are subject to strict legal scrutiny with respect to the circumstances of each particular case and the amount of fees that can be charged (by the natural parents, surrogate mothers, and attorneys).

If you wish to adopt a member of your extended family (for example, a cousin), some states allow the natural mother to place the child directly with you. You then need only to obtain the natural parents' consent and a petition for adoption, plus anything else required under the law in your state, to present to the court for final approval. However, most states require you to seek the adoption through a third party (that is, a lawyer or a medical professional). Many people inquire about available children through lawyers specializing in adoption; some use word of mouth; some even place ads in newspapers.

Private adoption is gaining popularity. The principal reasons seem to be that adoption agencies have long waiting lists of prospective adopting parents and they do not have the kinds of children most people desire (healthy white babies). Adoption agencies have often been criticized for being mainly interested in placing unwanted and hard-to-adopt children.

However, the process of private adoption does have its drawbacks. For example, the process raises serious questions about possible profiteering and other forms of impropriety by the people arranging the adoptions. If you are seeking to adopt privately, be sure to comply with all state and federal laws governing adoptions.

In many states, an attorney specializing in private adoption placement must be registered with the state as an adoption agency and must provide the same counseling services for prospective adopting parents that a regular adoption agency provides. Moreover, beyond the cost of payments needed to consummate the adoption, that attorney is *prohibited* from accepting a fee for placing a child. Legitimate costs might include the following:

- The cost of placing an ad in a newspaper to publicize your interest in seeking to adopt
- Reasonable legal fees for advice and services, for example, drafting required documents and representing you in court
- Reimbursement for filing fees and incidental court costs
- The natural mother's medical costs, if a prenatal adoption agreement was made with her

The failure to comply with such legal requirements can lead to the nullification of the adoption. In addition, criminal sanctions can be imposed where evidence of direct payment for the child is shown. Some natural mothers have been able to revoke consent by claiming that they were not properly counseled.

Thus you must take all necessary precautions in private adoptions to ensure that the natural mother of the child you are seeking to adopt has placed the child willingly after careful consideration of her needs and desires. You should also be sure that the child's natural father has, at minimum, been given legally adequate notice of the plans to put the child up for adoption (to avoid a challenge on the grounds of due process). Most important, be sure you have not overpaid for the adoption and that none of the money was used to "purchase" the child.

Your state or county department of social services can give you a good idea of "reasonable" expenses for a private adoption. In many states, the adopting parents and their attorney must present sworn affidavits to the court describing all fees, compensation, and other remuneration given and received in connection with the private adoption. This is why it is important to be sure that expenses are neither unreasonable nor improper.

Although many private adoptions fail because legal requirements are not followed, there is no reason why the process cannot be successfully accomplished. If you are aware of the requirements regarding counseling for the natural parents, consents, and fees, and comply with these rules, your chances of obtaining a child properly and legally will increase greatly.

The Legal Implications of Adoption

There are a variety of legal implications for you as the adopting parent and for the adoptee. The following are some of the important rights and obligations that arise with a consummated adoption.

1. *Change of name.* You may wish to have the adoptee's surname changed to that of your own to make the child "part of the family." This is a universal practice among adopting parents and is easy to do. Simply request that the change be made a part of the final adoption decree. (*Note:* This request should appear in the petition for adoption that is filed with the court.)

2. *Inheritance.* Under most circumstances, the child you adopt becomes your legal heir. State law varies as to what may and may not be inherited by and from an adopted person.

Some states restrict certain inheritance rights to biological heirs; others do not. Also, some states bar adoptive parents from inheriting, sharing, or receiving property inherited by the adoptee from his or her natural parents. Consult a lawyer for specific advice on this subject.

3. **The "sealed-records" controversy.** Most state adoption statutes provide for the sealing of all records pertaining to an adoption, including the original birth certificate. This is done to keep the facts surrounding the adoption secret and to protect the natural parents' right to privacy. The rationale is that when a child is placed for adoption, the decision is quite painful for the natural parents. Sealing the records, so the theory goes, is seen as a way of severing ties and closing emotional wounds. The sealed-records rule also protects the adoption process. Natural parents are more likely to put children up for adoption when they are assured their privacy will be protected. In addition, adopting parents are more likely to adopt when they know that they will not have to confront the natural parents as a consequence of the adoption.

Typically, access to sealed records can only be made upon a showing of "good cause." In other words, there must be strong genealogical, medical, or psychological justification for a court to order such records opened on behalf of the adoptee or adopting parents (for example, where there is a high risk of a hereditary disease which could be treated if the medical history of the natural parents were known).

Access to adoption records is *rarely* granted. Nonetheless, adopted persons have become increasingly active in their legal efforts to unseal adoption records. One such case involving the adopted child of former New York City mayor Jimmy Walker attracted national media attention. Mary Ann Walker, adopted daughter of the late ex-mayor, petitioned the court to unseal her adoption records. Ms. Walker was adopted in 1936 when she was 6 months old. The arrangements were made through Cradle in Evanston, Illinois, an adoption agency that catered to famous couples. Mayor and Mrs. Walker knew practically nothing about their daughter's natural parents; they knew only that she came from "intelligent and fine American people."

In March 1979, Ms. Walker wrote to Cradle asking for "nonidentifying" information—the circumstances of her birth and her lineage. She received some information, but was not given the names of her natural parents. She then went to court to obtain this information. After a hearing, a New York County surrogate judge denied the request. He cited a strong and clearly enunciated New York policy that granted access to such records only upon a showing of good cause or special interest. Mere curiosity was not enough.

The Adoptees Liberty Movement Association (ALMA) is a national organization spearheading the effort to ease access to adoption records. Recently ALMA failed in its attempt to have the New York "sealed-records" statute declared unconstitutional on the ground it violated the Fourteenth Amendment of the Constitution. ALMA's theory was that this law caused adoptees "psychological pain and suffering not experienced by nonadopted persons." The New York State Court of Appeals was not persuaded.

If you are an adopted person seeking facts about your natural parents, be aware that you will probably be unsuccessful in your quest (in light of these rulings and statutes). You do have the right to go to the agency that arranged the adoption and ask for "nonidentifying" information about the kinds of people your natural parents were (their occupations, nationality, etc.) However, positive identification of those parents will probably be prohibited.

If you desire more information on this subject, you may wish to contact ALMA at its New York headquarters:

Adoptees Liberty Movement Association
P.O. Box 154
Washington Bridge Station
New York, NY 10033

4. Open Adoption. A recent innovation in adoption practice designed to diminish the sealed-records problem is the concept of "open adoption." Here, an arrangement is made which allows the adoptee to have continuing contact with certain blood relatives. This is provided in an agreement. The agreement is introduced at the adoption proceeding. The judge carefully scrutinizes the document and weighs all the factors to determine whether this should be granted.

Often it is a good idea, particularly in cases where older children are familiar with their blood relatives. In a recent New York case, for example, a 12-year-old boy living in a foster home was due to be adopted. An investigation of the boy's background revealed he had regular contact with three other siblings who were also in foster care; there was a strong emotional bond between the children. Although New York law does not specifically authorize open adoptions, the judge was convinced that it was in the child's best interests for him to be allowed to continue his familial contacts. Thus the judge ordered this arrangement as a matter of judicial discretion.

If you are seeking to adopt a child with strong emotional ties to a natural family that cannot otherwise care for him or her, consider the possibility of framing an agreement to allow for an open adoption. Such an agreement may resemble the following:

Sample Agreement of Open Adoption*

[Adoptive mother] and [Adoptive father] agree to adopt [Child]. [Birth mother] and [Birth father] agree to consent to the adoption of [Child] by [Adoptive mother] and [Adoptive father].

It is further agreed that following finalization of the adoption it is in the best interests of [Child] that there be contact between him/her and the following members of his/her family: [Birth mother, birth father, etc.].

Such contact will consist of the exchange of pictures twice yearly and three annual visits between [Child] and [Birth mother] and [Birth father]. The birth parents will send pictures of themselves to the [Adoption agency] on or about [Date] and [Date] of each year. The adoptive parents will send pictures of [Child] to the agency on or about [Date] and [Date] of each year. The agency will send the pictures of the birth parents to the adoptive parents and the pictures of the child to the birth parents.

The visits will take place on or about [Date], [Date], and [Date] of each year at the offices of the agency. In the event the agency ceases

*This sample agreement is taken from the *Journal of Family Law*, Vol. 22, No. 1, University of Louisville, October 1983, pp. 90–91.

to do business in [State], the parties will select another mutually agreeable agency to receive communications from the parties and to provide a site for visitation.

The parties agree that this agreement shall remain in force until [Child] reaches his/her eighteenth birthday, unless such agreement shall become contrary to [Child's] best interest. In such an event the parties agree to attempt to reach an amicable resolution of the issues presented in accordance with the best interests of the child and if unable to do so will petition a court of competent jurisdiction to assist in resolution of any unresolved issues.

The parties to the agreement understand and intend that any disagreement or litigation as to the issue of visitation or other contact between the child and his/her birth family after the adoption is final shall not affect either the validity of the adoption or the custody of [Child].

Signed:

[Birth mother]

[Birth father]

[Adoptive mother]

[Adoptive father]

Specialized Adoptions

Mixed Adoptions

Many states incorporate racial, religious, and ethnic limitations in their adoption laws; this encourages the practice of matching parents and children of similar backgrounds. If you are interested in adopting a child of another race, religion, or nationality and your state imposes such a restriction, ask a lawyer to review the constitutionality of the limitation. Although there may be cultural arguments for promoting matched adoptions (for instance, to preserve the child's heritage), cases suggest your chances of adopting a culturally different child can be enhanced by demonstrating your willingness to develop the child's consciousness of his or her native culture.

Although most agencies presume it is better to place children with parents of the same race, courts in several states have declared that rules making race the dominant factor in placing children are unconstitutional. For example, one white couple from Maryland recently sought to adopt a mildly retarded 3-year-old black child. The couple filed suit after the Baltimore County Department of Social Services delayed their request for the adoption. The agency cited state policy requiring social-service agencies to make strenuous nationwide efforts to find suitable same-race parents for a child before considering an interracial adoption. The couple sued to overturn the policy and claimed it was unconstitutional. The case was settled before trial in favor of the couple, who the county agreed would make the most suitable parents, since they were both special-education teachers who had worked extensively with the child in the past.

Assert your rights if you wish to adopt a child with a background culturally different from your own. Be aware that courts in many states are easing the barriers to interracial and interreligions adoptions.

International Adoptions

If you experience difficulty in adopting a child, you may go to an adoption agency that specializes in placing children from foreign countries. Many of these agencies arrange adoptions from only one region—for example, Latin America—so you should decide which country or area you want a child from before looking for an agency that will help arrange the adoption.

When going to an international adoption agency, be sure to ask the representative about the amount of red tape you will have to endure to secure an adoption. This varies considerably from country to country. Also, be sure to ask about *your* qualifications. International adoption agencies operate by way of contact with a correspondent agency in the country of the child's origin. These foreign agencies have their own concept about what constitutes an appropriate adopting family. For example, many look favorably on families with traditional lifestyles. Thus it is wise to review your qualifications to be sure there will be no problem. You will also be required to undergo the same home investigation that is involved in domestic adoptions. In addition, be sure to inquire about the following:

• *Fees.* These should include all charges from the moment of your first consultation with an international adoption agency. Ask how much it will cost you in total to consummate a foreign adoption. Just to be safe, ask for a written estimate that itemizes all costs that may arise.

• *Risk of disease for the adopted child.* Many, if not most, of the children that are adopted from foreign countries come from impoverished homes. Medical care is inadequate and disease is common. You should inquire about the risk from disease before you decide you want to pursue international adoption.

• *The possibility of visiting the child's country before making the adoption.* It might be a good idea to visit the child in his or her own country to investigate economic, hygienic, and other conditions before going through with any adoption.

International adoptions are made in one of two ways: (1) by bringing the child into this country for adoption, or (2) by going to the child's country and consummating the adoption there. Either way, you must comply with the same preadoption requirements mandated for a domestic adoption—that is, file an adoption petition, obtain available consents, submit to a home investigation, appear before the court, and obtain a final order of adoption.

In addition, you must deal with the U.S. Immigration and Naturalization Service (INS) in order to secure the adopted child's entry into this country. In order to comply with INS regulations, you must go to the INS office in your area and file an I-600 form. The I-600 form is a petition to classify the prospective adoptee as an immediate relative in order to have the child brought to this country for adoption. The INS will evaluate your petition and send you written notification of its decision. If your petition is denied, you will have the right to appeal. If it is approved, you can move on through the rest of the adoption process.

If you are planning to adopt a child from another country but the child is not yet identified, the INS allows you to file what is known as an I-600A form. This is an application for a petition for "advance processing of an orphan," and it is filed under the following circumstances:

- The petitioner is unmarried and is traveling abroad to locate a child for adoption in the United States.

- The petitioner is unmarried and is traveling to a foreign country to locate and adopt a child while abroad.

- The petitioner and spouse are traveling abroad to locate a child for adoption in the United States.

- The petitioner and spouse are traveling to a foreign country to locate and adopt a child while abroad.

- The married petitioner or the married petitioner's spouse is traveling abroad to locate a child for adoption in the United States.

Under this advance-processing method, if you are given a favorable determination on your petition, you have one year to provide the INS with the exact identification of the child you locate abroad. If you fail to provide the INS with such identification, your petition will be considered abandoned and you will later have to submit a new application. If you *do* identify a child, you may then file the regular I-600 form to demonstrate that you have the complete package of documentary evidence and information required for the international adoption. Incidentally, when you first file with the INS (either the I-600 or the I-600A form), you will be required to pay a fee. This fee is *not* refundable if your application is denied. However, if you have filed an I-600A form and have located a child that you wish to adopt, there is no additional fee for following up with the regular I-600 form.

If the foreign child you wish to adopt is already in this country, make sure that he or she is not here illegally. A child present in the United States either illegally or as a nonimmigrant is ineligible for consideration under an INS orphan petition. However, if the child has legal immigrant status, there is no longer any reason to worry about ensuring that he or she has been in this country for the length of time normally necessary to qualify for naturalization. Since 1978, residence and physical presence requirements for children adopted from foreign countries have been abolished. As soon as the adoption is completed and all legal requirements have been met, the child is *automatically* a United States citizen, and is entitled to any and all rights that would accrue to any child born naturally to you.

Completing an international adoption is not difficult if you are aware of the rules and abide by them. Depending upon which country you adopt from, the process may even be accomplished more easily and more quickly than a domestic adoption.

For further information write:

American Public Welfare Association
1125 15th Street N.W., Suite 300
Washington, DC 20005

for a copy of the *National Directory of Intercountry Adoption Services*.

Special-Needs Adoptions

There is at present no shortage of "special-needs" children (those with physical or emotional handicaps or of another race). These children are hard to place, and they tend to be older when they are finally adopted. As a result, agencies have relaxed their criteria as to the age and occupation of the prospective adopting parents. For example, couples in their middle years willing to give the extra care and attention required are now getting the opportunity to adopt these children, couples who might have been denied the opportunity to adopt normal children.

Most states provide an economic incentive for the adoption of a special-needs child by offering subsidy payments to the adopting family. Subsidies range up to $100 a week. Eligibility for subsidized adoption is based more on the child's specific needs (for instance, medical services) than on the family's financial ability to care for the child.

According to the Model State Subsidized Adoption Act, which is the prototype for the actual state laws governing subsidized adoption, a special-needs child is a person who is difficult to adopt because of one or more of the following factors*:

- Physical or mental disability
- Emotional disturbance
- Recognized high risk of physical or mental disease
- Age
- Sibling relationship
- Racial or ethnic factors

To be eligible for the subsidy the child must be in the temporary foster care of the family that is seeking the adoption. Evidence must be presented which demonstrates that reasonable efforts were made to place the child without subsidy (that is, other potential adopting parents were contacted but declined) and that all other adoption procedures were followed (that is, petitions were filed, consents were obtained, investigations were conducted, etc.).

If you are interested in undertaking a subsidized adoption, contact your state or county department of social services for information. There are many special-needs children available, and you should be able to adopt one (or more) within a relatively short period of time.

For Further Information . . .

In undertaking any process having legal implications, there is nothing like being well informed about available options. If you wish to obtain additional information about the subject of adoption, there are a variety of organizations that can assist you with answers about every aspect of the adoption process

---

*Model State Subsidized Adoption Act and Regulations 2, U.S. Department of Health, Education, and Welfare, Pub. No. 76-30010, 1975.

and its implications for all parties involved. Your local department of social services may know of such organizations in your area. The following is a sampling of some of the larger associations. Do not hesitate to contact them.

Adoptees Liberty Movement
  Association
P.O. Box 154
Washington Bridge Station
New York, NY 10033

Adoptive Parents Committee
210 Fifth Avenue
New York, NY 10010

Child Welfare League of
  America
67 Irving Place
New York, NY 10003

Children's Aid Society
150 East 45th Street
New York, NY 10017

5 | Protecting the Family: Domestic Violence and the Law

Introduction

Family violence is a phenomenon that is reaching crisis proportions. Hardly a day goes by that we do not read a disturbing story about marital rape, child neglect, incest, child snatching, or spouse abuse.

This chapter will tell you how to deal with and reduce domestic violence. You will learn what to do, how to act, and how to fight back legally in the event you yourself are victimized or you discover an incident of child abuse.

These areas are discussed because they are the most common forms of private violence in the United States today. However, the law is changing rapidly to protect victims in these areas; no longer must you or your children suffer pain, humiliation, and mental anguish at the hands of a spouse or lover.

Read the information carefully. You will learn about the kinds of assistance that are available and how to obtain them. Most important, you will discover a variety of options you can use in acting quickly and correctly in the event of an emergency.

Child Snatching

Between 25,000 and 100,000 children are victims of child snatching each year. In most cases the abducted child is taken by the parent *not* entitled to legal custody; reunion of the child with the custodial parent is the exception, not the rule.

Animosity toward the ex-spouse rather than concern for the child is generally the motive for child snatching. Violence sometimes attends these incidents. Many cases involve children being carried away against their will, kicking and screaming in the process. After the abduction, the life of the child may be unstable; he or she may be moved from place to place because the abducting parent does not want to get caught. This disruption can cause long-term psychological and/or physical trauma.

The effects of child snatching are devastating upon the

custodial parent as well as the child, and it is important to act properly once it occurs. But by recognizing key warning signs, you may be able to prevent child snatching *before* it occurs. The following preventive and remedial measures should be reviewed if you think you and your child may become victims.

How to Prevent Child Snatching

1. *Recognize the possibility.* Child snatching can be avoided by recognizing the key signs that warn of the likelihood of an abduction. Signs include the flexibility of your ex-partner's lifestyle, the lack of roots he or she may have in the community, and the availability of financial or physical assistance from out-of-state family or friends. Most child snatchings occur right before or after divorce proceedings. Be aware that job dissatisfaction or creditors pressing your ex-spouse for payment of delinquent bills will increase the possibility of abduction and flight.

2. *Talk to the child's teachers, baby-sitter, and/or other guardian.* It is a good idea to talk to these individuals to remind them of your concern and solicit their help if your spouse reveals to them that a child snatching is being planned.

3. *Speak to a competent lawyer.* An experienced matrimonial lawyer will be able to advise you of your rights. (See Chapter 1 for guidelines in finding and working with a lawyer.) If a child-custody decree has not yet been granted and you feel a child snatching is imminent, your lawyer can take immediate action. This is done by going into court and asking the judge for temporary sole custody of the child, pending a full hearing for separation or divorce. Such an order, once granted, can serve as a deterrent to child snatching.

4. *Seek a child-custody decree.* A child-custody decree can protect your rights as the custodial parent in the event of a child snatching. For example, the decree may order the ex-partner to seek your written consent before taking the child on an extended trip or vacation. It can also contain a provision requiring the noncustodial parent to compensate you for expenses incurred in enforcing custody. Some decrees even re-

quire the noncustodial parent to post a bond before taking the child away and include provisions evidencing your right to obtain police assistance in the event of a problem.

You should also be aware that the federal Educational Rights and Privacy Act (ERPA) restricts an ex-partner from transferring a child's scholastic records to another school after a child snatching. However, to gain protection under this law, it is necessary to file a copy of the custody decree at your child's school *before* an abduction occurs. That is why it is best for you to obtain a decree of child custody as soon as possible. (See Chapter 7.)

Note: An experienced lawyer will ask for many favorable points in your custody decree. The preceding points are merely a few of the important items to be considered.

5. *Protect yourself by contract.* While a custody decree may protect your rights as a custodial parent after a child snatching, a separation agreement can address similar rights before a court issues a custody decree. Properly drafted separation agreements protect the rights of both parents with respect to custody and often inhibit illegal behavior.

The following clause, for example, illustrates the kind of provision that can protect both parties, but particularly the noncustodial father:

> Neither party shall remove the residence of the child beyond a radius of fifty (50) miles from the present residence without prior, written consent of the other party. If the Mother shall remove the residence of the child beyond said radius without the consent of the Father or the Court, such failure to obtain consent shall be presumptive of the right of the Father to obtain custody of the child, shall terminate further payments under this Agreement to the Wife for her support and maintenance and for that of the child and shall, in addition, entitle the Father to pursue all other remedies available to him under the circumstances.

Separation agreements containing penalties for violating custody arrangements often have a dramatic effect in reducing the risk of child snatching. Discuss this with your lawyer.

6. *Instruct your child to call you when he or she is away.* Small children should be told to call you or a trusted friend or relative in the event "anything happens." Abducting parents often tell children that the other parent has died, moved away, disappeared, remarried, or no longer cares. Reminding your child to call may disprove that and may help you discover where the child is being hidden.

7. *Take periodic photographs, fingerprints, and videotapes of your child.* Up-to-date photographs, videotapes and fingerprints will assist the police (or FBI) in identifying the child. Young children grow rapidly and their features change dramatically in a few years. Clear fingerprints will be particularly helpful in the event your child is abducted. Some companies do this for a modest fee. If you desire to take fingerprints yourself, call the nearest police station for advice. The police will tell you how to make and preserve the prints properly. You may also wish to read a helpful book by Michael Schaefer called *Child Snatching* (see bibliography). This book gives step-by-step instructions on how to take and preserve your child's fingerprints.

8. *Consider your legal options.* You and your child may be able to recover damages against your ex-partner in a lawsuit. Some courts award civil damages to custodial parents who are deprived of their custody rights after a child snatching. If you have exectued a separation agreement or obtained a judicial decree granting sole legal custody, it may be possible to recover:

- Expenses you have incurred in obtaining your child
- Money for the emotional distress you have suffered
- Money as compensation for the loss of companionship and society with your child
- Money to compensate your child for being held against his or her free will
- Punitive damages (that is, additional money paid to you to penalize the kidnapping ex-partner for willful, outrageous conduct)
- Trial expenses, court costs, attorney fees, and other

litigation-related expenses (for example, stenographer fees)

• Malpractice and negligence damages imposed against the abducting parent's attorney

The court can also increase the amount of damages awarded if your ex-partner fails to return the child within a specific time period.

Although a lawsuit will not guarantee a child's return, it may reimburse you for expenses incurred in attempts to regain custody of the child. Courts have allowed some custodial parents to recover compensatory damages (indemnifying the parent for actual expended costs) together with large punitive damage awards. In one recent case, for example, the custodial mother was awarded $65,000 in compensatory damages for the abduction of the child, and an additional $65,000 was assessed against the five individuals who assisted the husband in the child snatching. In a 1978 New York case, the custodial mother was awarded $14,950 for the loss of services of the child and her wounded feelings, $5,000 in legal fees, and $100,000 in punitive damages for intentional and malicious child snatching. The abducted infant was also entitled to recover damages for false imprisonment (calculated at the rate of $20 per day for each day the child was held), $5,000 for the actual imprisonment, and $50,000 in punitive damages against the abducting father.

Although courts are awarding damages for amounts expended in locating and regaining the child, such a lawsuit may not be worth much unless you have located the whereabouts of your ex-partner, his or her property, or other assets of significant value.

However, the primary reason for instituting a lawsuit for damages is its deterrent effect. In many cases, the existence of a money award obtained in your ex-partner's absence, coupled with the certainty that the court will increase the award as time passes, may cause the ex-partner to return the child. That is why you should remind your spouse or lover that you will institute a lawsuit in the event of a child snatching. This may cause your ex-partner to think twice before taking illegal action.

9. *Take proper steps to avoid the possibility that your ex-spouse can permanently leave the United States with your child.* The terms of a custody decree can prohibit the child's removal from the country or limit it to instances where your ex-partner must first obtain your written consent. Be sure to file a copy of the decree with the U.S. State Department if your spouse travels abroad frequently; this will help protect your rights.

If your spouse does take the child out of the country, you will have greater trouble instituting that child's return. The reason is that the United States government cannot force a foreign country to honor American custody court orders and decrees. Foreign laws vary widely and you may have no options other than contacting the Department of State and various American embassies and counsulates.

Thus, it is best to take precautions to avoid a child snatching to a foreign country. That is why, if possible, you should keep your child's passport and birth certificate in a safe place known only to you; this can hinder a child snatching to a foreign country. However, be aware that new passports and birth certificates can be issued once a claim is made that they are lost or stolen.

How to Proceed Once Child Snatching Has Occurred

There are several remedial steps to take after your child has been abducted.

1. *Stay calm.* Although this advice may seem impossible to follow, you must remain calm because you will need to make many important and well-reasoned decisions.

2. *Contact the police immediately.* Important leads tend to disappear as time passes. The faster you contact the police, the more quickly they will be able to gather leads and act upon them.

Don't forget to give the police the following information:

- Full name
- Nickname

- Signature and other handwriting
- Address and home phone number
- Citizenship
- Scars or blemishes
- Blood type
- Date and place of birth
- Medical history and current necessary prescriptions
- Social-security number
- Age, sex, race, height, weight, color of eyes
- Hair color
- School
- Grandparents' and other relatives' addresses
- Recent photographs, fingerprints, and/or videotapes

You may also wish to contact the data bank at the National Crime Information Center. The Center assists the FBI and police in locating abductors who travel from state to state.

3. *Check with friends, neighbors, ex-in-laws, and your spouse's boss.* Most child snatchers are not loners. Often they reveal their plans to trusted individuals before they act. You may gain information regarding your child's whereabouts through these people.

4. *Avoid committing illegal acts.* Some victims make threats to an ex-partner's family or friends or take the law into their own hands. Such illegal conduct can expose you to criminal and/or civil penalties and jeopardize your chances of obtaining permanent custody of the child, since some judges view illegal countermeasures as evidence of your unfitness as a parent and may revoke a previous award granting you custody, or may even deny custody.

5. *Consider filing kidnapping charges.* Congress passed the Parental Kidnapping Prevention Act in 1980. This legislation extended the Fugitive Felon Act to cases involving child snatching and has been instrumental in reducing the number of child snatchings and in apprehending fugitives from justice, since FBI agents can now assist state law-enforcement agents in returning abducted children to their custodial parents. Under this law they also have the authority to bring abducting parents back to the state where the child previously resided to face criminal charges.

In order to receive assistance from the FBI, the following three conditions must be met:

- Parental kidnapping must be a felony in the state where it occurred (see Table 5-1).
- That state must have begun a felony prosecution and issued a warrant.
- The local prosecutor must ask the U.S. attorney general for a federal "unlawful flight to avoid prosecution" warrant.

In order to determine whether child snatching is a felony in your state, thereby enabling the FBI to get involved, consult Table 5-1. This chart lists states that classify child stealing, child snatching, custodial interference, or parental kidnapping (abduction) as a felony. (*Note:* Many parents are not willing to involve the police or the FBI once a child snatching has occurred. Although this may be understandable, it is probably not wise.)

When you decide to press criminal charges against your ex-spouse for parental kidnapping, the local police and prosecutor will play a major role in the arrest and trial. Some people often confuse the respective duties of each.

The police perform the following important roles in child-snatching cases:

- They receive the complaint from the victimized spouse.
- They gather the necessary paperwork to support the charges.
- They obtain witness statements.
- They confer with and work closely with the prosecutor.
- They officially communicate with and work closely with other police departments, public agencies and the FBI.

Table 5-1

State Legal Codes Regarding Child Snatching

State	Law*	Comment
Alaska	ALASKA STAT. § 11.41.320 (1978)	Makes child snatching a felony if child is removed from the state
Arizona	ARIZ. REV. STAT. ANN. § 13.1302 (1978)	
Arkansas	ARK. STAT. ANN. § 41-2411 (1977)	Makes child snatching a felony if child is removed from the state
California	CAL. PENAL CODE § 278.5 (West Supp. 1982)	
Colorado	COLO. REV. STAT. § 18-3-304 (1978)	Makes child snatching a felony if child is removed from the state
Delaware	DEL. CODE ANN. tit. 11, § 785 (West Supp. 1982)	Makes child snatching a felony if child is removed contrary to a valid court order
Florida	FLA. STAT. ANN. § 787.04 (West Supp. 1982)	
Georgia	GA. CODE ANN. § 26-1312 (Supp. 1982)	Makes interstate interference with custody a felony if the child is either removed from the state or taken from another state and brought into Georgia
Hawaii	HAWAII REV. STAT. § 707-726 (Supp. 1981)	Makes child snatching a felony if child is removed from the state
Idaho	IDAHO CODE ANN. § 18-4501 to 4503 (1979)	Makes child snatching a felony if child is removed from the state
Illinois	ILL. ANN. STAT. ch. 38, § 10-5 (Smith-Hurd 1979)	

Indiana	IND. CODE ANN. § 35-42-3.3 (West 1979)	Makes child snatching a felony if child is removed from the state
Iowa	IOWA CODE ANN. § 710.6 (West 1979)	Makes child snatching a felony if child is removed from the state
Kansas	KAN. STAT. ANN. § 21-3422a (1981)	Makes aggravated interference with custody a felony
Louisiana	LA. REV. STAT. ANN. § 14.45 (West Supp. 1982)	
Maine	ME. REV. STAT. ANN. tit. 17A, § 303 (Supp. 1982)	
Maryland	MD. ANN. CODE art. 27, § 2A (Supp. 1982)	Makes child snatching a felony if child is removed from the state
Massachusetts	MASS. GEN. LAWS ANN. ch. 265, § 26a (West Supp. 1982)	Makes child snatching a felony if child is exposed to danger
Michigan	MICH. COMP. LAWS ANN. § 750.350 (Supp. 1982)	Makes child snatching a felony only when an adopted child is taken by the natural parent
Minnesota	MINN. STAT. ANN. § 609.26 (West Supp. 1982)	Makes child snatching a felony only if child is not returned within fourteen days
Mississippi	MISS. CODE ANN. § 97-3-53 (Supp. 1982)	
Missouri	MO. ANN. STAT. § 565.150 (Vernon 1979)	Makes child snatching a felony if child is removed from the state in violation of a custody order
Montana	MONT. CODE ANN. § 45-5-304 (1981)	
Nebraska	NEB. REV. STAT. § 28-316 (1979)	Makes child snatching a felony if child is taken in violation of a valid custody decree

(continued)

Table 5-1 (*Continued*)

State	Law*	Comment
Nevada	NEV. REV. STAT. § 200.359 (1979)	Makes child snatching a felony if child is taken in violation of a valid custody decree
New Hampshire	N.H. REV. STAT. ANN. § 633 (1973)	Makes kidnapping a felony
New Mexico	N.M. STAT. ANN. § 30-4-4 (1978)	Makes child snatching a felony if child is removed from the state
New York	N.Y. PENAL LAW § 135.50 (McKinney Supp. 1982–1983)	
North Carolina	N.C. GEN. STAT. § 14.320.1 (1981)	
North Dakota	N.D. CENT. CODE § 14-14-22.1 (1981)	Makes child snatching a felony if child is removed from the state; incorporates it into the UCCJA
Ohio	OHIO REV. CODE ANN. § 2905.04 (Page 1982)	Makes child snatching a felony if child is removed from the state
Oklahoma	OKLA. STAT. ANN. tit. 10, § 1627 (West Supp. 1981)	Incorporates child snatching into the UCCJA
Oregon	OR. REV. STAT. § 163.245,-.257 (1981)	
Rhode Island	R.I. GEN. LAWS § 11-26-1.1 (1981)	Makes child snatching a felony if child is removed from the state in violation of an existing custody decree
South Carolina	S.C. CODE ANN. § 16-17-495 (Law. Co-op Supp. 1982)	
South Dakota	S.D. CODIFIED LAWS ANN. § 22-19-10 (Supp. 1982)	Makes child snatching a felony if child is removed from the state

State	Citation	Description
Tennessee	Tenn. Code Ann. § 39-2-303 (1982)	
Texas	Tex. Penal Code Ann. § 25.03 (Vernon Supp. 1982)	
Utah	Utah Code Ann. § 76-5-303 (Supp. 1981)	Makes child snatching a felony if child is removed from the state
Vermont	Vt. Stat. Ann. tit. 13, § 2451 (Supp. 1981)	
Virginia	Va. Code § 18.2-47 (Cum. Supp. 1981)	Makes child snatching a felony if child is removed from the state by a parent; removal is punishable as contempt of court in any proceeding that may be pending
Wisconsin	Wis. Stat. Ann. § 946.71,-.715 (West 1982)	Makes child snatching a felony if child is removed from the state; makes interference by a parent with parental rights of the other parent a felony
Wyoming	Wyo. Stat. § 6-4-203 (Supp. 1982)	Makes child snatching a felony if child is concealed and whereabouts of the child are not revealed to the custodial parent

*The date inside the parentheses indicates the most recent version of the law in each state. Be sure to thoroughly research the law in your state; laws in this area are changing rapidly and the chart may not be up to date by the time you read it.

Source: *Hofstra Law Review*, Vol. 11, No. 3, Spring 1983, pp. 1107–1108.

The prosecutor performs the following important roles in child-snatching cases:

- He or she makes the decision to arrest the ex-spouse.

- He or she interrogates friends and relatives of the ex-spouse who might have information about the whereabouts of the child; concealed information may lead to a conspiracy charge against those who have knowledge but fail to disclose it.

- He or she requests necessary assistance from the police, public agencies, and the FBI.

- He or she issues legal process for the investigation.

Your responsibilities do not end once you file criminal charges. Often the parent filing charges is asked to help gather information and pursue leads to locate the ex-spouse. That is why it is important to know as much as possible about your ex-partner. For example, always keep a list of your spouse's banks, credit cards, property holdings, social security number, date of birth, names and addresses of friends and relatives, and other pertinent data such as military service history. Such a list will simplify the investigative process when or if it must be commenced.

Note: Be aware that even if you commence criminal charges and have a trial, you may not obtain a guilty verdict, since some juries sympathize with abducting parents.

6. *Consider instituting a civil lawsuit.*

7. *Contact an investigative agency to help you.* Private investigators can assist you in locating your abducted child. There are many reputable firms in your area; simply look in the Yellow Pages under the "Private Investigator" heading.

A skilled investigator will contact your ex-partner's bank and credit-card companies, investigate your ex-partner's employment history and job skills, and speak to his or her friends, relatives, neighbors, co-workers, and former employers. Usually the investigator will contact utility companies and school officials to determine if and where the child's records were transferred. The local post office will also be contacted to determine if a forwarding address was given, and the state Bureau of Motor Vehicles will be contacted to determine if a new driver's license or car registration was issued.

(*Note:* Although it is not advisable, you may wish to personally conduct your own investigation; the preceding hints give you some good places to start.)

To avoid future misunderstandings and problems, be sure you thoroughly investigate the reputation of the agency you are hiring. Inquire whether the firm is licensed and adequately bonded. This can be done by contacting your local Better Business Bureau or the consumer protection office. Any state department of consumer affairs or local Better Business Bureau will likely require that private investigative agencies be licensed. Some require that agencies post performance bonds and sign affidavits before they can be licensed. Contact these regulatory bodies to determine whether a particular firm is licensed. A license does not guarantee the reliability or competence of an investigative agency, but it is a step in the right direction. Don't forget to inquire whether any complaints or lawsuits have been lodged against the investigative agency in the recent past.

If you are hiring a private detective who practices alone, be sure to do a little investigating on your own. Check out the investigator's credentials and make sure he or she is licensed. Approximately forty-five states require private detectives to be licensed. At a minimum, this means that they are required to have some training or equivalent law-enforcement experience, pass a qualifying exam, and have no past criminal record. In addition, the state agency that monitors private investigators can tell you if any complaints have been filed against the detective. Don't forget to inquire about this.

Before hiring the investigative agency or private detective, it is also a good idea to ask for references. Ask for the names of other clients who have used the investigator's services; confirm all references after they are received.

Once you have hired the investigative agency or private detective, be specific about what you want. Inquire what costs will be involved. Be sure you know how much you will be charged for the work involved. Instruct the detective not to "snatch back" the child; this will complicate legal matters and may harm the child emotionally as well. Always confirm your agreement in writing to protect yourself. If you ask for and do not receive written confirmation of your agreement, send a letter to the agency that documents your understanding of the agreement. The following is an example.

Sample Letter Agreement

(Date)

Mr. Ronald Smith
ABC Private Investigator Service
Centerville, N.Y.

Dear Mr. Smith:

This will confirm that I have retained the services of your private investigative agency to assist me in locating my 6-year-old son who was taken from me by my former husband.

You agree to use your best efforts in locating the whereabouts of my ex-husband and son; however, you agree not to "snatch back" my child. Rather, the full extent of our agreement is for you to locate the whereabouts of these individuals and report this information to me for use by my attorney.

For your services, I shall pay you at the rate of $75 per hour. I have paid you an initial retainer of One Thousand Dollars ($1,000) to be applied against your hourly rate. In the event my child is returned to me or you discover his whereabouts before the retainer has been depleted, or I decide to discontinue your services for any reason, you agree to promptly return the unused balance within one (1) week from my written request.

I understand that your hourly rate does not include costs and expenses. These include, but are not limited to, long-distance phone calls, travel, parking, and photocopies made by you. They also do not include the fee for your assistant's time, for which you advise me I will be billed at the rate of $40 per hour.

Per our agreement, you shall confer with me on all expenses exceeding $100, which I shall approve *before* they are incurred. In addition, you shall bill me monthly with respect to all services performed and costs incurred and shall send me complete, accurate, itemized monthly statements with receipts to prove same.

As notice of your acceptance of this agreement, please sign this letter below where indicated and return a signed copy to me immediately.
I look forward to working with you.

Sincerely,

Allison Johnson

Accepted and agreed to:
ABC Private Investigator Service

By:_____
(Sent certified mail, return receipt requested)

8. Contact the Parent Locator Services agency in your state. The federal Parent Locator Service was originally established to locate absent parents who defaulted in making support payments to their spouses. It was then extended to assist in locating abducting parents. If your state is among those that utilize this service, you can receive assistance, provided an appropriate individual applies for relief on your behalf. Such persons include a judge of the local family court, a U.S. attorney, or an authorized state representative. Some of the parent locator services that use the federal Parent Locator Service in parental kidnapping and child-custody cases are listed below:

California
Child Support Management
  Branch
Department of Social Services
744 P Street
Sacramento, CA 95814

Colorado
Division of Child Support En-
  forcement
Department of Social Services
1575 Sherman Street
Room 423
Denver, CO 80203

Georgia
Office of Child Support Recov-
  ery
State Department of Human
  Resources
P.O. Box 80000
Atlanta, GA 30357

Minnesota
Office of Child Support
Department of Public Welfare
Space Center Building
444 Lafayette Road
St. Paul, MN 55101

Missouri

Child Support Enforcement
    Unit
Division of Family Services
Department of Social Services
P.O. Box 88
Jefferson City, MO 65103

New Jersey

Child Support and Paternity
    Unit
Department of Human Services
CN 716
Trenton, NJ 08625

Pennsylvania

Child Support Program
Bureau of Claims Settlement
Department of Public Welfare
P.O. Box 8018
Harrisburg, PA 17105

Texas

Child Support Enforcement
    Branch
Texas Department of Human
    Resources
P.O. Box 2960
Austin, TX 78769

Virginia

Division of Support Enforce-
    ment Program
Department of Social Services
8007 Discovery Drive
Richmond, VA 23288

Washington

Office of Support Enforcement
Department of Social and
    Health Services
P.O. Box 9162-FU-11
Olympia, WA 98504

Further information may be obtained from:

Federal Parent Locator Service
Department of Health and Human Services
Office of Child Support Enforcement
Rockville, MD 20852
(301)/443-4950

9. *Pursue your rights under the federal Educational Rights and Privacy Act.* Under this law, for example, you may be able to obtain the name, address, and telephone number of the school to which your child's records have been transferred. Speak to a lawyer about this.

10. *Pursue your rights under the Uniform Child Custody Jurisdiction Act.* This law has recently been enacted in many states to limit child snatching and provide remedies to parents who have been victimized. Together with the fed-

eral Parental Kidnapping Prevention Act of 1980, the law has significantly strengthened both children's and parents' rights. Don't forget to discuss these laws with your lawyer.

Spouse Abuse

Spouse abuse (and abusive relationships in general) continues to be a well-concealed social problem in this country. A look at some current statistics confirms this:

- As many as 6 million wives (including women who have never been legally married) are abused by their husbands or lovers each year. Only a small fraction of these incidents are reported.
- Battery, more than any other accident or crime, is the greatest cause of physical injury to women.
- Between 2,000 and 4,000 battered women die from attacks each year.
- According to the FBI, 40 percent of all murdered women die at the hands of their husbands and 10 percent of all murdered men are killed by their wives, many in retaliation for prior abuse.
- More than 30 percent of all police activity is in response to complaints of domestic violence, particularly wife beatings.
- Approximately 40 percent of all police injuries are incurred while responding to complaints of domestic violence; approximately 20 percent of all police deaths occur while responding to domestic-violence incidents.

The occurrence of spouse abuse in our society is not limited to low-income groups or to people of a particular ethnic background. Until recently, battering was considered a private family matter rather than a crime. Police and judges often tended to discourage battered women from bringing their cases into court. Now pressure from a changing society has caused officials' perceptions, as well as the law, to change. Because of the abolishment of interspousal tort immunity laws under which spouses were previously protected in many states, more women are now suing their husbands directly for their personal injuries. It has also become easier for women to press criminal charges against abusive husbands and make these charges stick.

There are many options to pursue if you are the victim of spouse abuse. These include family counseling, arrest, and divorce or separation. The following pages will outline the various steps you can take to remedy such abuse.

How to Protect Yourself from Spouse Abuse

1. *Act quickly and decisively.* It is often difficult to act properly in a situation of ongoing domestic violence. Many wives submit to abusive husbands because of social pressure or because of their own idealistic expectations. Others cannot afford to leave their husbands for economic reasons.

However, failure to act quickly and decisively may only prolong the misery and produce increasingly violent attacks. In addition, unfair as it may seem, failure to take action may create a legal presumption of acquiescence to the abuse if and when redress is finally sought in the courts. *Remember this.*

There are a number of persons and organizations to turn to for well-reasoned advice:

- *Friends.*
- *Your church or temple.*
- *Victims' services agencies.* Most large communities provide direct assistance for victims of family violence. Services are typically free and are often useful to women contemplating legal action (that is, those who need advice about how to hire a lawyer). The agencies are usually listed in the phone book under city or county government "Victim Services." Phone and schedule an appointment with an appropriate agency representative.
- *Crisis-intervention centers and marriage counse-*

lors. Although a visit to a crisis-intervention center or a marriage counselor may prevent future problems, it may be difficult to persuade your spouse to accompany you. Also, consultation fees are sometimes charged; be sure to ask up front whether fees are imposed. For your protection, ask for a written estimate of all charges.

• *Battered-women's shelters.* If your situation is serious, it may be necessary to leave your home and stay overnight in a battered-women's emergency shelter. Some cities maintain shelter programs through their department of social services. (Consult local government listings under this heading in the phone book.) Shelters are also run by private, non-profit organizations such as the YWCA. The YWCA has a network of more than 200 shelters with outreach and counseling services in thirty states. Information may be obtained by contacting the YWCA directly at its national headquarters in New York:

> The Young Women's Christian Association
> 610 Lexington Avenue
> New York, NY 10022
> (212)/755-4500

There are also several hundred smaller private shelters throughout the country. Information about them can be obtained from social-services departments, crisis-intervention centers, marriage counselors, family-court probation officers, court officers, and your local police.

Despite their advantages, battered-women's shelters do have several drawbacks. One problem deals with physical space and comfort. There has been an increased demand for existing shelters, and the people who run them are often unable to accommodate every battered woman who needs assistance. Thus it is conceivable that you may be unable to stay at a shelter even if you require immediate help.

Another problem arises from the lack of confidentiality of your records. Information indicating your stay at a shelter can be subpoenaed unless such records are protected from being disclosed by state law. Frequently, a traumatized victim will tell a therapist at the shelter, "I feel guilty," "I think maybe I asked for it," or "I want to get revenge." Defense lawyers representing husbands are learning how to use such statements in subsequent litigation. As a result, subpoenas directed to staff officials are a growing problem. However, some states are currently passing laws exempting shelter records from use in court.

2. Save evidence. Always have a friend, relative, or official take color photographs of your injuries as soon as possible to prove the extent of the abuse. Have the pictures signed and dated by the person who took them. Never overlook the value of color photographs; untouched pictures are admissible evidence in court and can be used to your advantage. For example, they will assist your lawyer in obtaining a divorce on your behalf on the grounds of cruel and inhuman treatment; and they may help you get court protection even if you do not want a divorce.

In addition, always seek immediate medical treatment after you are beaten. Ask the doctor or nurse to document your injuries in a written report. Be sure the name of the person who injured you is mentioned in the report. This is because a doctor's visit can help prove that your injuries were caused by the beating, and the medical records can be used in court to prove your case.

Other evidence should also be saved for possible future use. This may include torn or bloody clothing, pictures documenting damage to your house or car, and the testimony of eyewitnesses.

3. Never take the law into your own hands. In many states, a battered spouse who fights back must prove a reasonable apprehension of imminent danger and great bodily harm to prevail with a self-defense claim. Some lawyers use evidence of past beatings and threats to prove reasonable apprehension. Others argue that it is not an unreasonable response for a woman of slight build to use a lethal weapon (for example, a gun or knife) when a man attacks her with his fists.

Always remember that you face possible criminal charges and lengthy incarceration if you fight back. One Alabama woman was convicted and sentenced to life in prison for shooting her husband, despite her contention that he slapped her around and held her at gunpoint. A Wisconsin woman was convicted and sentenced to ten years in prison for shooting her husband. Her lawyer argued that the man beat her and was sexually abusing their 12-year-old daughter at the time of the shooting. However, the woman lost the case because she had never called the police to assist her.

Remember, never take the law into your own hands if you can help it; it is best to call the police for help if you are being threatened.

4. *Call the police.* You should call the police during or immediately after the attack or threat of attack. This is particularly true if you want the person who beat you to be arrested or if you want protection so that you can leave. This is your right whether or not you are married to your attacker.

In some states, if the police refuse to arrest the person, you have the right to make the arrest yourself; the police must then assist you in taking the accused to the police station and filling out the arrest forms. If the police refuse to help you because they say that the accused is your spouse or the parent of your children, write down the officers' names and badge numbers. Let them see you do this. Then report them to their commanding officer or to the civilian complaint review board.

In some states, you may also go to the police station to sign a complaint and request that the person who injured you be arrested. You might want to see the district attorney if you were seriously hurt and required hospital care and the police would not make an arrest.

5. *Seek legal assistance immediately.* An increasing number of battered women are turning to the legal system for help. This is perhaps the most viable alternative you should explore. Some people believe that taking legal action against an abusive spouse will make him angrier and worsen the situation. However, studies show that this fear is unfounded.

The threat to take legal action is the most effective remedy against the batterer, and court action appears to have a *strong* deterrent effect on abusive spouses.

Note: Spouse abuse is now considered a crime in most states, and district attorneys can prosecute husbands even when wives change their mind about pressing charges. Conviction rates for such cases are quite high—for example, 82 percent in Minnesota and 94 percent in New York.

In order to determine whether or not to seek legal assistance, consider your objectives. For example:

- Do you want to save the marriage?
- Do you want to punish your abusive spouse?
- Does your spouse pose a continuing danger of physical injury to yourself and your children?
- Does your spouse need psychological help; should you see that it is provided?
- Can you solve your problem through the legal system without spending a fortune?

If these are your objectives, legal intervention may help you accomplish them. To proceed with legal intervention may or may not require the services of a lawyer. *Without* a lawyer, you can go to a family or domestic-relations court and:

- Get counseling for yourself and your spouse
- Get sole and exclusive custody of your children
- Get an order for your spouse to support you and your children
- Get an order for your spouse to stop injuring you
- Get an order for your spouse to move out of the house
- Get an order for your spouse to refrain from any acts which make the home an improper place for your children
- Get an order for your spouse to stay away from you and your children
- Set a time and place for your spouse to visit with the children

- Get an order for your spouse to pay for your lawyer
- Get an order for custody, visitation rights, and child support

With the services of an attorney you can obtain all of the above through a family or domestic-relations court, and you can also:

- Obtain a decree of divorce, separation, or annulment of your marriage
- Obtain a decree for a share of the marital assets (for example, furniture, the family car, cash in the bank, etc.) and obtain maintenance (that is, alimony) once you have a divorce

Note: You may also obtain a criminal conviction for assault, battery, and/or harassment in criminal court.

The following strategies will assist you once the decision to take legal action has been made:

Obtain a temporary order of protection. The first legal step you should consider taking against an abusive spouse is to obtain a temporary order of protection from the family court in the county where you reside. This measure is designed to give you immediate relief; it is not a final solution to your problem. Still, such an order will maintain the peace while an attempt is made to iron out family difficulties. The order can keep a violent spouse away from you or the children at your home, school, or business for a specified period of time (which varies from state to state). In many states the order can be renewed by demonstrating need.

The advantage of a temporary order is that you can have your spouse arrested if its terms are violated. In most cases, the police must make the arrest if that is your wish. A temporary order of protection is a useful device because it can be tailored to meet your objectives; many times it has made abusive spouses mend their ways and thus it has saved marriages.

Temporary orders are not expensive to obtain. Usually all you pay is a small (for example, $4) filing fee. This is important to know, especially for those who are not financially independent.

If you have decided that your marriage is not worth saving, you can use the temporary order of protection as a means of proving grounds in a divorce or separation action, as well as in a civil lawsuit based upon assault or battery. A violation of the temporary order may also give you an immediate right to proceed in criminal court for permanent protection.

Remember the following strategies when obtaining a temporary order of protection:

- Contact the police for procedural information. They will furnish you with facts on how to obtain an order (for example, what court to go to, how to file, etc.).

- Speak to the clerk when you go to family or criminal court. A clerk can answer all of your questions, so be polite.

- Visitation periods for the spouse are a common feature of temporary orders of protection. Tailor this to your needs when appropriate. For example, if you perceive a threat to your children or fear that they may be victims of child snatching, insist on a plan that will give you as much control over visitations as possible.

- Establish other conditions for your spouse to follow. For example, the order can prohibit your ex-partner from living with you for several days or require him or her to seek medical treatment for a drug problem before being allowed back in the house.

- Speak to a lawyer's referral service for an explanation of all of your options (that is, points to include in the temporary order). Many communities have such advisory organizations that are willing to inform you, without charge, of your rights. *Take advantage of these organizations.*

- Speak to a lawyer. Although you can obtain a temporary order of protection without the services of a lawyer, it may be wise to retain a lawyer to help you get one. A lawyer specializing in matrimonial law will save you time and aggravation and steer you in the right direction. However, be sure you know how much this will cost before you retain an attorney. Be sure the lawyer gives you a retainer agreement that specifies all costs you will incur.

Consider obtaining a more permanent solution. While many battered spouses remedy their problems through the use of a temporary order of protection, others encounter continuing difficulty. If your problem is particularly severe, you should consider filing criminal charges and/or hiring a lawyer who will be able to guide you through the steps that are required for a permanent solution. (Consult Chapter 1 for more information on how to hire a lawyer and make him or her work effectively for you.) When consulting with a lawyer, be sure to discuss *all* the facets of your case. These include:

- The nature of the abuse (that is, the types of injuries you have suffered)
- Options of civil and criminal action
- Matters pertaining to the custody and safety of your children as well as yourself
- Conditions for reconciliation with your spouse, such as his or her promise to seek treatment for a drug- or alcohol-abuse problem
- The divorce or separation option
- Court costs, attorney fees, and the possibility of having your spouse pay for these costs
- Other matters of importance to you

The lawyer you hire will do a better job if you keep him or her well informed about your problems, conduct, and desires.

Before instituting a civil lawsuit or criminal prosecution, it may be advisable for your lawyer to send a cease-and-desist (that is, a warning) letter to your abusive spouse. The letter would advise him or her of the steps you intend to take if the unlawful conduct continues. Such a letter serves many functions. It demonstrates the seriousness of your resolve to seek help. It also notifies your spouse that you have retained a lawyer to represent you and implies that you mean business. The letter will document the problem and state the consequences if the violence continues. In the event the letter is ignored, you can then proceed to take legal action in either a criminal or civil court, where you would be in the advantageous position of being able to show the judge a copy of the letter to demonstrate your reasonableness before seeking a remedy through the court system. The letter might also contain an invitation to a conference in your lawyer's office in an effort to amicably resolve the problem. Thus a cease-and-desist letter is very useful.

The following is an example of the kind of letter a lawyer might send.

Sample Cease-and-Desist Letter

STEVEN MITCHELL SACK

ATTORNEY AT LAW

450 SEVENTH AVENUE, SUITE 1011

NEW YORK, N.Y. 10123

—

(212) 695-2535

(Date)

Harry Jones
1000 Main Street
Centerville, N.Y. 12345

Re: Barbara Jones v. Harry Jones

Dear Mr. Jones:

This office has been retained by your wife as a result of a series of beatings received from you during the month of January 1985.

Such conduct caused her to suffer severe humiliation and embarrassment, emotional distress, and physical discomfort from lacerations and other visible bruises.

You are hereby instructed to cease and desist perpetrating any conduct of a threatening nature upon her person. This includes verbal threats, abusive language, and physical contact.

In the event this request is ignored, your wife will immediately seek a temporary order of protection in the family court. This order may, among other things, prohibit you from remaining in your marital residence in the immediate future. Be assured that I will also recommend filing criminal charges as well as a civil lawsuit grounded in assault and battery.

I am hopeful all of this will not be necessary. Therefore, kindly have your attorney or yourself contact this office within the next several days so that we may discuss this problem rationally in an effort to resolve the situation in an amicable fashion.

Thank you for your attention in this matter.

Yours truly,

Steven Mitchell Sack

cc: Barbara Jones

(Sent certified mail, return receipt requested)

File criminal charges. If you desire to seek stronger action or to punish your spouse, you may wish to file a complaint in criminal court rather than in family court. You cannot use both courts to try the same issue in many states. That is why it is important to recognize what you are trying to accomplish. For example, if you want to help your spouse with his or her problem, commencing an action in family court is probably the best (that is, the less intimidating) way. Although many criminal-court judges incorporate nonpunitive orders (for example, a request to seek psychiatric treatment), these are often given in conjunction with jail sentences and fines. Family-court judges, however, rarely order imprisonment (although they can remove the case to criminal court if they believe that a spouse is dangerous and a significant amount of violence has arisen or is likely to arise).

In most states, removal of a case from criminal court to family court cannot be done without your consent. The potential may thus exist for your spouse to pressure you into dropping criminal charges. However, be aware that prosecutors are now generally investigating and proceeding with criminal cases of spouse abuse more often than ever before. They now have leverage to bring what were once considered harmless "family spats" into court and can order that the abuser attend a workshop to control his or her violent behavior as a condition of holding prosecution in abeyance.

Thus, do *not* be intimidated by your abusive spouse. Be candid with the police, the district attorney assigned to the case, and your lawyer. Remember, these people are on your side and will do all they can to help.

Many cities and counties have established a domestic-violence prosecution unit to help abused spouses. These units provide assistance ranging from the investigation and prosecution of criminal cases to the offer of shelter, counseling, and referral services. Warning letters are sometimes sent on behalf of victims who choose not to press criminal charges; criminal prosecution then follows if the violence does not end. For further information or assistance, contact your local domestic-violence prosecution unit.

A judge in criminal court may have the power to do the following:

- Set criminal charges against your spouse, ex-spouse, or lover
- Release the abusive spouse without bail on the promise to return to court for a hearing
- Release the abusive spouse with bail
- Give you a temporary order of protection protecting you and your children
- Adjourn the case on the spouse's promise not to hurt or threaten you
- Sentence the abusive spouse to probation pending medical or psychiatric evaluation
- Convict the abusive spouse of a crime

It is possible to obtain a temporary order of protection before your spouse is arrested; the order may even accompany an arrest warrant. A temporary order of protection can also be requested at the arraignment, even if your spouse has fled and the hearing is being held in his or her absence. After a conviction, the criminal court may issue an order of protection for as long as the court determines is necessary for your protection and that of your family or household members. Don't forget to ask for this if it seems appropriate in your case.

Note: If you decide to bring criminal charges, you can strengthen your case by being prepared. The following can help you prove your charges:

- Sworn affidavits from witnesses (for example, friends, relatives, neighbors who saw the beatings or observed lacerations and bruises on your body).

- Medical reports describing the number of visits and the injuries you received.

- A copy of the police report that documents the violent incident(s).

- Color pictures of your injuries. Always take color photographs of any injury immediately after a beating to prove the extent of your injuries. Months later, when your scars or bruises have healed, the pictures will demonstrate your injuries at their worst. *Never overlook this.* Untouched pictures are admissible evidence in court and are often used by judges or juries to award large verdicts.

Collect these items *before* visiting a lawyer or prosecutor. They can substantially improve your chances of success in the case.

Additional point: After you have obtained a temporary order of protection and a disposition of the case in either family or criminal court, it may then be necessary to obtain a permanent order of protection for yourself and your children. Such an order can direct the abuser to leave your household permanently and can award you sole custody of your minor children. In addition, the order can direct your spouse to pay you for losses suffered as a result of the abuse. These include medical expenses, loss of earnings or support, child support, attorney fees and court costs, and other out-of-pocket losses resulting from your injuries. Permanent orders of protection are very useful and should be obtained whenever the situation arises. Don't forget to speak to your lawyer or to the clerk of the court to inquire how to go about obtaining one.

When difficulties in a marriage include violence, it is important to confront the problem rather than sweep it under the rug. While no one wants to cause the breakup of a family, you must take the proper steps to protect yourself. Thus, if you are the victim of spouse abuse:

- *Act quickly and decisively.*
- *Communicate your problem to the appropriate individuals.*
- *Do not hesitate to use the legal system for help.*

Remember, your health and well-being, as well as the safety of your children, are at stake.

Marital Rape

Marital rape, like spouse abuse, is a hidden social problem. Until recently, marital rape was considered a consequence of a disobedient wife's refusal to perform her matrimonial duty, rather than a crime. Even today, thirty-eight states provide husbands with partial or complete immunity from prosecution. (See Table 5-2 for a state-by-state listing through 1981.)

Although some people tend to think of marital rape as a private family squabble, the victim often experiences the same violence and terror associated with being raped by a stranger. Many women who have been raped by their husbands suffer feelings of guilt and depression, experience loss of sexual interest, lose trust in people, and feel violent toward others.

If you are a victim of marital rape, you should remember that you have rights that can be enforced; no longer should you hide your head in shame and continue in the situation. The following strategies can protect you both legally and emotionally.

How to Protect Yourself from Marital Rape

1. *Act quickly and decisively.* More than 85 percent of all marital-rape cases include some form of physical violence. Thus it is essential to take action immediately. Do not wait for your husband to repeat his actions. Avoid allowing social, economic, or emotional pressures to cause you to delay taking corrective action. The failure to act may reduce your chances of success in a future lawsuit by raising doubts about your credibility. It may also give your husband the impression that you accept such conduct.

Table 5-2
Marital Rape Laws, State by State

CATEGORY	
1	*Absolute Exemption.* A husband can never be prosecuted for rape of his wife so long as the parties are married. The exemption still applies even if the parties are separated by court order. The exemption only ends when the parties are divorced; when the man is no longer *legally* the victim's husband.
2	*Partial Exemption.* A husband can be prosecuted for rape of his wife in some circumstances. Some states allow prosecution if the rape occurred after one spouse filed papers in court to end the marriage, or when the parties were not living together. The event or circumstance that ends the exemption differs from state to state.
3	*Cohabitant Exemption.* A man who is living with a woman that he is not legally married to cannot be prosecuted for raping her. Often this exemption is stated as a "defense," rather than a bar to prosecution. Thus, the district attorney may institute rape charges against the man, but he cannot be convicted of rape if he can prove he was living with the victim.
4	*Voluntary Social Companion Exemption.* This exemption may apply to husbands, cohabitants and social companions (i.e., dates). There is no requirement that the rapist live or have lived with the victim. Most states that have this type of exemption require that there have been past voluntary sexual relations between the defendant and victim in order for the exemption to apply. However, West Virginia does not require any past sexual activity.
5	*Silent Statute.* The law does not mention whether husbands may or may not be prosecuted for rape of their wives. It has been assumed, until recently, that husbands could *not* be prosecuted because of Hale's alleged "common law" marital rape exemption. However, recent lawsuits in New Jersey, Massachusetts and Florida have held that no "common law" exemption exists. Thus, it is not clear if husbands can be prosecuted for marital rape in these "silent" states. Whether marital rape is a crime in these states will depend on future judicial decision, or legislative interpretation of the statutes.
No Exemption	The marital rape exemption has been abolished; husbands can be charged with rape of their wives in all or most cases.
Rape Degrees	In some states, there are different "types" of rape, murder, assault, etc. In most states, the criminal laws punish rape more or less severely depending on the circumstances of the rape (e.g., whether a weapon was used; age, mental and/or physical condition of the victim; whether the assault involved illegal sexual penetration, conduct, contact or use of a foreign object). These differences in the law are called "degrees." It is not possible to give a uniform definition for each "degree" as each state bases its rape degrees on different factors. (The fact that the marital rape exemption may apply in some rape degrees and not others has political and practical significance. The law is saying that it will tolerate certain violence by husbands against

(continued)

Table 5-2 (*Continued*)

their wives that it will not tolerate between strangers. Practically, the different application of the exemption, based on the degree of rape charged, may decide whether marital rape cases will ever be prosecuted or what, if any, penalty will be imposed.)

Gender-Neutral Statutes

Traditionally, the law defined rape as a crime only men could commit. Thus, only husbands were granted the "immunity" or protection of the marital rape exemption. Today, many states have rewritten their laws in gender-neutral terms. Under these new rape laws, women can also be prosecuted for rape and the immunity granted under the marital rape exemption is extended to both spouses. The following chart does not incorporate these gender-neutral changes since it is intended to reflect reality rather than pure "legalese."

STATE	CATEGORY	STATUS OF MARITAL RAPE LAW	CITATIONS
Alabama	*1, 3*	Husbands and cohabitors can *never* be charged with rape of mate.	Title 13A-6-60(4), 13A-6-61
Alaska	*2*	Husband can only be charged with rape of wife if parties were living apart *or* he caused severe physical injury (besides the rape).	Stat § 11.41.445(a)
Arizona	*2*	Husband cannot be charged with wife rape while parties are living together.	R.S. § 13-1404-06
Arkansas	*5*	Statute only exempts husbands in statutory rape cases. Whether marital rape is a crime will depend on judicial decision or legislative interpretation of "common law" exemption.	Stat. § 41-1803, *et seq.*
California	*No Exemption*	Husband can be charged with crime of "spousal rape." Thirty-day reporting requirement.	Pen. C. § 262
Colorado	*2*	Husband cannot be charged with rape of wife while parties live together.	R.S. § 18-3-409
Connecticut	*No Exemption to First-Degree Rape; 1, 3*	Spouse/cohabitors *can* be charged with first degree rape; marital and cohabitor exemption for all other sexual assaults.	Pen. Code § 53a-67(b), as amended by H.B. 5247

Table 5-2 (*Continued*)

STATE	CATEGORY	STATUS OF MARITAL RAPE LAW	CITATIONS
Delaware	*3, 4*	"Voluntary social companion" of victim cannot be charged with first degree rape; this may exempt husbands, cohabitors and "dates." Cohabitors (and spouses living together) cannot be charged with rape of mate.	D.C.A. §§ 761-764, 772(b)
District of Columbia	*5*	Not known if "common law" exemption applies, making marital rape legal.	R.S.D.C. § 22-2801
Florida	*No Exemption*	Husbands can be charged with rape of wife, the same as a stranger. (*State v. Larry Smith*)	S.A. § 794.011
Georgia	*5*	Statute only exempts husbands in statutory rape cases. Marital rape *may* be legal under "common law" exemption; will depend on judicial decision or legislative interpretation of statute.	C.A. § 26.2001, 2018
Hawaii	*4, 2*	"Voluntary social companion" of victim cannot be charged with forcible (first degree) rape; this may exempt husbands, cohabitors and "dates." Husbands cannot be charged with "lesser" sexual assaults of wife while parties are living together.	R.S. § 707-730 to 732
Idaho	*2*	Husband cannot be charged with rape of wife *unless* parties have been living apart at least 180 days or legal action for divorce or separation started (petition filed).	C. § 18-6107
Illinois	*1*	Husband can *never* be charged with rape of wife.	A.S. Ch. 38 § 11-1

(*continued*)

Table 5-2 (*Continued*)

STATE	CATEGORY	STATUS OF MARITAL RAPE LAW	CITATIONS
Indiana	2	Husbands cannot be charged with rape of wife *unless* parties live apart and court action for separation or divorce started (petition filed).	S.A. § 35-42-4-1(b)
Iowa	*No Exemption to First- and Second-Degree Rape; 3*	Husbands *can* be charged with first and second degree rape of wife. Husbands and cohabitors *cannot* be charged with third degree sexual abuse of mate.	C.A. § 709.2 to 709.4
Kansas	1	Husband can *never* be charged with rape of wife.	S.A. § 21-3502
Kentucky	2	Husbands and cohabitors cannot be charged with rape of spouse *unless* court order of separation.	R.S. § 510.010 (3)
Louisiana	2	Husband cannot be charged with rape of wife *unless* court order of separation.	R.S.A. § 14.41
Maine	2, 3	Husbands and cohabitants cannot be charged with rape of mate while parties living together.	R.S.A. Title 17A § 251, 252
Maryland	2	Husband cannot be charged with rape of wife *unless* court order of separation.	A.C. § 27-464D
Massachusetts	*No Exemptions*	Husbands can be charged with rape of wife same as a stranger (no exemption). (*Commonwealth v. Chretien*)	A.L. Ch. 265 § 22; Ch. 277 § 39
Michigan	2	Husbands cannot be charged with rape of wife *unless* parties live apart and court action for separation or divorce started (petition filed).	M.S.R.C.C. Ch. 23 § 2340

Table 5-2 (*Continued*)

STATE	CATEGORY	STATUS OF MARITAL RAPE LAW	CITATIONS
Minnesota	*No Exemption*	Husbands can be charged with rape of wife under most circumstances.	S.A. § 609.349
Mississippi	*2, 5*	Husband cannot be charged with "sexual battery" of wife *unless* parties living apart. Separate "rape" statute does *not* exempt husbands; unknown if marital *rape* is a crime.	MCA § 97-3-95 to 103, (Supp. 1980)
Missouri	*2*	Husband cannot be charged with rape of wife *unless* court order of separation.	A.S. § 566.010:2
Montana	*2, 3*	Husbands/cohabitants cannot be charged with rape of mate while parties are living together.	R.C. § 45-5-506
Nebraska	*No Exemption*	Husband can be charged with rape of wife the same as a stranger.	R.S. § 28-319, 320
Nevada	*2*	Husbands cannot be charged with rape of wife *unless* parties live apart and court action for separation or divorce started (petition filed).	R.S. § 200.373
New Hampshire	*No Exemption*	Husband *can* be charged with rape of wife under most circumstances.	RSA 632-A:5 (H.B. 516, effective 8/81)
New Jersey	*No Exemption*	Husbands *can* be charged with rape of wife, same as a stranger (no exemption).	S.A. § 2C:14-5(b)
New Mexico	*2, 3*	Husbands/cohabitants cannot be charged with rape of their mates *unless* parties living apart or legal action for divorce or separation started (petition filed).	Stat. § 30-9-10, 11
New York	*2*	Husband cannot be charged with rape of wife *unless* court order of separation.	Pen. L. § 130.00

(*continued*)

Table 5-2 *(Continued)*

STATE	CATEGORY	STATUS OF MARITAL RAPE LAW	CITATIONS
North Carolina	2	Husband cannot be charged with rape of wife *unless* court order of separation or spouses living apart pursuant to written agreement.	G.S. § 14-27.8
North Dakota	2	Husbands cannot be charged with rape of wife *unless* court order of separation.	C.A. § 12.1-20-01, 02, 03
Ohio	2	Husband cannot be charged with rape of wife *unless* parties live apart and court action started (petition filed) or written separation agreement entered into.	ORC § 2907.01, 02
Oklahoma	1	Husband can *never* be charged with rape of wife.	S.A. Title 21 § 1111
Oregon	*No Exemption*	Husbands can be charged with rape of wife same as a stranger.	R.S. § 163.305
Pennsylvania	2, 3	Husbands/cohabitants cannot be charged with rape of mates *unless* parties living apart or written separation agreement entered into.	S.A. Title 18 § 3103
Rhode Island	2	Husband cannot be charged with rape of wife *unless* court order of separation.	G.L. § 11-37-1
South Carolina	2	Husband cannot be charged with rape of wife *unless* court order of separation.	C. § 16-3-658
South Dakota	1	Husband can *never* be charged with rape of wife.	C.L.A. § 22-22-1
Tennessee	2	Husband cannot be charged with rape *unless* court action for divorce or separation started (petition filed).	C.A. § 39-3702

Table 5-2 (*Continued*)

STATE	CATEGORY	STATUS OF MARITAL RAPE LAW	CITATIONS
Texas	*1, 3*	Husbands and cohabitor can *never* be charged with rape of wife/mate.	§ 21-02(a) § 21-12
Utah	*2*	Husband cannot be charged with rape of wife *unless* court order of separation.	Crim. C.A. § 76-5-402, 407
Vermont	*1*	Husband can *never* be charged with rape of wife.	S.A. Title 13 § 3252
Virginia	*5*	Unknown if marital rape is a crime.	Code 18.2-61, *et seq.* (effective 7/1/81)
Washington	*1*	Husband can *never* be charged with rape of wife.	R.C.A. Ch. 9A.44.010, *et seq.* (Supp., 1979)
West Virginia	*1, 3, 4*	Husbands and cohabitants can *never* be charged with rape of mate. "Voluntary social companion" cannot be charged with 1st degree sexual assault (date-rape exemption).	Code § 61-8B-1
Wisconsin	*2*	Husband cannot be charged with rape of wife *unless* parties live apart and court action for divorce or separation started (petition filed).	S.A. § 940.225(6)
Wyoming	*2*	Husband cannot be charged with rape of wife *unless* court order of separation.	S.A. § 6-4-307

Source: Diana Russell, *Rape in Marriage*, Macmillan, New York, 1982.
Reprinted with permission from the National Center on Women & Family.

2. *Communicate the problem.*

A wife can be repeatedly raped during her marriage and no one will know about it. It is important to communicate your problem; no one can assist you if you remain silent.

Marriage counselors, crisis-intervention centers, victims' services agencies, friends, and religious organizations can provide help. One excellent source of assistance is a rape-crisis center which may be located in your community (consult your local telephone listings).

If you are attacked, call a rape-crisis center immediately. Most rape-crisis centers maintain twenty-four-hour hotlines. Staff members can accompany you to the hospital or police station and assist you in preparing examination forms and police reports. Ask a counselor if you have a legal cause to file criminal charges and how you go about doing it. A positive answer may serve as a starting point for legal action.

3. *Explore your legal options.* State law varies considerably with respect to marital rape. In twelve states marital rape is now considered a crime. Other states impose certain conditions before making it a crime (for instance, in some states the rape must be accompanied by severe physical violence). An experienced matrimonial or criminal lawyer can provide you with a thorough explanation of your options. Schedule an interview with a lawyer if this seems appropriate in your case.

Several of the options to be considered are outlined below.

Consider obtaining a divorce or separation. If there is no chance of reconciliation, you may wish to obtain a divorce. The rape could be used to prove grounds (that is, cruel and inhuman treatment) for divorce. However, there are many factors to be considered when seeking a permanent dissolution of the marriage: the question of alimony or maintenance, division of marital assets, child support, child custody, and attorney fees and court costs. (See Chapter 6.)

If you are not sure you want a divorce, you may wish to first obtain a separation. A legal separation will give you time to attempt to resolve your difficulties and save the marriage. Your husband, for example, may consent to therapy, and you might reconcile your marriage if his therapy is successful.

Consider suing for your personal injuries. If you live in a state where interspousal tort immunity has been abolished, it may be possible to sue your husband for damages resulting from the rape. A lawyer specializing in matrimonial law will advise you whether it is worthwhile to consider commencing a civil lawsuit to recover damages for physical, psychological,

Table 5-3
Losses Recoverable in Proven Rape/Abuse Cases

Loss	Evidence
Injury-induced pain	Authorized drug prescriptions; medical reports; affidavits from nurses and attendants; color photographs of injuries
Pain and suffering	Authorized drug prescriptions; medical reports; affidavits from nurses and attendants; color photographs of injuries; testimony of medical experts, friends, and relatives
Shock, mental anguish, anxiety, embarrassment, humiliation	Authorized drug prescriptions; medical and psychiatric reports; affidavits from nurses and attendants; color photographs of injuries; testimony of medical experts, therapists, psychiatrists, friends, and relatives
Depression, neurosis, psychosis	Authorized drug prescriptions; medical and psychiatric reports; affidavits from nurses and attendants; testimony of medical experts, therapists, psychiatrists, friends, and relatives
Reduced sexual pleasure	Authorized drug prescriptions; medical and psychiatric reports; testimony of medical experts, therapists, and psychiatrists
Medical and drug expenses	Cancelled checks; receipts; unpaid bills
Inpatient and/or outpatient hospital care	Canceled checks; receipts; unpaid bills
Reduced earnings from work	Wage statements; affidavits from employer and fellow employees
Reduced profits from business	Books and records of your business; affidavits from partners and employees
Court costs, filing fees, witness fees, stenographic fees, legal fees	Canceled checks; receipts; unpaid bills

and emotional injuries as well as other losses attributable to the rape.

Table 5-3 lists the kinds of losses you may be able to recover as a result of a rape or abuse as well as the evidence needed to prove loss; don't forget to collect such evidence where appropriate.

Consider pressing criminal charges. You may decide to institute criminal charges against your spouse if you live in a state where marital rape is a crime. Table 5–2 indicates which states have a marital exemption for rape, which states limit the exemption, and which states consider marital rape a crime.

Note: Some states fall into more than one category. In addition, considerable legislation and litigation has occurred over the past few years; the table reflects the law as of July 1, 1981. Thus you should review the present law in your own state before taking action.

Many marital-rape cases are unsuccessful. Victims often face difficult procedural requirements, depending on state law. In some states, certain conditions (for instance, fear of earnest resistance or imminent danger) must be proved in order to make criminal charges stick. In one recent New York case, for example, a wife lost her case because she failed to prove she was not responsible for prompting her husband's advances. That is why it is best to have an experienced lawyer brief you on your chances of success before deciding to press criminal charges.

The following summarizes many of the major problems affecting women who file criminal charges against their husbands for rape:

- *Proving that there was a lack of consent.* Some people, including judges, believe that the institution of marriage obligates the wife to have sex at a husband's whim. To overcome such bias, a wife must prove that on a particular occasion, for good reason, she did not want to have sex and that her husband forced it upon her.

- *The jury's predisposition to doubt there was a rape.* Some experts believe this is often the biggest obstacle to overcome in a marital-rape case.

- *Proving that there is no other motive behind pressing charges.* To be successful, a wife must demonstrate that she is not pressing charges out of spite or to induce a more favorable divorce settlement.

- *Failing to provide other kinds of proof.* Many women fail to obtain prompt medical attention and/or to take color photographs of their injuries after a rape. This should always be done to strengthen a claim. A visit to a doctor or hospital can document the seriousness of your injuries and corroborate your story. Medical tests can be performed to prove the existence of semen in your body, thereby proving that a sexual act occurred. The test can also determine *when* the act occurred, if given within twenty-four hours.

- *Lack of witnesses and corroborated testimony.* This is a frequent problem because the act usually occurs when no one else is present. Some women lose their cases because they have no other evidence besides their own testimony (which a husband may refute).

There are some standard defenses used in marital-rape cases. You should be aware of them if you are to overcome them:

- *The victim was intoxicated.* Charges of marital rape are often defeated by the introduction of police reports or testimony supporting the presumption of intoxication or drug use at the time of the attack.

- *The rape was victim-precipitated.* Husbands often claim that they were teased or goaded into attacking the wife.

- *The victim delayed in reporting the rape.* Many wives wait too long before reporting the crime. Visible injuries then fade and the presumption of consent to the rape is sometimes created.

- *There is lack of evidence of battery.* If the wife delays in reporting the crime, if she is in good physical condition, if she cannot document her injuries or produce evidence (for example, color pictures or medical reports) that she was raped and/or beaten by her husband, prosecution for marital rape is not likely to succeed. That is why it is important to take color pictures of your injuries immediately, that is, when the bruises or lacerations are visible. You should also contact the police and seek prompt medical attention after the attack.

Do not be intimidated by your husband's lawyer if you decide to press criminal charges. Many states are recognizing the hardship on victims who come forward and file criminal charges. These states are making it easier for victims to testify. Some prosecutors are establishing special assault units to minimize the number of interviews victims must face. Other states have passed laws to improve conviction rates. In Minnesota, for example, victims no longer have to prove that they resisted, and their testimony needs no corroboration. In addition, the law links the severity of the punishment to the nature of the injury (thereby eliminating a judge's or jury's subjectivity and bias).

In an increasing number of states, defense attorneys representing husbands are prohibited from cross-examining rape victims about past sexual behavior as a means of attacking credibility. If your state has such a "rape shield" law, you need not fear the prospect of being embarrassed in a courtroom with such questioning. Ask your lawyer about this.

Child Abuse and Neglect

Child abuse, like other forms of domestic violence, is usually not reported to the authorities, yet it is known that the number of incidents is rising sharply. The Humane Association of America found that 413,000 cases of child abuse were reported to state and local authorities in 1976. By 1981 the figure had more than doubled to 851,000; in 1983 the number exceeded 1 million.

Other statistics illustrate the severity of the problem:

- The number of cases reported may be as low as 10 percent of the total number of child-abuse incidents.

- Only 5 percent of substantiated cases lead to criminal prosecution of the abuser.

- Twenty percent of substantiated cases result in removal of the abused child to a foster home. Most abusive parents do not lose custody of their children on a permanent basis.

- Reporting abuse does not always save the child. Approximately 25 percent of all child-abuse *deaths* involve children whose cases were already reported to the authorities.

How to Remedy Child Abuse

The information on the following pages will tell you what to do when you discover someone engaging in child abuse or neglect. Such strategies can help remedy the situation and may save a child's life.

1. *Seek the assistance of a child-protection agency.* The best source of assistance is through a local child-protection agency. These are listed in the phone book with local government agencies under "Social Services." Call the agency and describe the situation. A representative will determine if the case falls within the definition of child abuse and whether to commence an investigation.

Once an investigation is conducted, the agency will either label the case as "unfounded" or will verify the abuse and find assistance for the troubled family. This can include financial assistance, day care, and counseling for the abusive parent(s). One common arrangement is to place the family under "home supervision." This allows a family to stay together while a social worker makes regular visits to determine whether the children are being adequately cared for. Improvements are immediate in some cases. However, according to a study conducted by the U.S. Department of Health and Human Services, most parents require supervision, sometimes with weekly visits extending over several months.

If the child abuse is particularly acute or if the abusive parents refuse to take corrective action, stricter measures involving the legal system may be required.

2. *Institute child-protection proceedings.* Child-protection proceedings should be instituted immediately in severe abuse or neglect cases. Anyone in contact with the abused child can apply to the local family court for an order directing temporary removal of the child from the home. In fact, all fifty states have mandatory child-abuse reporting laws. These require health-care professionals, teachers, social workers, and law-enforcement officers to report child abuse to the appropriate child-protection agency in their county. Friends, neighbors, and relatives are also encouraged to report cases of child abuse. Under these laws, penalties can be imposed (including fines and other sanctions) for individuals who do not comply.

After temporary removal of the child has been effected, a petition for child abuse is then filed against the abusive parent or guardian in family court. In most states, only the child-protection agency is authorized to file such a petition and only after completing its investigation. A factual hearing is then conducted to determine whether the child is abused or neglected within the meaning of applicable state law. This can be a problem because it is often difficult to distinguish between legitimate parental discipline and unreasonable force.

State laws governing child abuse and neglect vary as to specifics but are all targeted toward identifying a general pattern of parental conduct that is neglectful or abusive. The signs which most family-court judges look at in determining whether there is child abuse or neglect include:

- Infliction of physical injury by nonaccidental means
- A substantial risk of injury or death
- Excessive corporal punishment
- Disfigurement or impairment
- Lack of proper supervision and guardianship
- Failure to provide adequate food, clothing, shelter, and medical care
- Abandonment

Parents often counter these charges with a variety of defenses; for example, they may claim:

- Legitimate parental action (discipline)
- Financial difficulties
- Religious prohibitions against medical treatment (in cases of child neglect)
- Premenstrual stress, temporary insanity, or limited wrongful behavior due to an adverse reaction to a drug prescription

Often a finding of child abuse or neglect will only be made when a combination of factors is present. In a recent New York family-court case, for example, a judge ruled that the presence of black eyes, bruises, and lumps on the child was insufficient in itself to demonstrate child abuse. However, the parents' failure to seek immediate medical care for the child after the beating resulted in a finding of neglect!

Individuals other than parents can also be brought into family court on charges of child abuse or neglect. This includes baby-sitters, lovers, siblings, and relatives. Where the parent is not committing the abuse, the family court will either order the parent to remove the offending person from the household or will remove the child from the home.

Proof of child abuse and neglect can be shown in a variety of ways. The most typical evidence involves injuries sustained by the child. This is often demonstrated by photographic proof of the injuries in addition to the testimony of a health-care professional (a doctor, nurse, or hospital attendant) who treated the child.

Most family-court judges are liberal in terms of the kinds of evidence they accept in determining neglect or abuse. As a result, they will base their findings on any written record or report introduced during the abuse proceeding. In many states, the child is represented at such proceedings by a court-appointed lawyer known as a guardian *ad litem*. The guardian *ad litem* represents the child's concerns and is responsible for voicing an opinion as to what is best for the child. The recommendation may even call for a solution the child may not want—such as separation from the parents. The use of court-appointed guardians *ad litem* usually works well to protect children.

After the fact-finding hearing is concluded, the case is

ready for disposition. The family-court judge weighs all the evidence and comes to a decision that is in the *best interests of the child*. The court may direct a temporary or permanent solution. One immediate solution may involve placing the child under foster care while the abusive parent undergoes therapy. Foster care sometimes causes an erosion of family ties, however, so a judge may decide to place the child in the temporary care of a relative (for instance, a grandparent) to increase the chance that family ties will be preserved.

When a judge finds severe child abuse or neglect (as in cases of torture, starvation, or rape), the court may recommend criminal prosecution of the abusive parent as well as permanent separation from the family. The family court may even order the transfer of a child-abuse case to criminal court, depending upon the seriousness and circumstances of the case; the extent of the harm to the child; the history, character, and condition of the abusive parent; and the attitude of the complaining party or victim toward criminal prosecution. The accused parent is then indicted for a number of charges, including common-law assault.

When termination of parental rights is an issue, the court carefully examines all the evidence at the fact-finding hearing. Judges are aware that although a permanent separation from abusive parents may protect the child physically, deep psychological and emotional damage may ensue. This is especially true for young children when the abuser is the mother. Thus the court will only permanently separate a parent and child when there is *clear and convincing proof* that the parent is unfit to care for the child and the child would be better off elsewhere.

Some judges seek a permanent solution for child abuse and neglect through adoption. Steps are taken in this area after it has been determined that the parents' rights in raising the child should be permanently severed.

3. *Consider divorce and custody proceedings.* Never be intimidated if your spouse is committing child abuse. Take immediate action to stop such conduct. Consult with a lawyer to explore the possibility of obtaining sole custody of the child(ren). If your spouse is a continuing danger to you and your children, you may wish to obtain a temporary order

of protection, even while taking immediate steps to help him or her.

4. *Make use of other available types of aid.* There are a number of programs and services designed to assist the abusive or neglectful parent:

- *Aid to Families with Dependent Children (AFDC).* If the child abuse stems from financial difficulties, your family may be eligible for welfare assistance. AFDC is available through your local department of social services and is co-sponsored by the federal government.
- *Food stamps.* While AFDC can help you with general financial problems, food stamps can help pay for your child's nutritional needs. Contact your local department of social services for eligibility information.
- *Medicaid.* An inability to cope with a child's poor health can lead to abuse and neglect. If you desire assistance to pay for your child's medical needs, contact a Medicaid representative through your local department of social services.
- *Day care.* Separation of the abused child and parent for part of the day may protect the child while freeing the parent for counseling. There are a variety of privately and publicly funded day-care centers in your area. Consult the Yellow Pages (or government listings) under "Day Care."
- *Marriage counseling.* Contact a marriage counselor if the abuse or neglect is rooted in marital difficulties. Consult the Yellow Pages for a marriage counselor near you. *Don't forget to discuss fees up front; for your protection, obtain a written estimate of charges.*
- *Parental education programs.* Child abuse and neglect often occur because parents have not learned proper homemaking skills. Some child-protection agencies sponsor home-supervisor programs where a social worker is sent to the troubled home to train the parent in essential skills.

5. Contact a child-abuse-prevention organization. There are many organizations actively working to overcome the problem of child abuse and neglect. These organizations serve as sources of information about existing programs for abused children and their parents. If you want to know more about what you can do to prevent child abuse, contact any (or all) of the following organizations:

Children's Aid Society
105 East 22nd Street
New York, NY 10010
(212)949-4800

New York Foundling Hospital
1175 Third Avenue
New York, NY 10021
(212)472-2233

Legal Aid Society
Family Law Unit
11 Park Place
New York, NY 10007
(212)406-0730

Society for the Prevention of
   Cruelty to Children
161 William Street
New York, NY 10038
(212)233-5500

National Center on
Child Abuse and Neglect
400 Sixth Street, S.W.
Washington, DC 20213
(202)245-2857

Child abuse and neglect are problems which are attracting national attention. The various laws and organizations in your state have come a long way toward protecting children. If you are aware of a child-abuse or child-neglect situation, take advantage of the network of services and programs in your area. Obtain legal assistance when necessary.

6 Breaking Up: Divorce, Separation, and the Law

Introduction

Statistics reveal that approximately one out of every two marriages entered in 1985 will end in divorce. This is a dramatic turnaround from previous generations, when most couples typically stayed together, through thick and thin, for life. Divorce rates have been rising steadily all over the country as traditional attitudes toward marriage have been altered and as women have sought greater independence and freedom.

The law has tried to keep pace with this phenomenon by making it easier for couples to obtain a divorce. Now divorce accounts for close to 50 percent of all civil litigation filings in the courts today; divorce cases have become more common than commercial and corporate cases. No-fault divorce laws passed in many states have eliminated the need to prove improper conduct by one or both spouses (which used to be essential in obtaining a divorce), thereby eliminating the need to air one's "dirty laundry" in open court. More states are simply rubber-stamping prearranged divorces; one state even recognizes divorce by registration—neither party needs to appear in court!

However, although the divorce decree is easier to obtain, equitable-distribution and community-property laws have made the focus *economic* in nature. No longer does the wife have to think only in terms of alimony. How to value and divide assets and property produced during the marriage, including the value of pensions, of a wife's homemaking services, and of professional degrees, has made the process quite complicated, with tremendous financial consequences for the divorcing couple.

This chapter will make you aware of what you are legally entitled to receive in a property settlement when the marriage is ended. You will learn the factors a court looks at when evaluating various forms of property. I will also discuss what constitutes separate property, property not subject to distribution and division.

After reading the information contained herein, you will have a better understanding of how divorce laws in this country work and how to get what you are due. I also discuss the processes of separation and annulment, for in some cases a separation agreement can help you avoid expensive divorce litigation. Of course, I also tell you how to work effectively with your lawyer for maximum results in your divorce case.

The Legal Implications of Dissolving a Marriage

Marriage is a civil contract between two people that all states have an interest in preserving. Almost any adult has the legal capacity to get married. Once married, a unique legal status is created, the obligations of which cannot be transferred or assigned, and which can only be dissolved by divorce or through annulment. In most states, it may also be altered by a decree of separation.

The law in each state governs marriage, divorce, annulment, separation, and related matters. The legislature of each state decides how a marriage can be dissolved; for example, many states provide for divorce merely on a showing of "incompatibility," "irreconcilable conflict," or "breakdown of the marriage." In other states, there must be a showing of grounds— for example, cruel and inhuman treatment, abandonment of one spouse by another for a requisite period of time, living apart for a sufficient period of time, imprisonment for more than a specified term, or adultery. Some states also allow other "no-fault" events like living apart under a separation agreement or decree for more than one year; this automatically ripens into a divorce after papers are filed in court.

Table 6-1 is a state-by-state compendium of current grounds for dissolving the marriage relationship.* The chart is current as of January 1, 1986. Column (1) shows the states which have "irretrievable marital breakdown" as the sole ground (except for mental incompetence) for divorce. Several states have simply added "breakdown" or "irreconcilable differences" to

---

*Accolades are given to noted authorities Doris Jonas Freed and Timothy B. Walker for the research undertaken in preparing this table and for permission to reprint several other tables throughout this book.

Table 6-1
Grounds for Divorce

	(1) Irreconcilable Differences or Irretrievable Breakdown Sole Ground	(2) Irreconcilable Differences or Breakdown Added to Traditional Grounds	(3) Incompatibility as Grounds	(4) Living Separate and Apart as Grounds	(5) Judicial Separation or Maintenance as Grounds	(6) Mutual Consent Divorces
Alabama		√	√	2 years		
Alaska			√			
Arizona	√					
Arkansas				3 years		
California	√					√
Colorado	√					√
Connecticut		√		18 months¹		√
Delaware		√	√	6 months		
Florida	√					√
Georgia		√				
Hawaii	√			2 years	Any period	√
Idaho		√		5 years		
Illinois		√²		√²		√²
Indiana		√				
Iowa	√					
Kansas			√			
Kentucky	√					
Louisiana				1 year		
Maine		√				
Maryland				1 year³		
Massachusetts		√⁴				
Michigan	√					
Minnesota	√					
Mississippi		√				
Missouri		√		1 year⁵		
Montana	√			180 days		
Nebraska	√					
Nevada			√	1 year		
New Hampshire		√				
New Jersey				1½ years		
New Mexico		√				
New York					1 year	
North Carolina				1 year		
North Dakota	√					
Ohio				1 year		√
Oklahoma			√			
Oregon	√					√
Pennsylvania		√		3 years⁶		

Table 6-1 (*Continued*)

	(1) Irreconcilable Differences or Irretrievable Breakdown Sole Ground	(2) Irreconcilable Differences or Breakdown Added to Traditional Grounds	(3) Incompatibility as Grounds	(4) Living Separate and Apart as Grounds	(5) Judicial Separation or Maintenance as Grounds	(6) Mutual Consent Divorces
Rhode Island		✓		3 years		
South Carolina				1 year		
South Dakota		✓				
Tennessee		✓		3 years		
Texas				3 years		
Utah					3 years	
Vermont				6 months		
Virginia				1 year[6]		
Washington	✓					✓
West Virginia		✓		1 year		
Wisconsin	✓			1 year		
Wyoming		✓				
Washington, D.C.				6 months[7]		
Puerto Rico				2 years		
Virgin Islands	✓					

1. Eighteen months living separate and apart *and* incompatibility.
2. Irretrievable breakdown *and* two years living separate and apart; if both parties consent, the period becomes six months.
3. Voluntary twelve consecutive months or two-year uninterrupted separation.
4. Separation agreement also required.
5. One year by mutual consent or two years living separate and apart.
6. Living separate and apart for one year is sufficient, six months if there is a separation agreement and there are no children.
7. Six months by voluntary separation, one year living separate and apart.

Source: Family Law Quarterly, Vol. XIX, No. 4, Winter 1986.

traditional divorce grounds. These states are indicated in column (2).

Other states use the "incompatibility" standard; they are indicated in column (3). Still other states allow divorce after a period of "living separate and apart," either instead of or in addition to the no-fault grounds. These states, with durational requirements for such a ground, are seen in column (4).

Still other states provide for conversion of judicial separation or separate maintenance decrees into divorce. These states and the durational requirements for conversion are indicated in column (5). Finally, a small, but growing number of states provide for "paper" dissolutions or dissolution by affidavits only where there is mutual consent to the divorce. This procedure makes it relatively simple to obtain a divorce, and this recent trend is incorporated in the laws of those states listed in column (6).

The fifty states also have different concepts with respect to who gets what when a divorce is obtained. Typically, the manner in which property is divided and distributed upon divorce is characterized by three different methods, and states are categorized accordingly as community-property states, equitable-distribution states, and common-law states.

The community-property states recognize marriage as a community of which each spouse is a member and to which each contributes equally through his or her labors. All property acquired during the marriage is regarded as community property in which both parties share equally, no matter who owns legal title to the property. The following is a list of states whose laws govern the distribution of property upon divorce according to community-property principles:

Arizona	New Mexico
California	Puerto Rico
Idaho	Texas
Louisiana	Washington
Nevada	

Note: Each community-property state has its own peculiar rules under which marital property can be divided. For further information, contact an experienced lawyer.

Most states follow the equitable-distribution rule. Under the laws in these states, each spouse is a partner to the marriage and the assets and property the partnership produces. Judges are empowered to distribute marital property *equitably*—not necessarily equally—after considering the following factors:

- The duration of the marriage
- The respective age and health of the parties
- The parties' preseparation standard of living
- Contribution of each party toward the acquisition, preservation, or appreciation of the marital property

- Contributions of the homemaker spouse
- Present and prospective earnings of each party
- Vocational skills of each party
- Desirability of the custodial parent working or remaining at home to care for the children

Typically, both equitable-distribution and community-property states do not consider *fault* in rendering a distributive award. Thus, for example, it may not matter if the husband has committed adultery when deciding what share of marital property he should keep. However, some states do consider economic dissipation of marital assets a factor in awarding less property to one spouse. An example of this would occur where, for example, one spouse is accused of mismanaging the couple's investments, running a couple's business into the ground, or creating huge gambling debts.

Finally, a few states are called common-law states because they do not include the value of homemaking services, companionship, professional degrees, or pensions in making decisions of property. In these common-law states, the courts have no general or equitable power to distribute property upon divorce; *title* alone controls. Thus, for example, if a husband buys a house and puts it under his wife's name, it's hers. If he owns all the stock in a business, it's his, and the wife is not entitled to share in the ongoing profits of the business, the appreciated value of the business during the marriage, or anything else; the wife cannot receive a nickel for it upon divorce (except in narrow instances where it is affected by gift law or where a lawyer can imply a constructive trust, tracing equitable title back to the property).

Obviously, common-law states have created tremendous inequities for spouses, particularly women, and the trend is for states to change their laws, becoming either equitable-distribution or community-property states. Obviously, it is very important to know how the law in your state deals with distribution of property upon divorce. This should be the first question you ask your lawyer.

Table 6-2 is a state-by-state listing of property distribution upon divorce. As you can see, community-property states

Table 6-2
Property Distribution

	A: Community-Property States		B	C: Equitable-Distribution Common-Law States		
	(1)	(2)		(1)	(2) Only marital	(3) Gifts, inheritances
	"Equal"	"Equitable"	Title states	All property considered	property considered	are excluded
Alabama					✓¹	Yes¹
Alaska				✓		
Arizona	✓	✓²				
Arkansas					✓³	
California	✓⁴					
Colorado					✓⁵	Yes⁵
Connecticut				✓		No
Delaware					✓	No
Florida				✓		
Georgia					✓	No
Hawaii				✓		No
Idaho	✓					
Illinois					✓	Yes
Indiana				✓		No
Iowa				✓		Yes⁹
Kansas				✓		No
Kentucky					✓	Yes
Louisiana	✓					
Maine					✓	Yes
Maryland					✓	Yes
Massachusetts				✓		
Michigan					✓	No
Minnesota					✓	Yes
Mississippi			✓⁶			
Missouri					✓	Yes
Montana				✓		No
Nebraska					✓	No
Nevada		✓				
New Hampshire				✓		No
New Jersey					✓	Yes
New Mexico	✓					
New York					✓	Yes
North Carolina					✓	Yes
North Dakota				✓		No
Ohio				✓		No
Oklahoma					✓	Yes
Oregon				✓		No
Pennsylvania					✓	Yes

Table 6-2 (*Continued*)

	A: Community-Property States		B	C: Equitable-Distribution Common-Law States		
	(1)	*(2)*		*(1)*	*(2)*	*(3)*
	"Equal"	"Equi-table"	Title states	All property considered	Only marital property considered	Gifts, inheritances are excluded
Rhode Island					✓	Yes
South Carolina		✓[7]		✓	✓	
South Dakota				✓		Unclear
Tennessee					✓[5]	Yes
Texas	✓[8]					
Utah				✓		
Vermont				✓		
Virginia					✓	Yes
Washington	✓					
West Virginia					✓	Yes
Wisconsin	✓				✓	Yes
Wyoming				✓		
Washington, D.C.					✓	Yes
Puerto Rico		✓			✓	Yes
Virgin Islands					✓[9]	Yes

1. Unless property used for the common benefit of both parties.
2. Statute says equitable but case law indicates this is equal.
3. Equal unless such division is inequitable.
4. Unless one party has misappropriated community property deliberately.
5. Except as to increase in value.
6. But see *Reeves v. Reeves*, 410 So. 2d 1300 (Miss. 1982).
7. But see *Parrott v. Parrott*, 292 S.E. 2d 182 (S.C. 1982).
8. Unless court finds equal division would be inequitable.
9. Personal property only.

Source: Family Law Quarterly, Vol. XIX, No. 4, Winter 1986.

and their distribution theories are indicated in columns A(1) and (2). Common-law-title states, which have no general or equitable power to distribute property upon divorce, except as to jointly held property, are listed in column B. Equitable-distribution states are defined in column C, with subdivisions: (1), listing those states that consider all property for distribution; (2), listing those states that distribute only marital property; and (3), listing those states that exclude distribution of gifts or inheritances received by one spouse during the marriage (because it is not considered marital property).

What Is an Annulment?

A marriage can be annulled depending on the proof of certain facts. If a marriage is annulled, it is considered void (that is, it never happened in the eyes of the law). This is important to certain people because an annulment does not carry the stigma of divorce. In some religious circles, it is easier to remarry after obtaining an annulment than after getting a divorce.

A man and woman must be legally capable of entering into a valid marriage. This means, for example, that if the marriage cannot be consummated sexually (one of the parties is incurably incapable of having sexual intercourse), if both parties to the marriage are minors, or if the marriage is obtained because one party deliberately concealed important information from the other before the wedding, the marriage may be annulled by direction of the court.

Most annulments are obtained on the grounds of *fraud*. In such a case the annulment is granted because concealed facts exist which, if known, would have caused the other party to cancel the wedding. For example, if one party to a marriage concealed a prior marriage, the inability or unwillingness to have children, or a serious criminal record or illness, that might be grounds for an annulment.

I recently represented a man who married a woman he had known for six days. A week after the marriage ceremony, he realized he had made a mistake and came to me for help. I informed him it was best to seek an annulment rather than a divorce in view of the brief duration of the marriage. His wife was shocked when she was served with legal papers. However, after lengthy negotiation between the parties and respective counsel, we all agreed it was in their best interests to obtain an uncontested annulment because it was cheaper and quicker, and avoided the stigma of divorce.

Thus, depending upon the length of the marriage and other factors, it may be wise to consider obtaining an annulment, rather than a divorce. Speak to your lawyer about this if it is applicable in your case.

What Is a Separation?

When a couple separates, they remain married but cease living together. Separations are often the first step toward a formal dissolution of marriage. However, they need not lead to divorce. Sometimes couples decide to live apart but remain legally married for religious, economic, or moral reasons. This means that they cannot remarry or disinherit the other spouse; they are still married in the eyes of the law.

When a couple mutually agrees to live apart on a permanent basis, the parties typically deal with questions concerning property rights, support, child custody, and other matters by signing a written separation agreement or obtaining a judicial decree of separation (which by its terms resolves these points). If both parties sign a valid separation agreement, it acts as a contract which binds both parties for as long as they live apart or until both spouses agree to change the agreement in some way.

An action for separation (that is, a separation decree) is commenced from a lawsuit in court. This differs from a separation agreement, which is usually prepared and reviewed by each party's lawyer. Neither the separation decree nor the separation agreement dissolve the marriage; that can only be done by obtaining a divorce or annulment. However, obtaining a separation decree or signing a separation agreement modifies marital relations and regulates the duties and obligations each spouse owes to the other. (Remember, though, the parties may get back together at any time if they wish.)

Some states require proof of grounds in order to grant a decree of separation. Other states recognize the mere living apart for a period of time (for example, one year) as sufficient to constitute a legal separation. It is important that you know the law in your state.

The following is a checklist of the advantages and disadvantages of obtaining a legal separation.

Advantages of Obtaining a Legal Separation:

- It allows the parties additional time to resolve their marital difficulties.

- It prepares the parties for the emotional trauma of divorce.
- Agreements with respect to child support, spouse support, custody, and other items can be more easily modified than in divorce.
- Legal obligations, including inheritance, pension rights, and death benefits, are still maintained.
- It is easier to prove grounds for a separation than for a divorce in those states which still require proof.
- Because of the perceived sanctity of marriage, courts are more willing to grant a judgment of separation than a divorce.

Disadvantages of Obtaining a Legal Separation:

- It can be seen as merely postponing the inevitable.
- As opposed to a divorce, it may leave a nonworking spouse with less means of support and no property-distribution benefits.
- The parties may incur double legal expenses—once for the separation, once for the divorce.
- Legal obligations, including inheritance, pension rights, and death benefits, are still maintained.

Separation Agreements

If you desire to obtain a legal separation, it is best to incorporate your rights, duties, and obligations in a written separation agreement. Most people are unaware that separation agreements are also used prior to a divorce; once the divorce decree is obtained, the terms of the separation agreement are usually merged into, and become a part of, the final divorce decree. Judges will not disturb the parties' intentions in the separation agreement unless they are unfair, unconscionable, or not in the best interests of the children.

The circumstances and formalities of executing separation agreements are governed by rules similar to those applying to prenuptial agreements. For example, there must be full disclosure and fair provision of assets. The contract should be prepared and reviewed by two lawyers to avoid any appearance of bias or partiality. Here, the skill and experience of both lawyers is required to ensure that the agreement is fair, just, and reasonable to both parties and their children. It is recommended that the agreement be in writing and clearly drafted; be notarized, with each party signing an acknowledgment; represent the exchange of all information concerning the couple's assets and net worth; and contain provisions for modifications in the event of changed circumstances. All of these factors will increase the chances that the agreement is deemed valid and enforceable by the courts.

Most people are unaware of the kinds of clauses that are included in separation agreements. I have included here one of my master separation agreements for illustration purposes *only*. Since your own particular case will be unique, you should never use a sample agreement such as this one. It is important that you retain a lawyer to represent you and to draft a document to suit your particular needs.

Sample Master Separation Agreement

PREAMBLE

AGREEMENT, made and entered into at _____, County of _____, State of New York, on this _____ day of _____, 19__, by and between _____, residing at _____, New York [hereinafter referred to as the "HUSBAND" and/or "FATHER"], and _____, residing at _____, New York [hereinafter referred to as the "WIFE" and/or "MOTHER"].

WITNESSETH

WHEREAS, the parties hereto were duly married to each other at _____, New York on _____ and there are _____ children the issue of said marriage, to wit: _____, born _____; _____, born _____; and _____, born _____, and there are no expectant additional issue of the marriage; and

WHEREAS, certain unhappy and irreconcilable differences have arisen between the parties, as a result of which they have separated and are now living separate and apart from each other; and

WHEREAS, it is the intention of the parties to continue to so live separate and apart from each other, and it is the desire to enter into an agreement, under which their respective financial and property rights, the care and custody of their unemancipated children and all other respective rights, remedies, privileges and obligations to each other, arising out of the marriage relation, or otherwise, shall be fully prescribed and bounded thereby; and

WHEREAS, the parties hereto have been fully, separately and independently apprised and advised of their respective legal rights, remedies, privileges and obligations, arising out of the marriage relation or otherwise, by counsel of their own choice and selection, and each having, in addition thereto, made independent inquiry and investigation with respect to all of the same, and each having been fully informed of the other's assets, property, holdings, income and prospects; and

WHEREAS, the parties hereto each warrant and represent to the other that they, and each of them, fully understand all the terms, covenants, conditions, provisions and obligations performed or contemplated by each of them hereunder, and each believes the same to be fair, just, reasonable and to his respective individual best interests,

NOW, THEREFORE, in consideration of the premises and of the covenants and promises contained herein, the parties hereto mutually agree as follows:

ARTICLE I: SEPARATE RESIDENCE

It is, and shall be, lawful for the parties hereto at all times to live separate and apart from each other and to reside from time to time at such place or places as each of such parties may see fit and to contract, carry on and engage in any employment, business or trade, which either may deem fit, free from control, restraint, or interference, direct or indirect, by the other in all respects as if such parties were sole and unmarried.

ARTICLE II: NO MOLESTATION

Neither party shall, in any way, molest, disturb or trouble the other or interfere with the peace and comfort of the other or compel or seek to compel the other to associate, cohabit or dwell with him or her by any action or proceeding for restoration of conjugal rights or by any means whatsoever. Neither party shall directly or indirectly make statements to each other, or any other persons, which are derogatory of the other party.

ARTICLE III: SEPARATE OWNERSHIP

Except as otherwise expressly set forth herein, each party shall own, free of any claim or right of the other, all the items of property, real, personal and mixed, of any kind, nature or description and wheresoever situated, which are now in his or her name, control or possession, with full power to him or to her to dispose of the same as fully and effectually in all respects and for all purposes as if he or she were unmarried.

ARTICLE IV: MUTUAL RELEASE AND DISCHARGE OF GENERAL CLAIMS

Subject to the provisions of this agreement, each party hereby releases and forever discharges the other of and from all cause or causes of action, claims, rights or demands whatsoever, in law or in equity, which either of the parties hereto ever had, or now has, against the other, except any or all cause or causes of action for divorce, annulment or separation, and any defenses either may have to any divorce, annulment or separation action now pending or hereafter brought by the other.

ARTICLE V: RESPONSIBILITY FOR DEBTS

(a) The Wife represents, warrants and convenants that she has not heretofore, nor will she hereafter, incur or contract any debt, charge, obligation or liability whatsoever for which the Husband, his legal representatives or his property or estate is or may become liable, except as otherwise specifically set forth in this agreement. The Wife agrees to indemnify and hold the Husband harmless of all loss, expenses (including reasonable attorneys' fees) and damages in connection with or arising out of a breach by the Wife of her foregoing representation, warranty and covenant.

(b) The Husband represents, warrants and covenants that he has not heretofore, nor will he hereafter, incur or contract any debt, charge, obligation or liability whatsoever for which the Wife, her legal representatives or her property or estate is or may become liable and that he shall assume and be solely liable for all liabilities and obligations for which the parties are or may be jointly liable, except as otherwise specifically set forth in this agreement. The Husband agrees to indemnify and hold the Wife harmless of loss, expenses (including reasonable attorneys' fee) and damages in connection with or arising out of a breach by the Husband of his foregoing representation, warranty and covenant to the Wife.

ARTICLE VI: MUTUAL RELEASE AND DISCHARGE OF CLAIMS IN ESTATES

Each party hereby releases, waives and relinquishes any and all rights which he or she may now have, or may hereafter acquire, as the other party's spouse under the present or future laws of any jurisdiction (a) to share in the estate of the other party upon the latter's death; and (b) to act as executor or administrator of the other party's estate. This provision is intended to, and shall constitute, a mutual waiver by the parties to take against each other's Wills, now or hereafter in force, under the present or future laws of any jurisdiction whatsoever. The parties intend, by the aforedescribed waiver and release, to relinquish any and all rights in and to each other's estate including the right to set off any and all distributive shares and all rights of election presently provided for under New York law or any other jurisdiction. However, the foregoing shall not bar a claim on the part of either party against the other for any cause or causes arising out of a breach of this agreement during the lifetime of the deceased party against whose estate such claim may be made.

ARTICLE VII: CUSTODY AND VISITATION

(a)   The parties shall have joint custody of the unemancipated children of the parties, irrespective of whether the children shall reside with the Mother or the Father and each shall be responsible for the supervision, control and care of the children. The arrangement will afford both parties ample opportunity to enjoy the children's society and to participate in a harmonious policy best calculated to promote the interests of the children.

(b)   The parties acknowledge that the children's wishes are to be considered in connection with the exercise of visitation rights, and each party agrees that he shall encourage the children in anticipating periods of visitation with the other.

(c)   Each of the parties hereto agrees to keep the other informed at all times of the whereabouts of the children when with the Father, or the Mother, respectively, and they mutually agree that if either of them has any knowledge of any illness or accident, school problems or other circumstances affecting the children's health or general welfare, the Father or the Mother, as the case may be, will promptly notify the other of such circumstances.

(d)   The parties shall consult with each other with respect to the children's education, illnesses and operations (except in emergencies), health, welfare and other matters of similar importance affecting the children whose well-being, education and development shall, at all times, be the paramount consideration of the Father and Mother;

(e)   Each party agrees that, in the event of acute illness of the children at any time, the other party shall have the right of reasonable visitation with the children at the place of confinement;

(f)   Each parent shall be entitled to complete, detailed information from any pediatrician, general physician, dentist, consultant or specialist attending the children for any reason whatsoever and to receive, upon request, copies of any reports given by them, or any of them, to the other parent;

(g)   Each parent shall have the right of reasonable, unhampered telephone communications with the children and shall provide to the other parent a telephone number for that purpose;

(h)   From the date hereof, the children shall reside with the Mother. The Father shall have liberal visitation rights. While the children are residing with the Mother, the Father shall have the right to visit the children outside of the Mother's residence during two (2) weekday (Monday through Thursday) evenings per week and two (2) weekends (Friday between 7:00 and 9:00 p.m. through Sunday between 7:00 and 9:00 p.m.) per month in accordance with arrangements mutually made with the Father and the children on reasonable prior notice by the Father to the Mother;

(i)   Notwithstanding the foregoing, the children shall reside with the Father for a period of up to two (2) full weeks during each and every Summer.

(j)   Notwithstanding the foregoing, the Mother shall have the right to visit the children on Mother's Day if at the time they are residing with the Father; and the Father shall have the right to visit with the children on Father's Day if at that time they are residing with the Mother. For at least four (4) hours on the children's birthday, the parent with whom the child is not then living shall have the right of visitation in accordance with arrangements mutually made with the visiting parent and the child on reasonable prior notice by the visiting parent to the parent; the parties alternate visitation on major holidays from year to year;

(k)   If either party shall fail to comply with any of the provisions of this Article, the other party shall have the right to initiate a proceeding in the Supreme Court or the Family Court of the State of New York, in New York County, for such relief as may be appropriate under the circumstances;

(l)   Although the parties hereby acknowledge that nothing herein contained shall be construed as an obligation or duty on the part of a party to exercise rights of visitation, nevertheless they acknowledge the need for planning activities for the children and further acknowledge that disappointing a child may have serious, adverse effects upon the child. Accordingly, each party agrees that on all occasions when he or she does not plan to exercise rights of visitation or expects to be early or late in so doing or intends to return the children at an earlier or later hour, as much advance notice as reasonably possible will be given to the other party in order that appropriate plans will be made for the children;

(m)   The parties shall exert every reasonable effort to maintain free access and unhampered contact between the children and each of the parties and to foster a feeling of affection between the children and the other party. Neither party shall do anything which may estrange the child from the other party or injure the children's opinion as to the Mother or Father or which may hamper the free and natural development of the children's love and respect for the other party;

(n)   Each party covenants, represents and warrants not, at any time or for any reason, to cause the children to be known or identified or designated by any name other than _____ and both parties covenant, represent and warrant that they will not initiate or permit the designations of "Father" and/or "Mother" or their equivalent, to be used by the children with reference to any person other than the parties hereto;

(o)   In no event shall the children be adopted without express, prior written consent of each of the parties;

(p)   Nothing herein shall bar or limit the parties from discussing and agreeing upon modifications of the provisions set forth in this Article;

(q)   Reference herein to "child" shall refer to the unemancipated children of the parties;

(r)   Should either party die or become seriously incapacitated mentally or physically while the children are still of minor age, the guardianship and custody of the minor children shall remain wholly and exclusively with the other party;

(s)   It is the parties' intention to exercise fully all rights of visitation as herein provided but the exercise thereof shall be entirely optional, and failure to exercise such right on any particular occasion shall not be deemed or construed or constitute a waiver of a right thereafter to full compliance with the provisions hereof;

(t)   Neither party shall remove the residence of the children beyond a radius of fifty (50) miles from their present residence without prior, written consent of the other party. If the Mother shall remove the residence of the children beyond said radius without the consent of the Father or the Court, such failure to obtain consent shall be presumptive of the right of the Father to obtain custody of the children and to terminate further payments under this agreement to the Wife for her support and maintenance. In addition, it shall entitle the Father to pursue all other remedies available to him under the circumstances.

ARTICLE VIII: SUPPORT AND MAINTENANCE OF THE WIFE AND CHILDREN

(a)   The Husband shall pay to the Wife for her support and maintenance, the sum of _____ per week, due in advance on Saturday of each week. Said payments shall continue for a period of _____ years from the execution date of this Agreement; however, all payments shall cease prior to the end of said ____ year period in the event of the death of either the Husband or the Wife, or in the event that the Wife remarries. At the end of said ____ year period, the Husband shall pay the Wife for her support and maintenance the sum of _____ per week for an additional period of _____ years; however, all payments shall cease prior to the end of said _____ year period in the event of the death of either the Husband or the Wife, or in the event that the Wife remarries. At the end of said _____ year period, the Husband shall pay the Wife for her support and maintenance the sum of _____ per week for an additional period of _____ years; however, all payments shall cease prior to the end of said _____ year period in the event of the death of either the Husband or the Wife, or in the event the Wife remarries.

(b)   The parties hereby acknowledge that the aforesaid payments made by the Husband to the Wife as support and maintenance shall constitute taxable income to the Wife and be a tax deductible expense to the Husband, and the sums indicated herein have been computed with such tax consequences in mind and in consideration of the relative tax burdens and benefits upon the parties based upon the respective incomes of the parties;

(c)   Remarriage of the Wife as used in this Agreement shall be deemed a remarriage of the Wife regardless of whether such marriage shall be void or voidable or terminated by divorce, annulment or otherwise.

(d)   All payments by the Husband to the Wife under this Article shall be made by check or money order and forwarded to the Wife at her residence or at such other place as she shall designate in writing to the Husband;

(e)   Upon the happening of any event which shall result in the change or cessation of any payments to the Wife hereunder, such change or cessation shall be effective as of the date of such event with an appropriate apportionment for the payment (if any) for that month;

(f)   There shall be no liability on the part of the Husband or his estate for any support payments or performance of any other obligations under this Agreement from and after the death of the Wife or the death of the Husband, except for those obligations accrued but not performed prior to the date of death, anything to the contrary in this agreement notwithstanding;

(g)   The Wife acknowledges that she is in good health and is capable of earning an adequate salary as a _____ and that she has sufficient means for her own support from her share of the joint property distributed between the parties. Accordingly, she waives and renounces any and all claims against the Husband for support or maintenance exceeding those amounts specified in this Agreement and for any other property, either joint or separate, owned by or due to the Husband, and agrees that she will not at any time demand or apply therefor for said additional support, maintenance or property, and will hold the Husband harmless therefrom.

ARTICLE IX: ADDITIONAL SUPPORT

(a)   In addition to the support provided in Article VIII hereof, the Father agrees to furnish at his own expense Blue Cross, Blue Shield and major medical insurance (or other equivalent) for the benefit of the children of the parties until the remarriage of the Wife and/or emancipation of the children and to pay all reasonable medical, dental, orthodontia and drug expenses (hereinafter collectively called "medical expenses") of the children of the parties. The Mother shall advise the Father of any medical insurance which may be furnished to her by an employer in order that the Father need not duplicate coverage for the children. If the Mother is required to pay for such coverage of the children, the Father may elect to utilize said coverage for the children and shall promptly pay for or reimburse the Mother for such expense or to provide his own coverage. For uninsured medical and dental expenses, the parties shall share said costs equally, provided he or she, as the case may be, shall have given consent for such expenses, which consent will not be unreasonably withheld (unless medical or dental treatment is required in such short time that it is impossible or impractical to obtain such consent).

(b)   The Mother agrees that she will promptly fill out, execute and deliver to the Father all forms and provide all information in connection with any application he may make for reimbursement of medical, dental and drug expenses under any insurance policies which he may have. He shall promptly refund to the Mother any medical expenses paid for by her either directly or if insured, out of the proceeds of an insurance claim which the Husband shall file promptly.

(c)   The Father will furnish to the Wife at her request documentation and other proof of his compliance with the provisions of this Article, and the Wife, in addition, is hereby authorized to obtain direct confirmation of compliance or non-compliance with any insurance carrier.

(d)   In addition to the foregoing, the Father shall pay promptly one-half (1/2) of all reasonable expenses for the tuition, fees, transportation and outfitting of the children at a summer camp, or for summer or vacation travel or similar summer or vacation activity, if the children desire to pursue such activity and if the Father consents thereto, which consent will not be unreasonably withheld. The Mother agrees to consult with the Father regarding each such activity and to consider such suggestions and comments which he deems shall be in the best interests of the children. In no event will the Father be required to pay for any of the said expenses incurred for the participation of the Mother in such activity or activities.

(e)   It is understood that the Father's obligation for the support of the children herein shall be suspended during any period when the children are in summer camp or other activities which necessitate the children staying away from home at the Father's expense.

(f)   In addition to the foregoing, if the children of the parties have been recommended by a teacher, guidance counsellor or other educational adviser or administrator to obtain tutoring help with respect to any academic lessons or courses, the Father agrees to pay promptly for one-half (1/2) of the reasonable cost of such tutoring.

(g)   In addition to the foregoing, if the children of the parties desire to attend religious school or receive private religious training, the Father agrees to pay promptly for one-half (1/2) of the reasonable cost of such education or training. Both parties shall encourage the use of financial aids, grants, loans and scholarships to help defray expenses, and they agree to cooperate with each other and the child toward that end. The expenses referred to in this subparagraph shall include, but shall not be limited to, application and testing fees, tuition, required books, uniforms, materials and supplies, reasonable transportation and incidental expenses.

ARTICLE X: EMANCIPATION EVENT

The children shall be deemed, for the purposes of this agreement, to have become emancipated upon the earliest happening of any of the following events:

(a) Attaining the age of 21 years;

(b) Marriage of the child, even though such marriage may be void or voidable, and despite any subsequent divorce, annulment or other termination thereof;

(c) Entry of the child into the military service;

(d) Engaging in full-time employment whereby the child is fully self-supporting;

(e) The child establishing a permanent residence away from either party. Residence at a camp, boarding school, college or travel shall not be deemed a change in the permanent residence of a child sufficient to constitute emancipation.

ARTICLE XI: LIFE INSURANCE

(a) The Husband's life is insured by _____ for the face amount of _____ of which the Wife has heretofore been sole beneficiary. The Father agrees that he will provide and maintain, at his own expense, said life insurance policy insuring his life for the benefit of the children of the parties until they are emancipated and shall furnish proof thereof upon the reasonable request of the Wife.

(b) The Father will not pledge, hypothecate or encumber the policy by loan or otherwise during such period.

(c) The dividends payable under said policy shall belong exclusively to the Father who shall have the option of accepting payment thereof or applying same in reduction of premiums.

ARTICLE XII: TAXATION

(a) It is the intention of the parties that for Federal, State and local income tax purposes, payments made in accordance with Article VIII of this agreement shall entitle the Husband to take the children as his dependents.

(b) The parties agree that regardless of their marital status, the parties shall file separate tax returns from this day forward.

(c) Each party agrees to cooperate fully with the other in the event of any audit or examination by a taxing authority of the said joint tax returns and agrees to furnish to the party being examined or his, or her, designees, promptly and without charge, such papers, records, documents and information as may be reasonably appropriate in connection with such audit or examination.

ARTICLE XIII: LEGAL REPRESENTATION

The parties represent to each other that the Wife has been represented by _____ _____ and the Husband has been represented by *STEVEN MITCH-ELL SACK, ESQ., 450 Seventh Avenue, New York, New York,* as their respective attorneys. Both attorneys will be paid separately by their respective clients. Both parties represent and warrant that they have dealt with no other attorney for which services the other is or may become liable and will indemnify and hold the other party harmless of all loss, expenses (including reasonable attorneys' fees) and damages in the event of a breach by one party of said representation and warranty.

ARTICLE XIV: POSSIBLE INVALIDITY

In case any provision of this agreement should be held to be contrary to, or invalid under, the law of any country, state or other jurisdiction, such illegality or invalidity shall not affect in any way any other provisions hereof, all of which shall continue, nevertheless, in full force and effect; any provision which is held to be illegal or invalid in any country, state or other jurisdiction shall, nevertheless, remain in full force and effect in any country, state or jurisdiction in which such provision is legal and valid.

ARTICLE XV: INDEPENDENT COVENANTS

Each of the respective rights and obligations of the parties hereunder shall be deemed independent and may be enforced independently irrespective of any of the other rights and obligations set forth herein.

ARTICLE XVI: FULL DISCLOSURE

Each party has made independent inquiry into the complete financial circumstances of the other and is fully informed of the income, assets, property and financial prospects of the other. Each has had a full opportunity and has consulted at length with his or her attorney regarding all of the circumstances hereof and acknowledges that this agreement has not been the result of any fraud, duress or undue influence exercised by either party upon the other or by any other person or persons upon the other. Both parties acknowledge that this agreement has been achieved after full disclosure, competent legal representation and honest negotiations.

ARTICLE XVII: DIVISION OF PROPERTY

The parties acknowledge that all items of real property, personal property fixtures and furnishings, wherever they may be, have been previously divided to the satisfaction of both the Husband and the Wife upon the signing of this Agreement, and that neither will make any claim against the other with respect to the aforesaid property.

ARTICLE XVIII: MODIFICATION AND WAIVER

Neither this agreement nor any provision hereof shall be amended or modified or deemed amended or modified, except by an agreement in writing duly subscribed and acknowledged with the same formality as this agreement, except as expressly provided herein. Any waiver by either party of any provision of this agreement or any right or option hereunder shall not be deemed a continuing waiver and shall not prevent or estop such party from thereafter enforcing such provision, right or option, and the failure of either party to insist in any one or more instances upon the strict performance of any of the terms or provisions of this agreement by the other party shall not be construed as a waiver or relinquishment for the future of any such term or provision, but the same shall continue in full force and effect.

ARTICLE XIX: LEGAL INTERPRETATION

This agreement and all of the rights and obligations of the parties hereunder shall be construed according to the laws of the State of New York as an agreement made and to be performed within said State.

ARTICLE XX: RECONCILIATION AND MATRIMONIAL DECREES

This agreement shall not be invalidated or otherwise affected by a reconciliation between the parties hereto, or a resumption of marital relations between them unless said reconciliation or said resumption be documented by a written statement executed and acknowledged by the parties with respect to said reconciliation and resumption and, in addition, setting forth that they are cancelling this agreement, and this agreement shall not be invalidated or otherwise affected by any decree or judgment of separation or divorce made in any court in any action which may presently exist or may hereafter be instituted by either party against the other for a separation or divorce. Each party agrees that the provisions of this agreement shall be submitted to any court in which either party may seek a judgment or decree with such specificity as the court shall deem permissible and by reference as may be appropriate under law and under the rules of the court. However, notwithstanding such incorporation, the obligations and covenants of this agreement shall survive any decree or judgment of separation or divorce and shall not merge therein, and this agreement may be enforced independently of such decree or judgment.

ARTICLE XXI: CHANGE OF ADDRESS

The parties hereby agree that each will notify the other by registered or certified mail, return receipt requested, of any change of address, and/or telephone number, within _____ days of the date of such change.

ARTICLE XVII: IMPLEMENTATION

The Husband and Wife shall, at any and all times, upon request by the other party or his or her legal representatives, promptly make, execute and deliver any and all such other and future instruments as may be necessary or desirable for the purpose of giving full force and effect to the provisions of this agreement, without charge therefor.

ARTICLE XXIII: ENTIRE UNDERSTANDING

This agreement contains the entire understanding of the parties who hereby acknowledge that there have been and are no representations, warranties, covenants or undertakings other than those expressly set forth herein. The parties agree that a memorandum of this agreement shall be executed upon the signing hereof and the same may be filed in the Office of the appropriate County Clerk.

IN WITNESS WHEREOF, the parties hereto have hereunto set their respective hands and seals the day and year first above written.

_____

_____

STATE OF   )
)   ss.:
COUNTY OF   )

On the _____ day of _____, 19__, before me personally came _____ to me known to be the individual described in and who executed the foregoing instrument and she did duly acknowledge to me that she executed the same.

_____

STATE OF   )
)   ss.:
COUNTY OF   )

On the _____ day of _____, 19_____, before me personally came _____ to me known to be the individual described in and who executed the foregoing instrument and he did duly acknowledge to me that he executed the same.

_____

What Is a Divorce?

Once a couple has decided they no longer wish to continue their marriage and are not interested in obtaining a legal separation, either or both spouses must file certain documents in court to obtain a divorce. A divorce is a formal court proceeding in which a marriage is dissolved. The laws governing divorce vary from state to state, and each state can grant divorces only to its own residents—by definition, people who have lived within the state for a minimum period of time, usually six months.

Each state has its own requirements for obtaining a divorce. For example, although the trend is moving toward granting divorces without a showing of "fault," some states still require proof of adultery, abandonment, cruel and inhuman treatment, bigamy, or imprisonment by the "moving party," the plaintiff, in order to grant a divorce. In these states you cannot obtain a divorce merely on the basis of "irretrievable breakdown of the marriage" or "irreconcilable differences" or simply by mutual consent. You must present witnesses, including yourself, to prove your allegations of fault. (For example, if you were seeking a divorce on the grounds of cruel and inhuman treatment, you might have to prove that you were physically assaulted or humiliated in front of witnesses on more than one occasion.) This can be done through the use of oral testimony, documents, photographs, and other evidence. The "responding party," the defendant, then has the opportunity of contesting such charges and/or countersuing for divorce.

It is necessary to speak to an experienced lawyer to learn more about your options and rights. While some people are able to obtain a divorce on their own, this is *not* recommended where the couple has acquired marital assets (including a house and other property), liquid assets (stocks, bonds, and savings), or other assets. The last decade has brought a major change in the focus of contested divorce cases; now the emphasis at the time of the breakdown of the marriage is "How much can I get out of this mess?" rather than "Whose fault is it?" Most people are unaware of the kinds and amount of property distribution they are entitled to. For example, some states allow wives to receive a share of their husbands' professional practices, businesses, and pensions (as well as benefits derived from homemaking services). Only an experienced lawyer can tell you what constitutes marital assets subject to distribution in your state, how they are located, and how much they are worth.

What Are You Entitled to upon Divorce?

1. *Distribution of assets.* When I am retained by a client seeking a divorce, I first require a detailed marriage history that sets forth specific data (the date and place of marriage, the names and ages of children of the marriage, the dates of acquisition of major marital assets, etc.) and the events that form the basis of a client's complaint. This is done by filling out certain forms I have prepared, including:

- The economic history of the marriage (who bought what with whose money?)
- A financial affidavit (listing the assets of the marriage)
- A preseparation standard-of-living questionnaire
- A current breakdown of monthly living expenses
- An additional questionnaire, which ascertains the amount of time spent in homemaking services, where key financial documents can be located, etc.

All of this information assists me in putting together an accurate picture of both spouses' income and the value of their assets prior to entering settlement discussions. Acquiring this information is necessary in attempting to resolve the divorce by settlement.

As I mentioned earlier, both spouses are allowed to share assets acquired during the marriage in both community-property and equitable-distribution states. In most states, marital property is defined as "all property acquired by either or both spouses during the marriage and before the execution of a separation agreement or the commencement of a matrimonial action, regardless of the form in which title is held."

This means that, depending on the state, a spouse would be entitled to receive either an equitable (fair) or an equal share of the present value of the following:

- Life insurance policies, including their cash values
- Annuities
- Pensions
- Profit-sharing plans
- Keogh and IRA plans
- Closely held businesses
- Professional licenses and degrees
- Tax-shelter investments
- Real estate acquired during the marriage
- *Inter-vivos* trusts
- Patents, copyrights, and royalties

- Bank accounts
- Leasehold interests and mortgages
- Stocks and bonds
- Stock options
- Household furniture and furnishings
- Art objects, coins, jewelry, antiques, collectibles
- Oil and mineral rights
- Promissory notes, tax refunds, security deposits
- Value for homemaking services
- Other assorted items

In order to recover your fair share though, you would first have to determine the existence of these assets and then determine their value. This would be done by your lawyer after you provided him or her with detailed information or with sources of information as to the existence of such assets. For example, I typically ask clients to produce copies of the following for my examination:

- Tax returns
- Insurance policies
- Bank records
- Stock-brokerage records
- Registry of deeds and mortgage records
- Employment records
- Pension, profit-sharing, and retirement plans

After I am satisfied that I have uncovered the existence and discovered the location of all assets, it is then essential to evaluate how much these marital assets are presently worth. Often the assistance of experts such as brokers, accountants, and appraisers is required in this process.

I also examine the economic history of the marriage to determine the amount and types of assets that are *separate* property, not subject to division upon divorce. Separate property is typically defined as "property acquired before marriage or property acquired by bequest, devise or descent, or gift from a party other than the spouse." In some states, separate property also includes:

- Compensation for personal injuries
- Property acquired in exchange for or the increase in value of separate property, except to the extent that such appreciation is due in part to the contributions or efforts of the other spouse
- Property described as separate property by written agreement between the parties

As you can see, what constitutes separate or marital property, and the value of each asset, is often a difficult legal question. In fact, some divorce trials take more than several weeks to resolve these issues. The following hypothetical example will illustrate some of the problems:

Jonathan married Debra in 1980. At the time of the marriage, Jonathan was a first-year law student and Debra was a registered nurse earning $30,000 annually; her earnings enabled Jonathan to attend school full-time. Jonathan had $100,000 in the bank; Debra had $5,000. The parties received $10,000 in wedding gifts.

The couple purchased a house in 1981 with a down payment of $25,000. Five years later, after Jonathan had graduated from law school and become a licensed attorney, he had an affair with another woman; Debra sued him for divorce.

Is Jonathan's adultery grounds for divorce? Yes. However, fault is not to be considered in determining the amount of assets to be distributed upon divorce (fault *is* considered, though, when one of the parties dissipated assets by gambling, poor investments, etc.), and some states don't require proof of fault regardless.

Is Debra entitled to half the value of the house? Maybe, if the parties reside in a state that recognizes community property. If they live in a equitable-distribution state, Debra would receive a fair share of the house, depending upon the unique facts of the case. However, if the initial down payment had been $100,000 (contributed by Jonathan), Debra would have a weaker argument in claiming the house was marital property, unless she spent considerable time and effort remodeling the house and thereby measurably increasing its value.

Is Debra entitled to a cash payment for the value of Jonathan's professional degree? Maybe, especially since her earnings paid for his education expenses. However, there might be considerable difference of opinion as to what Jonathan's license is presently worth, depending on state law.

Note: The right to treat professional degrees as marital property, subject to valuation and division upon divorce, varies on a state-by-state basis. For example, the New York Court of Appeals recently ruled that a medical license is property subject to division upon divorce and awarded $188,000 to a wife who helped support her husband through medical school. However, most states do *not* recognize professional degrees as marital property. Table 6–3 is a current listing (as of January 1, 1986) of those states which do allow for such distribution.

2. *Maintenance payments.* A husband (and in rare cases, a wife) is liable for the support of his spouse and/or children. If the parties cannot agree, the court will determine the amount. This payment is called "maintenance" (formerly called "alimony") and can be made payable on a temporary or permanent basis.

Maintenance is made in such an amount as justice requires, having regard to the circumstances of the case and of the reasonable needs of the parties. It is also based on the spouse's ability to pay and other factors.

The amount and duration of maintenance is generally determined according to the following guidelines:

- The income and property of each spouse, including marital property distributed in the action
- The duration of the marriage and the age and health of both parties
- The present and future capacity of the person having need to be self-supporting
- The presence of children of the marriage in the respective homes of the parties

Table 6-3
Consideration of Spousal Contribution to Professional Degrees

	States with case law discussions	States with statutes requiring consideration of this situation*		States with case law discussions	States with statutes requiring consideration of this situation*
Alabama	✓		Nevada		
Alaska			New Hampshire	✓	
Arizona	✓		New Jersey	✓	
Arkansas	✓		New Mexico	✓	
California	✓	M & P	New York	✓	M & P
Colorado	✓		North Carolina		P
Connecticut	✓		North Dakota	✓	
Delaware	✓		Ohio	✓	M & P
Florida	✓	M	Oklahoma	✓	
Georgia			Oregon		M
Hawaii			Pennsylvania	✓	M & P
Idaho			Rhode Island		
Illinois	✓		South Carolina		
Indiana	✓	M & P	South Dakota	✓	
Iowa	✓	M & P	Tennessee		M & P
Kansas			Texas	✓	
Kentucky	✓		Utah		
Louisiana			Vermont		P
Maine			Virginia		M
Maryland			Washington	✓	
Massachusetts			West Virginia		P
Michigan	✓		Wisconsin	✓	M & P
Minnesota	✓		Wyoming	✓	
Mississippi			Washington, D.C.		
Missouri	✓		Puerto Rico		
Montana			Virgin Islands		
Nebraska		P			

*M = maintenance; P = property division

Source: *Family Law Quarterly*, Vol. XIX, No. 4, Winter 1986.

- Where practical and relevant, the standard of living established during the marriage
- The tax consequences to each party
- Contributions of the party seeking maintenance to the career or career potential of the other party and value of services as a spouse, parent, wage earner and homemaker
- The wasteful dissipation of family assets by either spouse
- Other factors the court finds to be just and proper

In most states, maintenance is usually paid only for a brief period of time (perhaps no more than five years) after the divorce. This is because the emphasis has shifted to giving nonworking spouses a larger share of marital assets in one lump-sum payment and then terminating any continued involvement between the parties. In some states, maintenance is awarded only until a recipient has become able to support himself or herself (this is called "rehabilitative maintenance").

You should also know that although maintenance awards are increasingly no-fault-oriented, some states still provide that marital misconduct is a bar to maintenance, and others—for example, Florida, Georgia, Kentucky, and Pennsylvania—consider fault grounds including adultery, cruel and inhuman treatment, etc., as a relevant factor. In addition, several states provide for modification or termination of alimony upon proof that the spouse receiving such payments is cohabiting with an individual other than the former spouse (column 1 in Table 6-4).

Table 6-4 illustrates these points in greater detail on a state-by-state basis.

3. *Social-Security, Accident, and Health-Insurance Benefits.* A divorced party is entitled to receive social-security benefits based on an ex-spouse's earnings. You may also be able to participate in your divorced spouse's accident- and health-insurance plans according to the law in several states. Speak to an experienced attorney about this if it is applicable in your case.

4. *Attorney fees.* You may also be entitled to attorney

Table 6-4
Alimony Considerations

	(1) Marital fault not considered	(2) Marital misconduct is bar to alimony	(3) Cohabitation ends or modifies alimony	(4) Marital fault is a factor in determining alimony
Alabama		√	√	
Alaska	√			
Arizona	√			
Arkansas	√			
California	√		√	
Colorado	√			
Connecticut				√
Delaware	√			
Florida				√
Georgia		√	√	
Hawaii	√			
Idaho		√		
Illinois	√		√*	
Indiana	√			
Iowa	√			
Kansas	√			
Kentucky				√
Louisiana		√	√	
Maine	√			
Maryland	√		√*	
Massachusetts	√			
Michigan				√
Minnesota	√			
Mississippi	√			
Missouri				√
Montana	√			
Nebraska	√			
Nevada	√			
New Hampshire				√
New Jersey	√			
New Mexico	√			
New York	√		√	
North Carolina		√		
North Dakota				√

Table 6-4 (Continued)

	(1) Marital fault not considered	(2) Marital misconduct is bar to alimony	(3) Cohabitation ends or modifies alimony	(4) Marital fault is a factor in determining alimony
Ohio	✓		✓ (permissive)	
Oklahoma	✓			
Oregon	✓			
Pennsylvania			✓	✓
Rhode Island				✓
South Carolina	✓			
South Dakota				✓
Tennessee			✓	✓
Texas				
Utah			✓	
Vermont	✓			
Virginia		✓		
Washington	✓			
West Virginia		✓		
Wisconsin	✓			
Wyoming	✓			
Washington, D.C.				✓
Puerto Rico		✓	✓	
Virgin Islands	✓			

*Insofar as it changes economic status.
Source: Family Law Quarterly, Vol. XIX, No. 4, Winter 1986.

fees incurred in connection with your divorce. I frequently request reimbursement for this item, particularly when I represent female, nonworking spouses. Don't forget to ask for this if it is applicable in your case.

Strategies to Protect Yourself in Divorce Proceedings

The following strategies should always be considered and used if you are involved in divorce proceedings. Failure to follow some of these points could cost you money and aggravation, while utilizing these strategies can maximize the amount of money you will obtain in settlement and help you work more effectively with your lawyer.

1. *Know the laws in your state with respect to obtaining a divorce and distributing property and other assets.*

2. *Hire an experienced, competent lawyer to represent you.* The more money your marital estate is worth, the more there is riding on the competence and skill of your lawyer. The best divorce lawyers are well-trained in financial analysis, tax aspects of divorce, and business litigation. For example, they know how to properly evaluate the present worth of a pension, closely held business, or professional degree. They can also speak intelligently with experts such as accountants and financial advisors. Choose a lawyer whom you trust and feel comfortable with, one who possesses ample litigation and business experience. Choose a lawyer who spends at least 30 percent of his or her practice on divorce-litigation matters.

3. *Try to obtain copies of pertinent business records before commencing divorce proceedings.* Financial documents, including tax returns, net-worth statements of closely held businesses, correspondence, and banking records, frequently have a habit of disappearing after legal proceedings begin. Thus it is a good idea to collect this information well before the commencement of legal action. By collecting as much information as possible about your spouse's finances and businesses, you will enable your lawyer to gather appropriate evidence and properly evaluate your case. (*Note*: If possible, try not to get caught collecting the evidence.)

4. *Be sure your lawyer spends sufficient time investigating your marital history.* A competent lawyer learns thoroughly all the pertinent facts of a case. If you get the feeling that your lawyer is careless or irresponsible, make him or her work harder. If you are still not satisfied, shop around for another lawyer before it is too late.

5. *Recognize the value of your homemaking services if you are a nonworking wife; conversely, be prepared to offer evidence demonstrating your wife's self-centered, nonproductive drain on the family partnership if you*

Table 6-5
Factors in Property Distribution and/or Maintenance

	(1) States which recognize nonmonetary contributions	(2) States with specific statutory guidelines	(3) Marital Fault a Factor			(4) Economic misconduct considered
			Fault excluded	Fault or respective merits may be considered	State statutes silent re: fault	
Alabama				✓		
Alaska	✓	✓	✓			
Arizona	✓	✓	✓			✓
Arkansas	✓	✓			✓	
California	✓	✓	✓			✓
Colorado	✓	✓	✓			✓
Connecticut	✓	✓		✓		✓
Delaware	✓	✓	✓			✓
Florida	✓	✓		✓		✓
Georgia	✓	✓		✓		
Hawaii		✓		✓		
Idaho		✓		✓		
Illinois	✓	✓	✓			✓
Indiana	✓	✓	✓			✓
Iowa	✓	✓	✓			
Kansas	✓	✓	✓			✓
Kentucky	✓	✓	✓			
Louisiana		✓		✓		
Maine	✓	✓	✓			✓
Maryland	✓	✓				
Massachusetts	✓	✓	✓[1]			
Michigan				✓		
Minnesota	✓	✓	✓			✓
Mississippi	✓			✓		
Missouri	✓			✓		
Montana	✓	✓	✓			✓
Nebraska	✓	✓			✓	
Nevada					✓	
New Hampshire					✓	
New Jersey[2]						
New Mexico					✓	
New York	✓	✓		✓		✓
North Carolina	✓	✓		✓		
North Dakota	✓			✓		
Ohio	✓	✓			✓	
Oklahoma					✓	
Oregon	✓	✓	✓			
Pennsylvania	✓	✓		✓[3]		✓

(continued)

Table 6-5 (Continued)

	(1) States which recognize nonmonetary contributions	(2) States with specific statutory guidelines	(3) Marital Fault a Factor — Fault excluded	(3) Fault or respective merits may be considered	(3) State statutes silent re: fault	(4) Economic misconduct considered
Rhode Island	✓	✓		✓		
South Carolina					✓	
South Dakota	✓	✓	✓			✓
Tennessee	✓	✓		✓[3]		
Texas					✓	
Utah					✓	
Vermont	✓	✓		✓		✓
Virginia	✓	✓		✓		
Washington		✓	✓			
West Virginia	✓	✓		✓[3]		✓
Wisconsin	✓	✓	✓			
Wyoming					✓	
Washington, D.C.	✓	✓		✓		✓
Puerto Rico					✓	
Virgin Islands			✓			

1. Fault excluded if divorce is granted on grounds of irretrievable breakdown.
2. These categories are not applicable to the New Jersey statute.
3. Fault excluded for property settlement, *not* for alimony.

Source: *Family Law Quarterly*, Vol. XIX, No. 4, Winter 1986.

are a husband. An increasing number of states recognize the contributions of the spouse who is homemaker, parent, and maintainer of the well-being of the family. These are considered nonmonetary contributions to the economic assets of the marriage in determining property distribution and/or maintenance.

Table 6-5 (column 1) lists states that currently recognize nonmonetary contributions.

6. *Assist your lawyer in developing a realistic approach to your case.* Present a good image. Avoid doing things for spite, such as clearing out safe-deposit boxes, closing checking and savings accounts, tapping phones, and withholding visitation of the children, unless absolutely necessary or unless a trial is unlikely.

7. *Be prepared to trace all marital assets and pur-*

chases, including what was purchased, when, the source of funds, etc. This will be extremely helpful to your lawyer.

8. *Establish evidence to support your side of the case in matters of employability.* For example, be prepared to show that your spouse is a healthy individual, college-educated, etc., and to demonstrate any health or employment problems of your own. Courts have wide discretion in determining the amount and duration of maintenance payments. Thus great care should be taken to establish your spouse's ability to enter the job market and be self-sustaining and/or your inability to do the same.

9. *Never underestimate the value of experts in your case.* Experts are playing a large role in matrimonial cases these days. If your lawyer is not using an expert, be sure to question him or her about this.

10. *Be sure your lawyer properly advises you as to what is considered marital property subject to division upon divorce.* In one of my recent cases, the opposing lawyer failed to advise his client (the wife) that she was entitled to receive a portion of her husband's pension. I advised my client that this oversight would probably be grounds for a malpractice suit if the wife ever found out about it. Don't leave everything up to your lawyer. Question what you are entitled to receive and be sure you get adequate explanations. If you have doubts, feel free to obtain a second opinion. There is nothing wrong in doing this and it may relieve your anxieties.

11. *Never agree to pay more than you can afford.* I have observed that some husbands, out of guilt or fear, agree to pay more money in settlement than they can afford. Later they find that they are giving so much money in child support, maintenance, and other expenses that they have no money to support themselves.

Be realistic. Recognize that you will need ample funds for your own life after the divorce. This may include, for example, sufficient money to pay for rent, food, clothing, entertainment, automobile expenses, etc. In fact, your lawyer should request an itemized monthly expense sheet from you that reflects your current and estimated future financial needs. (See sample in Chapter 8.) This chart can then act as a practical guideline in formulating a reasonable settlement. Remember, there is life after divorce for you as well!

12. *Be aware of the tax consequences of divorce and be sure that your lawyer has considered all tax angles when structuring the settlement.* This is important and is frequently overlooked. (See Chapter 10.)

7 | Placing the Kids: Child Custody and the Law

Introduction

Fortunately, most people learn about child-custody disputes only by watching television documentaries and movies such as *Kramer v. Kramer*. However, more Americans are being personally exposed to this problem as the number of divorces has skyrocketed over the last two decades. In 1960, for example, courts decided the custody of over 400,000 children. In 1970, the number exceeded 870,000. Now, with more than 1 million children experiencing the divorce of their parents annually, some experts are calling for the creation of special courts so that judges, with the assistance of trained psychiatrists and social workers, can preside solely over child-custody-related disputes, unhampered by crowded court calendars and other matters.

Too often, the children become the victims of divorce. Most contested custody cases are emotionally and financially draining on the parties involved. In many cases, parents become so hateful to each other that the children are used as pawns in a battle; in essence, they become the spoils of divorce. Psychological, physical, and legal problems arising from these fierce battles are causing such harm to children that many courts have recognized a child's "bill of rights" and are designating court-appointed lawyers (sometimes referred to as guardians *ad litem*) to protect the children's rights and voice their interests and concerns at formal hearings.

Critics of the present system argue that the method of determining custody for children of divorced parents is essentially no system at all. These commentators point out that many cases are decided by the whim of judges who fail to consider a child's best interests. For example, in one recent Pennsylvania case, a court awarded custody of a 13-year-old girl to her mother, despite the child's stated preference for her father. The decision was made without consideration of a court-ordered psychiatric evaluation.

Others proclaim that fathers are being treated too kindly by the courts. For example, women's organizations are springing up throughout the United States to fight back against a perceived gradual erosion of the "tender-years" doctrine that has made it easier for fathers to gain custody, especially when they have financial resources mothers cannot match. In addition, grandparents, stepparents, and other extended members of the family are petitioning the courts to be awarded custody and visitation rights in preference to those of the natural parents—a request unheard of only a few years ago.

So many changes in the law are occurring in this area that even lawyers are finding it difficult to keep pace with the trends. (Example: In 1985 courts grappled with legal issues ranging from a lesbian mother's visitation rights to whether a father with herpes should forfeit custody!)

This chapter will explore the areas of child custody and related subjects. In addition to learning the general legal principles of custody, you will discover how successful lawyers win custody cases for their clients and will read of many of the problems encountered in custody trials. I will discuss the difference between joint and sole custody and define the occasions when each should be utilized. Also, I will provide a checklist of items to consider in negotiating a custody arrangement with your spouse and will explain factors the court looks to in modifying custody from one parent to the other.

If you are currently involved in a custody or support battle, or anticipate engaging in one in the future, the following material will enable you to better evaluate your chances of success and assist both you and your lawyer in gaining desired results.

General Principles of Child Custody

Years ago the law stated that the father was the exclusive custodian of a couple's children. However, when women became emancipated in the nineteenth century, the law recognized that both spouses had equal rights to the custody of their children; upon divorce custody was awarded to the spouse most fit (that is, emotionally and financially stable).

Judges in most states have come to recognize that children too have rights in divorce and custody proceedings. For example, some have incorporated a Bill of Rights for children into their court proceedings. This Bill of Rights, as adopted from Wisconsin Supreme Court decisions, has spread to use throughout the United States and provides the following:

The Child's Bill of Rights

I. The right of the child to be treated as an interested and affected person and not as a pawn

II. The right to grow up in the home environment that will best guarantee an opportunity to achieve mature and responsible citizenship

III. The right to the day-by-day love, care, discipline, and protection of the custodial parent

IV. The right to know the noncustodial parent and to have the benefit of such parent's love and guidance through adequate visitation

V. The right to a positive and constructive relationship with both parents, with neither parent permitted to degrade the other in the child's mind

VI. The right to have moral and ethical values inculcated by precept and example, and to have limits set for behavior so that the child may develop self-discipline early in life

VII. The right to the most adequate level of economic support that can be provided by the efforts of both parents

VIII. The right to the same opportunities for education that the child would have had if the family unit had not been broken

IX. The right to such periodic review of custodial arrangements and child support orders as the parents' circumstances and the child's benefit require

X. The right to the recognition of the fact that children involved in a divorce are always disadvantaged parties, and the law must take affirmative steps to assure their welfare

Some states, including Wisconsin and New Hampshire, have recognized representation by attorneys to be essential to the protection of children's rights, and appoint guardians *ad litem* to represent them in certain divorce cases. This has expedited the settlement of many divorce cases, since when an impartial lawyer for the children presents evidence to the court, neither parent can distort the truth as easily.

Judges are also protecting children through novel decisions. One recent Michigan case which employed the services of a guardian *ad litem* made national headlines. Rather than force the children to leave the home to live with either their mother or father, the judge granted custody of the *parents' house* to the children, allowing both parents to live with them on a month-to-month rotation! The judge required the parents of the boys (aged 15, 13, and 11) to share the costs of maintaining the household, and stipulated that their house could not be sold until the last of the three boys graduated from high school.

Table 7-1 summarizes current state guidelines with respect to custody laws. As can be seen in the table, the law now generally states that a judge must make determinations of custody according to the *child's best interest and overall welfare*. What constitutes a child's "best interest" depends upon the facts and circumstances of each particular case. Custody issues, more than most litigated matters, are determined primarily by their unique patterns; judges are supposed to carefully weigh *all* of the significant factors relevant to a child's welfare and best interests.

In determining what constitutes a child's best interests, judges are theoretically *not* supposed to consider the following:

- Whether the parents agreed by contract with whom the child would live
- The "tender-years" doctrine, whereby custody of a young child is automatically granted to the mother, particularly if the young child is a girl
- Which parent fights the harder to gain custody of the child

The judge will typically focus on the following:

- The atmosphere and stability of the respective parent's home
- The amount of care, affection, and concern demonstrated by each parent to the child
- The child's stated preference, particularly when he or she is relatively mature (for example, 13 or older)

Table 7-1
Custody Laws

	(1) States with statutory custody guidelines	(2) States which consider the children's wishes	(3) States with joint custody laws		(1) States with statutory custody guidelines	(2) States which consider the children's wishes	(3) States with joint custody laws
Alabama	✓	✓		Nevada	✓	✓	✓
Alaska	✓	✓	✓	New Hampshire		✓	✓
Arizona	✓	✓		New Jersey			✓
Arkansas				New Mexico	✓	✓	✓
California	✓	✓	✓	New York			
Colorado	✓	✓	✓	North Carolina			✓
Connecticut		✓	✓	North Dakota	✓	✓	
Delaware	✓	✓	✓	Ohio		✓	✓
Florida	✓	✓	✓	Oklahoma		✓	✓
Georgia		✓		Oregon	✓		✓
Hawaii	✓	✓	✓	Pennsylvania			✓
Idaho	✓	✓	✓	Rhode Island			
Illinois	✓	✓	✓	South Carolina			
Indiana	✓	✓	✓	South Dakota		✓	
Iowa	✓	✓	✓	Tennessee		✓	✓
Kansas	✓	✓	✓	Texas		✓	✓
Kentucky	✓	✓	✓	Utah		✓	
Louisiana	✓	✓	✓	Vermont	✓		
Maine	✓	✓	✓	Virginia	✓	✓	
Maryland			✓*	Washington	✓	✓	
Massachusetts			✓	West Virginia		✓	
Michigan	✓	✓	✓	Wisconsin	✓	✓	✓
Minnesota	✓	✓	✓	Wyoming	✓		
Mississippi			✓	Washington, D.C.	✓	✓	
Missouri	✓	✓	✓	Puerto Rico			✓
Montana	✓	✓	✓	Virgin Islands			
Nebraska	✓	✓					

*Case law only.
Source: *Family Law Quarterly*, Vol. XIX, No. 4, Winter 1986.

- The ability and availability of each parent to care for the child
- The financial standing of each parent and the financial capability of each to support the child

- The morality of each contesting parent and past conduct toward the other
- Whether or not the child will be forced to relocate or suffer other disruptive changes
- A parent's compliance with court rules and orders
- A parent's religious beliefs that may seriously threaten the child's welfare

In principle, custody awards are not aimed at either rewarding or punishing parents, since the court's paramount concern is for the child's ultimate welfare. Judges are supposed to consider all of the above factors in making a determination of custody. In addition, courts traditionally take the view that the children of the marriage should not be split up (for example, the son with the father and the daughter with the mother) or shuttled back and forth between divorced parents (for example, six months with the father, six months with the mother) merely to appease both of them. (This is sometimes referred to as "split custody.")

Nor are judges willing to modify (reverse) earlier decisions of custody merely because of changes in marital status (for example, if the noncustodial parent remarries) or improvements in economic circumstances (for example, if the noncustodial parent wins a $500,000 lottery), at least so long as the custodial parent is not shown to be unfit.

Examples of unfitness for mothers typically include incidents of open lesbianism in front of the child, immoral conduct, alcoholism or habitual drug use, history of child abuse or neglect, serious physical or mental impairments, or the inability to provide a suitable home environment for the child. Many of these same factors are used by contesting mothers to prove the unfitness of the father. Other factors might be a past history of child and wife beatings, failure to pay child support, and an extensive criminal record.

Frequently, neighbors, baby-sitters, household employees, schoolteachers, clergy, and relatives are requested to testify on behalf of one of the contesting parents. In addition, since the testimony of a psychiatrist, psychologist, or therapist is often crucial in determining whether the parent is fit or what is in the child's best interest, the opinions of such experts are usually given great weight by a judge.

Finally, the expressed preference of a child who is sufficiently intelligent and mature are factors to which weight must be given. In the absence of any grave disability (for example, the unfitness of the specified parent), a child's stated preference will be given consideration if it appears that the best interests, welfare, and development of the child will be served by awarding custody to the preferred parent. Thus, the child, the object of the dispute, may be called to testify at the trial. This is usually done *in camera* (in the judge's chambers) outside of the presence of the contesting parents and their attorneys, although a stenographic record of the interview is usually taken. *In camera* interviews protect the child from the rigors of cross-examination and reduce the chances of alienating him or her from either of the parents, who may not approve of the testimony.

Now you can see why child custody cases are often so lengthy and complex; each parent typically parades experts and friendly witnesses to prove that he or she is the most competent, caring, and loving parent, the one best suited for custody. Trials sometimes last more than a week, and money is often spent needlessly in the process.

Strategies to Avoid Custody Litigation

I personally offer the following recommendations to clients seeking to avoid complex custody battles and the harm that frequently occurs to their children in the process.

1. *Try to settle custody disputes privately before the divorce.* Courts are not bound by the parents' agreements concerning custody and visitation, and are free to modify them, particularly if the agreement is not in the child's best interest. Thus it is wise to discuss and settle the question of your child's "best interest" before resorting to expensive and time-

consuming litigation and court intervention.

If you and your spouse cannot resolve your differences and save your marriage, the least you can do is attempt to work out, by mutual agreement, the manner in which your children will be cared for.

The following is a comprehensive checklist of points which should be initially explored by parents about to commence divorce proceedings. Once an amicable meeting of the minds is reached concerning a majority of these points, they can then be incorporated into a written agreement. Usually, a lawyer will assist you in the process.

- What type of custody (that is, joint or sole) is desired?
- With whom will the child principally reside?
- What form of visitation rights will the noncustodial parent receive? (How many visits per week? When? Is notice to the custodial parent required before each visit?)
- Can visitation take place in the custodial parent's home or must the child be taken from the house?
- How much extended visitation (for example, vacations) with the noncustodial parent will be permitted?
- Is the custodial parent permitted to move the child to relocate or must he or she live within a certain geographic territory (for example, within a 50-mile radius) of the noncustodial parent? What happens if the child is moved? Can the other parent cut off support or regain custody?
- If the custodial parent is permitted to move to another state with the child, who will pay for the traveling expenses incurred when the child visits his noncustodial parent?
- How much decision-making power and authority does the custodial parent have regarding the child's education, health, religious training, vacations, trips, etc.? Does the noncustodial parent have the right

to be notified of said matters before the decisions are made? If so, does he or she have input or veto power?

- Are there circumstances where custody will change? If so, when? (When the noncustodial parent remarries?)

- Do both parents agree not to alienate the affections of the children? What actions may the injured parent take if this is not followed?

- If the children are to be in the ex-wife's custody, are they permitted to assume the name of the wife's second husband if she remarries? May they call the second husband "father"? May he legally adopt them?

- If the children are to be in the father's custody, and he remarries, may the children call the second wife "mother"?

- If the noncustodial parent contributes child support may he or she suspend support payments when the children visit him or her on extended vacations?

2. *Confirm your agreement in writing.* Once these and other terms are clarified and agreed upon, the next step is to crystallize them in writing. Agreements regarding custody are typically incorporated into a master separation agreement with separate sections for custody and child support. The separation agreement is then approved by a judge during divorce proceedings.

Alternatively, the parties may use a simple agreement with respect to these issues only. This is frequently done when the parents have not decided how they intend to distribute the marital assets (which will be the subject of litigation), property, and other finances of the marriage, but have agreed on matters affecting the children.

The following text was taken from one of my comprehensive separation agreements to illustrate the manner in which many of the foregoing points can be specified in writing. Remember, it is used for illustrative purposes only, and should not be actually used in your own matter without the assistance of a qualified attorney. (*Note*: The provisions in the agreement call for both parents to exercise joint legal custody, with physical custody of the children to remain with the mother. Of course, the agreement could be easily changed to indicate that both sole legal and physical custody remain with one of the parents.)

Sample Article in a Separation Agreement

CUSTODY AND VISITATION

(a) The parties shall have joint custody of the unemancipated children of the parties, irrespective of whether the children shall reside with the Mother or the Father and each shall be responsible for the supervision, control and care of the children. The arrangement will afford both parties ample opportunity to enjoy the children's society and to participate in a harmonious policy best calculated to promote the interests of the children.

(b) The parties acknowledge that the children's wishes are to be considered in connection with the exercise of visitation rights, and each party agrees that he or she shall encourage the children in anticipating periods of visitation with the other.

(c) Each of the parties hereto agrees to keep the other informed at all times of the whereabouts of the children when with the Father, or the Mother, respectively, and they mutually agree that if either of them has any knowledge of any illness or accident, school problems or other circumstances affecting the children's health or general welfare, the Father or the Mother, as the case may be, will promptly notify the other of such circumstances.

(d) The parties shall consult with each other with respect to the children's education, illnesses and operations (except in emergencies), health, welfare and other matters of similar importance affecting the children whose well-being, education and development shall, at all times, be the paramount consideration of the Father and Mother;

(e) Each party agrees that, in the event of acute illness of the children at any time, the other party shall have the right of reasonable visitation with the children at the place of confinement;

(f) Each parent shall be entitled to complete, detailed information from any pediatrician, general physician, dentist, consultant or specialist attending the children for any reason whatsoever and to receive, upon request, copies of any reports given by them, or any of them, to the other parent;

(g) Each parent shall have the right of reasonable, unhampered telephone communications with the children and shall provide to the other parent a telephone number for that purpose;

(h) From the date hereof, the children shall reside with the Mother. The Father shall have liberal visitation rights. While the children are residing with the Mother, the Father shall have the right to visit the children outside of the Mother's residence during two (2) weekday (Monday through Thursday) evenings per week and two (2) weekends (Friday between 7:00 and 9:00 p.m. through Sunday between 7:00 and 9:00 p.m.) per month in accordance with arrangements mutually made with the Father and the children on reasonable prior notice by the Father to the Mother;

(i) Notwithstanding the foregoing, the children shall reside with the Father for a period of up to two (2) full weeks during each and every Summer.

(j) Notwithstanding the foregoing, the Mother shall have the right to visit the children on Mother's Day if at the time they are residing with the Father; and the Father shall have the right to visit with the children on Father's Day if at that time they are residing with the Mother. For at least four (4) hours on the child's birthday, the parent with whom the child is not then living shall have the right of visitation in accordance with arrangements mutually made with the visiting parent and the child on reasonable prior notice by the visiting parent to the parent; the parties alternate visitation on major holidays from year to year;

(k) If either party shall fail to comply with any of the provisions of this Article, the other party shall have the right to initiate a proceeding in the Supreme Court or the Family Court of the State of New York, in New York County, for such relief as may be appropriate under the circumstances;

(l) Although the parties hereby acknowledge that nothing herein contained shall be construed as an obligation or duty on the part of a party to exercise rights of visitation, nevertheless they acknowledge the need for planning activities for the children and further acknowledge that disappointing a child may have serious, adverse effects upon the child. Accordingly, each party agrees that on all occasions when he or she does not plan to exercise rights of visitation or expects to be early or late in so doing or intends to return the children at an earlier or later hour, as much advance notice as reasonably possible will be given to the other party in order that appropriate plans will be made for the children;

(m) The parties shall exert every reasonable effort to maintain free access and unhampered contact between the children and each of the parties and to foster a feeling of affection between the children and the other party. Neither party shall do anything which may estrange the child from the other party or injure the children's opinion as to the Mother or Father or which may hamper the free and natural development of the children's love and respect for the other party;

(n) Each party covenants, represents and warrants not, at any time or for any reason, to cause the children to be known or identified or designated by any name other than _____ and both parties covenant, represent and warrant that they will not initiate or permit the designations of "Father" and/or "Mother" or their equivalent, to be used by the children with reference to any person other than the parties hereto;

(o) In no event shall the children be adopted without express, prior written consent of each of the parties;

(p) Nothing herein shall bar or limit the parties from discussing and agreeing upon modifications of the provisions set forth in this Article;

(q) Reference herein to "child" shall refer to the unemancipated children of the parties;

(r) Should either party die or become seriously incapacitated mentally or physically while the children are still of minor age, the guardianship and custody of the minor children shall remain wholly and exclusively with the other party;

(s) It is the parties' intention to exercise fully all rights of visitation as herein provided but the exercises thereof shall be entirely optional, and failure to exercise such right on any particular occasion shall not be deemed or construed or constitute a waiver of a right thereafter to full compliance with the provisions hereof;

(t) Neither party shall remove the residence of the children beyond a radius of fifty (50) miles from their present residence without prior, written consent of the other party. If the Mother shall remove the residence of the children beyond said radius without the consent of the Father or the Court, such failure to obtain consent shall be presumptive of the right of the Father to obtain custody of the children and to terminate further payments under this agreement to the Wife for her support and maintenance. In addition, it shall entitle the Father to pursue all other remedies available to him under the circumstances.

Since the courts have authority to decide all matters pertaining to the general welfare of children, custodial agreements between parents are subject to close judicial scrutiny. To be workable and lasting, a custody arrangement must be consistent with the children's welfare. For example, even if the parents agreed that the child was forbidden to visit his or her mother (in return for a large sum of money paid by the father to the mother), and this arrangement was discovered by the court, the private agreement between the parents would be deemed unenforceable.

In addition, courts are free to modify a prior agreement between the parties where circumstances have markedly changed (for example, the custodial parent becomes unfit or substantially less fit than at the time the arrangement of custody was agreed to, or one of the parents relocates to a distant state for the sole purpose of depriving the noncustodial parent of visitation rights). However, without a showing of changed circumstances, an agreement between the parties concerning custody, maintenance, and education of the child which are clearly in the child's best interests will not be overturned.

Thus it is important that you consult a lawyer experienced in custody matters to be certain that your intentions are clearly drafted and are fair to the child. This is essential and should not be done on your own.

3. *Understand the difference between joint and exclusive custody and decide which is best for you and your children.* Judges, lawyers, and mental-health professionals have created a concept which permits both parents to have an equal role in raising their children. Known as "joint custody" or "co-parenting," it provides that each parent share in the parental authority and day-to-day responsibilities regarding the children. This differs from the traditional concept of exclusive or sole custody, where the child resides with one parent who has the sole authority to make decisions regarding the child's education, health, religious training, and vacations, while the noncustodial parent merely has rights of visitation.

Many people have the mistaken belief that joint legal custody involves joint physical custody (for example, the child lives six months with the mother and then six months with the father). This is not so, as such arrangements are typically frowned upon by the courts. (The view is that shifting from parent to parent is disruptive to the child.) Rather, although the child typically resides exclusively with one parent (as in the sole-custody situation), both parents share equally in all major decisions affecting the child, and if the parents fail to agree, the issue may then be resolved in court or under binding arbitration.

While the concept of joint custody sounds reasonable, it doesn't always work in practice. Generally, the determination of whether a joint-custody arrangement is in the child's best interest depends on whether the parents are able to cooperate and agree on important decisions affecting the child. Joint custody carries with it the underlying assumption that the parties are willing to share as partners in raising the children and are capable of reaching amicable solutions concerning their children.

In essence, joint custody rarely works where parents are vindictive, spiteful, or harbor resentment towards each other. Rarely is it the best solution in contested custody matters or where the parents have shown an inability to cooperate.

It is important to know this critical legal distinction and understand whether you and your spouse will be able to enter into this arrangement to your child's benefit *before* agreeing to it. Remember, joint custody sounds good, but it does not work for everybody.

4. *Avoid using your children as pawns.* This is essential to their well-being. Parents frequently lose sight of the fact that in divorce the children are usually the losers. It is they who are deprived of the full-time guidance and direction that two parents can give them and which is so necessary for their moral, spiritual, and character growth. Continuing anger or bitterness toward your former spouse can injure your children far more than the separation itself.

Refrain from voicing criticism of the other parent. Do not force or encourage your child to take sides. Both parents should strive for agreement in decisions pertaining to the children, especially discipline, so that one parent is not undermining the other parent's efforts.

Do not use visitations as an excuse to continue arguments with your spouse. The visit should not be used to check on the other parent. Do not use your children as spies to gain information.

5. *Obtain a complete legal appraisal of your rights to custody if you cannot come to terms with your ex-spouse.* Most judges frown upon endless and spiteful litigation in custody matters. However, courts do recognize situations where litigation is essential in protecting the rights of children and their parents.

I deplore situations where clients want me to commence custody proceedings merely to get even with the other spouse. However, there have been instances where it is clearly in the child's best interest to reside with one parent over the other.

I use the following guidelines when interviewing potential clients in custody matters. You should review these guidelines, both before and after you visit a lawyer, to determine if you have a valid case.

- What are the client's objectives? Are his or her motives sincere?
- Has an earnest effort been made toward an amicable resolution? If so, why have negotiations broken down?
- Why is my client better qualified as the custodial parent?
- What witnesses will be able to verify this? What will their testimony be?
- Has my client remarried? If so, what kind of relationship does the child have with the new spouse? Have the newly married couple considered the change that custody will have on their marriage?
- What is the child's stated preference? Is the child of sufficient age and maturity that his or her desires will carry weight with the court?
- What are the relative strengths and weaknesses (in terms of financial disparity, age, and general health) of the contesting parents?

These points have to be discussed before your lawyer can give you a valid determination of the chances of success with your case. And there are other considerations: For example, it is important that you be appraised of the financial costs involved. Many custody-case outcomes hinge on the testimony of psychiatrists and other experts. Can you afford their fees? Some lawyers ultimately receive more than $50,000 in fees for their services in custody cases. Experienced practitioners may charge upwards of $5,000 to initially take the case, with additional costs incurred on an hourly rate. Thus, be sure you have the financial resources to back up your will to win.

If the child in question is very young, ask the lawyer whether your state has abolished the "tender-years" doctrine. For most of the century, this doctrine assumed that young children were better off living with their mothers unless the mothers were proved unfit. Now such a doctrine has been replaced by a focus on "the best interests of the child." A recent nationwide study of contested custody disputes reported that this changed legal standard has resulted in more fathers being awarded legal custody than ever before; in fact, two-thirds of the disputes cited in the study were decided in favor of the fathers. No longer is the mother automatically assumed to be the better parent for young children; *be aware of this.*

6. *Recognize that it is not easy to obtain a modification of an earlier custody agreement or court decree.* Your lawyer should also advise you that it will not be easy to modify a prior arrangement. The reason is that judges are reluctant to do so unless there has been a *significant* change of circumstances since the custody determination and unless it is in the best interests of the children to modify the custody arrangement.

To be successful, the parent making the request for a court modification (usually the noncustodial parent) must prove the above two factors. This requires a full hearing with both sides submitting opposing evidence. In some cases, courts have reversed custody decisions on the basis of:

- Denial of the noncustodial parent's visitation privileges
- Remarriage of either of the parties
- Changed circumstances or the custodial parent's lack of fitness

In one recent New York case, for example, a father sought the custody of his daughters, aged 11 and 8, from his wife whom he had divorced six years earlier. Originally, the couple agreed on joint custody with the children residing with the mother. The father petitioned the court after learning that the mother permitted a male friend to sleep with her openly in front of the children and that she left the children unattended for long periods of time. The elder daughter expressed a strong desire to live with her father, while the younger daughter said she wanted to continue living with her mother, but not if it meant being separated from her sister. The father won the case.

However, despite cases such as the above, it may be difficult to modify a previous ruling unless you can establish clear and convincing proof of a change of circumstances. Be sure you obtain an unbiased opinion of your chances from your lawyer.

7. *Know your rights with respect to visitation.* Courts have traditionally ruled that the right of the noncustodial parent to visit the child is practically absolute. Simply stated, a parent may not be deprived of his or her right to reasonable and meaningful access to the children of the marriage unless exceptional circumstances have been presented to the court. This means that a judge cannot revoke visitation privileges unless the child's welfare is in danger. For example, it is judicial error to deny visitation rights because the noncustodial parent has failed to make support payments or because the parents are unable to solve their differences. Even unwed fathers are entitled to visitation privileges, *unless it is not in the child's best interests.*

Contact an attorney immediately if the custodial parent is denying you access to your child or is flouting court-ordered visitation benefits (for example, not allowing you to visit your children on the days previously agreed to, shortening or canceling the visitation period without notice, etc.). This should be done particularly if you learn that your former spouse intends to move the children to a distant place; the law states that nothing should deprive the child of access to either parent (particularly where there is an agreement for joint custody, liberal visitation rights, or a territorial restriction in the agreement). Many noncustodial parents are regaining custody on this issue.

Tips on Winning a Contested Custody Case

In order to win a contested custody case, proper planning is essential. Cases are often lost because of the inability of counsel to prepare a case properly or because of failure to produce necessary experts (for example, psychiatrists) to help prove the case.

The following rules may prove helpful in establishing a successful case.

1. *Avoid making yourself look like the "bad guy."* Some parents commit acts which place their cases at a disadvantage. For example, they deliberately move their children to a distant location, thereby depriving the noncustodial parent of visitation rights. Others incite judges with their testimony. One woman was reported to have told a judge in open court of her preference for and indulgence in extramarital sex experimentation. The judge ruled that the best interests of her teenage girls would not be served by "awarding their custody to one who proclaims, and lives by, such extraordinary ideas of right conduct."

The more sincere and practical you appear, the better your chances of success.

2. *Try to make a good impression during the trial.* The way you present yourself at a child-custody hearing is crucial. The judge will be looking for signs demonstrating that you are the parent better suited for custody; looking and acting the part won't hurt your chances.

Always be properly attired, preferably in business clothes. Talk directly to the judge and respond to questions in a straightforward manner. If the judge asks you a question while you are speaking, stop immediately. Then answer the question honestly and to the point. Show respect; always refer to him or her as "Your Honor" or "Judge." Listen to the judge's instructions and *never argue*. Try to be diplomatic rather than emotional. Outbursts in the courtroom are inappropriate. Melodrama of that kind will never impress a judge.

3. ***Never force your child to live with you against his or her will.*** This is not fair to the child. Besides, the expressed preferences of a mature child will carry weight with a judge; don't forget this.

4. ***Be sure to introduce witnesses at the trial to support your claim.*** Ask the witnesses to recall, in advance of the trial, specific incidents which illustrate why you are better suited for custody and more dedicated to the child. Let the witness know where in the total sequence of the trial his or her testimony will come in. In addition to discussing the strategy of the case, it is a good idea to prepare the witness for cross-examination by the opposing lawyer so that he or she will know what to expect while on the stand.

One final point: Since an award of custody is essentially a decision in the behavioral discipline, it is clear that the testimony of a child psychiatrist/psychologist is important, if *not critical*. Thus, try to obtain a well-respected, well-qualified professional who has rendered opinions for child-custody cases in the past.

5. ***Work up a game plan.*** In order to be awarded custody, you will have to demonstrate your ability to care for the needs of your child. Thus it is important to develop a reasonable, workable routine that will demonstrate your capabilities to the judge. Be prepared to show, for example, where the child will live, how he or she will be transported to and from school, and who will care for the child when he or she is not in school and you are not physically present. In addition, the judge will probably seek answers to questions such as:

- Does the child have adequate room and sleeping accommodations?
- Does the child have a good relationship with *your* friends, relatives, and neighbors?
- Do you and the child have common interests?

Clients often fail to realize that the little things (like how much time you spend with the child) are more important than all the material possessions the child will gain by living with you. Develop and implement a practical game plan with this in mind.

Really get to know your child. Study and learn how to a be a better parent. Become active in the business, religious, and social activities of your church or synagogue; take the child(ren) with you to these activities whenever possible. It is also a good idea to devote some of your free time to civic endeavors such as Little League, Girl Scouts, etc. This type of involvement often impresses a judge as to your sincerity and your ability to care for the needs of your child.

6. *Prepare a detailed and factual list of provable reasons why the other parent should not be awarded custody or that there should be no change in custody.*

7. *Be prepared to show and prove that the child's life would be disrupted by a change of custody.* For example, it is frequently a good idea to prepare a list of close playmates, school friends, and social activities which the child enjoys and participates in.

8. *Prepare color photographs to prove your claim.* I frequently advise clients to take color photographs which help prove that life with you is more beneficial for the child. For example, it is a good idea to take pictures which show where the child lives, goes to school, plays, etc. The value of this evidence should never be overlooked.

9. *Maintain an open attitude toward visitation for the other parent.* This will demonstrate your desire to conduct yourself properly in the best interest of the child. I have found that such conduct is generally noted and given some weight by the court.

10. *Be a good loser.* Ultimately, only one parent wins a custody battle. If you lose, you must remember that you are still a parent and are still vital to the child's future development.

Some Final Considerations

Custody and Visitation Rights of Grandparents, Stepparents, and Extended Family Members

Although the custody and visitation rights of grandparents, stepparents, and members of the extended family have not been uniformly applied throughout the United States, courts are granting them certain privileges, particularly when it is in the best interests of the children to do so.

Some courts have granted visitation rights, and even exclusive custody, to grandparents after it was shown that the grandparents had established a close relationship with the children, the parents had died, and/or it was in the best interests of the children.

Recently, there has been a proliferation of grandparent-visitation statutes, and bills concerning this issue have been introduced in Congress. Some of these laws allow grandparents to petition state courts for visitation privileges following the dissolution of a marriage. Other courts are specifying that stepparents can stand in the place of parents when questions of child abuse, neglect, financial support, medical consent, and inheritance arise.

Recognize that any person who has a close and meaningful relationship with a child, one that benefits the child, may have a valid reason to petition a court for visitation rights and/or for custody and may intervene in any proceeding where the child's custody is being considered. For example, in a unique case in New York recently, a judge ordered that a natural father forfeit custody of his daughter to the child's maternal aunt. In the case, the 12-year-old daughter believed that her mother's death was caused in part as the result of her parents' divorce and her father's remarriage two months later. The child formed the opinion that the stress imposed upon her mother by the divorce exacerbated her illness and accelerated her death. The judge ruled that such fears were not entirely unfounded and ruled that the child was better off residing with her aunt.

Change of a Child's Surname

In the majority of cases, courts will not grant applications for changes in a child's surname unless it is in the child's best interest. This is because courts view such changes as disruptive to the child's sense of the family unit, and traditionally regard a change in a child's surname as having significant consequences. The issue of name change sometimes arises in postdivorce proceedings when one parent, usually a former wife, allows the child in her custody (despite the noncustodial father's objection), to use a hyphenated name that incorporates the father's name with her maiden name or allows the child to adopt the surname of a stepparent.

One recent California case listed the following factors in its determination of whether to allow a change of surname:

- Whether the child's health, education, and welfare would be negatively affected by the selection of a different surname
- The length of time the child has used the surname
- The effect the name change might have on the father-child relationship

Each case is decided according to its own particular facts. For example, one New York judge rejected a mother's application for permission to change the child's surname, even though the father had defaulted in his child-support payments. Other judges have granted the change where the father abandons or neglects the child.

It is interesting to note that in many cases where mature children (for example, 16- to 18-year-olds) have changed their surname without the approval of their fathers, judges have ruled that the fathers can stop making support payments since this constitutes a forfeiture of the right to receive parental support.

8 | Getting Your Due: Child Support and the Law

Introduction

The natural parent has a continuing duty to provide support for an unemancipated child. This means that if a parent is possessed of sufficient means (or is able to earn such means) he or she will be required to pay a fair and reasonable sum for the child's support until the child reaches 18 years of age (21 in some states), marries, permanently abandons the marital home, moves out, or gains full-time employment and becomes fully self-supporting.

This general proposition of law is recognized in virtually all states. However, it is wrought with numerous questions:

- What amount of support is considered fair and reasonable?
- Is a stepparent liable to provide support?
- What happens if one parent is unable to pay his or her fair share?
- What recourse does a parent have to enforce child support from the parent who fails this obligation?
- Under what circumstances can the amount of child support be modified by the court?
- Is a parent liable for college education costs, too?

The following sections will attempt to provide answers to questions such as these.

What Is Fair and Reasonable Support?

In most states, the amount of support given to a child depends upon the following factors:

- The particular circumstances of each case
- The financial abilities of each parent

- The parents' prior standard of living
- The best interests of the child
- The physical health of the child
- The child's educational or vocational needs and aptitudes
- The emotional health of the child
- Tax consequences to the parties, where practical and relevant

Both parents are generally equally liable to provide support according to their respective means and responsibilities, although some states make the father *primarily* liable and the mother *secondarily* liable. In those states, for example, if the father is unable to pay support, or fails to pay, then the responsibility falls directly on the mother. In addition, although historically the primary responsibility for child support is on the father, a mother's financial situation and assets may be viewed by the court when considering the amount of the father's liability for support.

Frequently, the parties to a divorce will specify the amount of child support to be paid. This is usually done in the separation agreement signed by both parents. The following articles are taken from one of my master separation agreements:

Sample Article in a Separation Agreement

ALLOWANCE FOR THE SUPPORT, MAINTENANCE AND EDUCATION OF THE CHILDREN

1. As and for the support, maintenance and education of each child, the Husband shall pay to the Wife the sum of _____ per week, per child, payable on each and every Friday of each week commencing on _____, 19__.

2. The aforementioned _____per week, per child, payment for each child shall continue with respect to each such child until an Emancipation Event as is hereinafter defined shall have occurred to any such child. Upon the occurrence of any such Emancipation Event, the Husband shall no longer be responsible for the payment of such _____ weekly amount of the particular child so emancipated.

3.   During the period that support payments are paid for the Children or either of them, the Husband shall be exclusively entitled to list them or either of them, as the case may be, as his dependents on his income tax return and the Wife shall not be entitled to list either of them as her dependents on her tax returns.

4.   All obligations under this Article shall terminate in the event of the death of the Wife or the death of the Husband. The parties contemplate that in the event of the death of the Wife, then with respect to such of the children concerning whom an Emancipation Event has not previously occurred, the Husband shall have such obligation as is imposed by law with respect to the support of any such child or children. In the event of the death of the Husband, all obligations set forth in this Article shall terminate.

Sample Article in a Separation Agreement

ADDITIONAL SUPPORT

(a)   In addition to the support provided herein, the Father agrees to furnish at his own expense Blue Cross, Blue Shield and major medical insurance (or other equivalent) for the benefit of the children of the parties until the remarriage of the Wife and/or emancipation of the children and to pay all reasonable medical, dental, orthodontia and drug expenses (hereinafter collectively called "medical expenses") of the children of the parties. The Mother shall advise the Father of any medical insurance which may be furnished to her by an employer in order that the Father need not duplicate coverage for the children. If the Mother is required to pay for such coverage of the children, the Father may elect to utilize said coverage for the children and shall promptly pay for or reimburse the Mother for such expense or to provide his own coverage. For uninsured medical and dental expenses, the parties shall share said costs equally, provided he or she, as the case may be, shall have given consent for such expenses, which consent will not be unreasonably withheld (unless medical or dental treatment is required in such short time that it is impossible or impractical to obtain such consent).

(b)   The Mother agrees that she will promptly fill out, execute and deliver to the Father all forms and provide all information in connection with any application he may make for reimbursement of medical, dental and drug expenses under any insurance policies which he may have. He shall promptly refund to the Mother any medical expenses paid for by her either directly or if insured, out of the proceeds of an insurance claim which the Husband shall file promptly.

(c)   The Father will furnish to the Wife at her request documentation and other proof of his compliance with the provisions of this Article, and the Wife, in addition, is hereby authorized to obtain direct confirmation of compliance or non-compliance with any insurance carrier.

(d)   In addition to the foregoing, the Father shall pay promptly one-half (1/2) of all reasonable expenses for the tuition, fees, transportation and outfitting of the children at a summer camp, or for summer or vacation travel or similar summer or vacation activity, if the children desire to pursue such activity and if the Father consents thereto, which consent will not be unreasonably withheld. The Mother agrees to consult with the Father regarding each such activity and to consider such suggestions and comments which he deems shall be in the best interests of the children. In no event will the Father be required to pay for any of the said expenses incurred for the participation of the Mother in such activity or activities.

(e)   It is understood that the Father's obligation for the support of the children herein shall be suspended during any period when the children are in summer camp or other activities which necessitate the children staying away from home at the Father's expense.

(f)   In addition to the foregoing, if the children of the parties have been recommended by a teacher, guidance counsellor or other educational adviser or administrator to obtain tutoring help with respect to any academic lessons or courses, the Father agrees to pay promptly for one-half (1/2) of the reasonable cost of such tutoring.

(g)   In addition to the foregoing, if the children of the parties desire to attend religious school or receive private religious training, the Father agrees to pay promptly for one-half (1/2) of the reasonable cost of such education or training. Both parties shall encourage the use of financial aids, grants, loans and scholarships to help defray expenses, and they agree to cooperate with each other and the child toward that end. The expenses referred to in this subparagraph shall include, but shall not be limited to, application and testing fees, tuition, required books, uniforms, materials and supplies, reasonable transportation and incidental expenses.

Although it is desirable to settle the issue of child support without the necessity of court intervention, it doesn't always happen that way. When the parties to a divorce cannot agree on the amount of appropriate support, the court will fix such an amount either prior to, during, or after the divorce is finalized. The general rule used by the court is to require the parents to supply the necessities of food, shelter, and maintenance for the children as may be reasonable with respect to the parents' means and financial capabilities.

Even when the parents agree on a certain sum and include this in their separation agreement, the court may modify the amount when it believes this to be in the best interests of the child. In one recent New York case, for example, the court commented that a modification of child support should be permitted in the event the amount specified in a separation agreement is not fair and reasonable when entered into, does not provide for a fair allocation of continuing responsibility, or fails to provide for the future needs of the children. In that case, the court then proceeded to redetermine support based upon the current needs of the children.

There are other situations which may cause a court to modify an agreement of child support. This may happen when an unanticipated or unreasonable change in circumstances occurs (for example, serious illness affects the child) or when a parent is shirking the legal obligation of support. Some states have allowed the father to stop paying child support if the mother denies him visitation rights. Thus, if you are a noncustodial father who is being hassled by your former wife regarding visitation, speak to a lawyer immediately; you may be able to legally stop paying support until unhampered visitation is resumed.

In certain situations, fathers may also stop paying support when their children abandon or deny them the love, affection, and respect they are entitled to as a parent. Again, if you are a parent who is experiencing this unfortunate situation, speak to a lawyer immediately; you may be able to legally stop paying child support until your child "comes around."

Although it may be difficult to calculate the precise amount of child support needed to adequately provide for the child (while at the same time not placing an undue hardship on the parent making such payments), there are certain guidelines I have found to be helpful in this regard. The first step is to prepare an accurate living-expense sheet to calculate ordinary living expenses for you, your ex-spouse, and the children. When this is filled out properly and honestly, you will have a better idea of how much child support and alimony is typically required. The form can also tell you how much you can afford to pay and still maintain an appropriate standard of living for yourself.

I use the following living-expense sheet to calculate a client's financial position. Feel free to adapt this for your own use; special circumstances (for example, extraordinary medical expenses or education costs) should also be included in your computations if that is appropriate.

Living Expense Sheet

For: _____

(Designate Husband, Wife, Children or any combination)

	Per Week	Per Month	Per Year
A. Housing expenses			
1. Rent			
2. Mortgage payment			
3. Property taxes (if not included in mortgage payment)			
4. Appliance and house service contracts			
5. Home repairs			
6. Gardening expense			
7. Exterminator			
8. Fuel oil			
9. Gas and electric			
10. Water			
11. Sewer			
12. Garbage collection			
13. Telephone			
14. Cable television			
15. Homeowners' association			
16. Tips to doormen, mailmen, etc.			
17. Snow removal			
18. House insurance			
19. Household help			
B. Food			
C. Cleaning and household supplies			

D. Laundry and dry cleaning

E. Clothing
   1. Clothing for self
   2. Clothing for children
   3. Clothing for spouse

F. Medical expenses not covered by insurance
   1. Doctors for self
                for spouse
                for children
   2. Dentists for self
                 for spouse
                 for children
   3. Hospital
   4. Psychotherapy
   5. Medicine (drugs)
   6. Vitamins
   7. Medical specialists
   8. Orthodontia
   9. Allergy expense
   10. Other _____
       _____
       _____

G. Auto expenses
   1. Gasoline and oil
   2. Maintenance and repairs
   3. Loan payments or rental
   4. Registration
   5. Insurance
   6. Depreciation
   7. Parking and tolls

H. Other transportation expenses
   1. Commutation
   2. Taxis and buses
   3. Other

I. Child-care expenses

    1. Lunch money
    2. Allowances
    3. Baby-sitter
    4. Grooming
    5. Summer camp
    6. Religious education
    7. Tutoring
    8. Lessons (music, dancing, etc.)
    9. Pet expense
   10. Education expenses

J. Personal expenses

    1. Tobacco
    2. Grooming
    3. Cosmetics
    4. Lunches
    5. Entertainment (includes dinners out)
    6. Vacations
    7. Club dues and expenses
    8. Religious dues and expenses
    9. Gifts and presents
   10. Hobby expenses
   11. Sports expenses
   12. Education expenses
   13. Books, magazines, records, etc.
   14. Charitable contributions (other than religious)

K. Business expenses

    1. Dues (union, etc.)
    2. Subscriptions, books
    3. Other reimbursed expense (specify)
    4. Retirement plan

L. Insurance

    1. Life insurance
    2. Medical insurance
    3. Accident insurance
    4. Disability insurance
    5. Other (specify)

M. Obligations

    1. Alimony
    2. Child support
    3. Loans (other than auto)
    4. Others (specify)

N. Recreation expenses (not
    otherwise mentioned above)

    1. Other real estate
    2. Boat expenses
    3. Airplane expenses

Please assemble and bring to the office the following items:

1. All income tax returns for the past five years
2. All bank books, certificates of deposit, and bank statements for the past three years
3. Listing by expense category of all checks written for the past two years with separate totals for each category for each year
4. Deeds to real estate
5. Loan books
6. Insurance policies
7. Retirement plan and statements
8. Recent paycheck vouchers or envelopes
9. Other _____

After I have obtained a conservative monthly figure of need for the appropriate party involved, it is then relatively easy to calculate the divorced parents' support obligations. This is sometimes done by a mathematical formula that determines each parent's contribution. Many courts first determine the reasonable needs of the children, based on the particular circumstances of the parties and the reasonable ability of each parent to pay child support, making allowances for the parents' reasonable living expenses. (You may have already done this using the preceding sample sheet.) These figures are then plugged into an equation, which considers the amount of each parent's income that is available for support, divided by the sum of both parents' income that is available for support, multiplied by the amount of the children's needs. After the court has calculated each parent's obligation, it can offset the amount by support provided directly to the children or determine what portion should go directly to the other parent.

This formula has been used by the Pennsylvania Supreme Court in an effort to remedy a "total lack of organization" in weighing the relevant factors in child-support cases. Using it will give you a better idea of the type of award a court may render if you and your ex-spouse cannot agree on the amount of child support to be paid. Speak to an experienced attorney for further details if you cannot resolve this issue in an appropriate fashion.

When Does Child Support Stop?

The responsibility of paying child support ends when the child becomes emancipated. The following article, taken from one of my separation agreements, illustrates the kind of criteria that can be applied in determining an emancipation event:

Sample Article in a Separation Agreement

EMANCIPATION EVENT

The children shall be deemed, for the purposes of this agreement, to have become emancipated upon the earliest happening of any of the following events:

    (a)   Attaining the age of 21 years;

    (b)   Marriage of the child, even though such marriage may be void or voidable, and despite any subsequent divorce, annulment or other termination thereof;

    (c)   Entry of the child into the military service;

    (d)   Engaging in full-time employment whereby the child is fully self-supporting;

    (e)   The child establishing a permanent residence away from either party. Residence at a camp, boarding school, college or travel shall not be deemed a change in the permanent residence of a child sufficient to constitute emancipation.

As I mentioned previously, some courts in certain states have ruled that noncustodial parents are not responsible for continuing to pay child support when their mature children refuse to maintain a relationship with them, change their surname, or refuse to give love and affection.

What Is the Liability of Stepparents, Grandparents, and Others in Providing Child Support?

In most states, a stepparent is not legally responsible for paying support unless he or she has adopted the child. Even if a stepparent volunteers or makes an oral promise to support the child while the child is residing in the stepparent's home, that obligation is not enforceable and can be terminated at the stepparent's discretion. For example, in a recent Oklahoma case, the court ruled that a husband was not responsible for supporting the child of his wife who had been impregnated by another man, even though the husband was aware that the child was not his at the time of the marriage. (*Note*: If, with the husband's consent, a child is conceived through artificial insemination by the sperm of an anonymous donor, the husband may have the duty of supporting the child.)

Grandparents, also, are not legally responsible for providing child support unless they have adopted the child. Thus, the duty to provide support typically extends to the natural parents and to no one else, except in special circumstances.

Is a Parent Legally Obligated to Pay for College?

Generally, parents are not legally responsible for paying the costs of a college education or of special training for their children. However, in cases where this is an issue, a court will look at:

- The educational background of the parents
- The environment in which the child grew up
- The child's academic ability
- The economic status and occupations of the parents

Often a combination of these factors will demonstrate a finding of special circumstances where the child is expected to attend college. In addition, the facts of the case may indicate that a parent's actions reflected the desire that the child attend college and the assumption that the parent would pay for it (for example, a parent makes specific promises in front of witnesses or the parties acknowledge their intentions to pay for college education in their separation agreement).

Thus, in most states, whether or not a parent (usually the father) will be ordered by the court to pay for the child's private school, college, or professional educational expenses is an issue of fact to be determined by all the circumstances. Certainly where the parent is capable of paying such support, and has encouraged the child to obtain a college or special degree, the court will be more willing to order that said payments be made.

Of course, the obligation to pay college costs does not necessarily mean that the child must attend a private college. Thus, if you are seeking to obtain support from an ex-spouse for college education or other related expenses, *try to be reasonable with your demands*. It is often difficult to predict how much money courts will award in this area; being reasonable may save you unnecessary legal expense and aggravation and may help you achieve support for your child's college education.

How Do You Obtain Child Support?

If you and your ex-spouse cannot agree on the amount of child support, or if you believe special circumstances have occurred which warrant a modification of the amount previously awarded, you must petition the court for an order of child support. Although this can be done without a lawyer, it is not advisable; speak to a lawyer immediately to protect your rights and those of your children in this area.

What Do You Do If Your Ex-Spouse Fails to Pay Child Support?

Child-support delinquency has become a national epidemic. In 1981, it was reported that only 53 percent of full court-ordered payments due to children were received by custodial parents; 28 percent of qualifying children received nothing. According to the federal Office of Child Support Enforcement, more than 6 million women sought enforcement of delinquent court-ordered child-support payments through the agency in 1981, an increase of 50 percent over the 4 million requests handled in 1979 (the first year the agency compiled such statistics). Experts suggest that these figures do not include the 3 million other women who have given up or who are trying to collect arrears through attorneys and other private channels.

Some experts believe divorced women have only a 10 to

20 percent chance of being paid on time and in full. There are many reasons why; one of the factors appears to be the high rate of remarriage for husbands, who are then unable to properly support the children from their first marriage. In addition, some custodial parents are simply reluctant to cooperate with the federal and state agencies set up for child-support enforcement.

However, most people are unaware that the federal government has enacted tougher laws and instituted more diligent collection activities to deal with this growing problem. Now there are ways to fight back, provided you know how. The following strategies were derived in part with the assistance of Elaine M. Fromm, author of the useful handbook, *Child Support Enforcement in Maryland*, and president of the Organization for the Enforcement of Child Support, a nationwide goup. The information given below will tell you how to act promptly and effectively once an ex-spouse fails to pay the required support, and should help you lessen your chances of being exploited.

1. ***Contact an action group in your state.*** Protest groups have been formed throughout the United States to fight against the difficulties frequently encountered in collecting delinquent child-support payments. These groups advise members of all laws that might help them collect, offer practical strategies, and provide names of local attorneys who specialize in handling similar matters. In addition, some of these groups lobby for tougher laws and pressure local politicians for assistance.

The Organization for the Enforcement of Child Support is a nonprofit, tax-exempt organization which seeks to enhance the enforcement of child support. It was formed in 1979 as an educational, self-help group of volunteers. The members study federal, state, and local child-support laws and procedures, monitor changes, and disseminate this information to the public through newsletters, printed literature, telephone contacts, public meetings, the media, and workshops.

In one recent workshop conducted by the association, for example, experts including lawyers, judges, and others explained:

- How to obtain a court order for support
- How to identify and discover what real and personal property is available for attachment
- How to collect from the spouse who is self-employed
- What to expect in court

This group presently has more than 20 chapters throughout the country. You would do well to contact the organization for more information and for the location of affiliated groups in other states. Contact Elaine Fromm, Organization for the Enforcement of Child Support, 119 Nicodemus Road, Reistertown, MD 21136; send a self-addressed stamped envelope if you desire a reply.

2. *Attempt to resolve the problem through mediation.* One option that is available and beneficial in some cases is family mediation. Family mediation is a process in which a trained professional guides structured discussions between family members and encourages them to reach an agreement that is acceptable to all parties concerned and with which both parties are willing to comply.

Mediation attempts to foster cooperation between the parties and set the stage for an amicable agreement. However, it is not for everyone. If the custodian of the children is significantly unequal in financial and/or emotional strength, he or she may do better being represented by an attorney rather than participating in the mediation process. In addition, a mediator who is not a lawyer may not be as knowledgeable of the tax consequences involved in a support agreement.

For more information about the pros and cons of mediation, see Chapter 9.

3. *Contact an attorney who specializes in this area.* Another way to attempt to prevent or minimize future problems with child-support enforcement is to choose a lawyer with whom you can discuss your needs and who can represent your interests in working out all aspects of the agreement (custody, visitation, child support, division of property, and other financial arrangements).

A good attorney can provide the best enforcement services if he or she is sufficiently experienced in the domestic-relations field. Such private attorneys can give as much time to a case as necessary to do an effective job. The biggest drawback, however, is expense, particularly if the child-support case is contested and the lawyer is charging you by the hour. I have witnessed some contempt actions where the amount of money recovered for the custodial parent barely covered attorney fees. However, some judges do allow your lawyer's fee to be paid by the other spouse, provided you request it through a petition filed with the court.

See a lawyer even if you think you are unable to afford the fees. Explain your financial condition. Ask for a reduced fee and ask about having the court order the noncustodian to pay all or some of your legal expenses and court costs. Some attorneys will take your case on a contingency fee basis. For more information about the types of fee arrangements that are available, questions to ask the lawyer at the initial interview, and steps to take to make your lawyer work more effectively for you, see Chapter 1.

4. *Contact a legal clinic for assistance.* Services offered in a legal clinic may be less personal than those given by a lawyer in private practice. However, the costs involved are much lower. One problem with legal clinics is that several different lawyers may work on your case, which may weaken your chances of success. *Remember this.*

5. *Contact a local chapter of the Child Support Enforcement Administration.* Services available from the Child Support Enforcement Administration include:
- Receipt, disbursement, and record-keeping of child-support payments
- Assistance in locating absent parents
- Referrals to the state attorney general's office and other enforcement agencies
- Implementation of state tax-refund intercept programs, the federal Tax-Refund Offset program, and unemployment intercept certifications
- Assistance in establishing support orders by consent when possible
- Assistance in enforcement
- Referrals to the IRS for collection services

Check to see if there is a local chapter of the Child Support Enforcement Administration (CSEA) in your state; if so, contact them immediately for assistance.

6. *Contact a local branch of your state attorney general's office.* Many state attorneys are empowered to prosecute nonsupport and paternity cases, and some employ staff attorneys for this purpose.

7. *Contact a local branch of your state's Legal Aid Society.* The Legal Aid Society provides statewide services to low-income clients in selected cases. You may wish to contact the Legal Aid Society for further assistance if you are living on modest funds.

8. *Know your rights.* There are basically two court systems to turn to for redress: criminal and civil. It is possible to proceed with civil litigation *and* criminal prosecution at the same time in some states. When a civil order exists and it is not being honored, a criminal action may be entered. You should contact a lawyer, the Legal Aid Society, or your state attorney general's office for further information.

The following remedies may be used for civil enforcement:

- *Wage liens.* In a civil case, you may request a wage lien when the person ordered to pay support is more than thirty days behind in payments. Many states do not have wage-lien statutes, however, so check to see if this is applicable in your state.

- *Garnishment.* Garnishment is a remedy used to attach a portion of a debtor's income to satisfy a debt, including settlement of arrears in child-support cases. There are limitations, however, on the amount of a debtor's income that can be taken through garnishment. Typically, you cannot garnish more than 50 percent of a person's weekly salary, up to a maximum of $200.

  Garnishment can be applied to all earnings except federal employee workers' disability benefits; earnings that can be attached include annuities, pensions, social security, nonfederal disability income, unemployment compensation, railroad retirement,

individual retirement accounts (IRAs), wages, retirement of armed services personnel, and federal
employees' wages and retirement.

- *Garnishment of military pay.* Federal law authorizes legal process against members of the U.S. military forces for garnishment of pay to collect child
  support (and alimony) arrears. This law provides a
  limit of 50 percent on the amount subject to garnishment, or similar process, for child support (and
  alimony) arrears for a person supporting a second
  family and 60 percent for a person who is not. The
  amounts are increased by an additional 5 percent in
  each situation if there are outstanding arrears more
  than twelve weeks old.

  For further information about the rights of military spouses and former spouses, contact:

  Mary Wurzel, President
  EXPOSE
  P.O. Box 11191
  Alexandria, VA 22312
  (703)/941-5844

- *Attachment of your spouse's real and personal property.* This is done by obtaining a court order which
  gives you the right to attach the respondent's assets
  to collect the obligation. Typically you request that
  the court file the *support judgment* (in the amount
  of money which the court determines is owed to you)
  as a lien in any county where the debtor has real
  estate, a bank account, a car, or other intangible
  assets.

  A judgment remains in effect for a limited period
  of time, typically six to twelve years. After you obtain
  a judgment, you must then take additional court action to enforce it. For example, a support judgment
  usually becomes final after thirty days. You must
  then record the final judgment and pay a small sum
  of money to the clerk of the court to obtain a *writ*.
  Once you obtain a writ, you can then contact the

sheriff, marshall, or other licensed individual to physically attach the property of the debtor, secure a voluntary wage lien, or obtain a lump-sum payment. (*Note*: In many states, the person obtaining the writ must pay for storage and auction costs.) A debtor is more likely to be amenable to payment of arrears when faced with imminent loss of a valued possession.

- *Assistance from the Internal Revenue Service.* The Child Support Enforcement Administration in your state may apply to the IRS for full collection process after other means of collection have failed. The IRS may enforce a levy for child-support obligations against income or assets of the noncustodian. Property may be seized and sold for payment of the delinquency. The IRS typically charges about $125 for this service. For further information, contact your county child-support agency.

  In addition, the IRS is allowed to intercept federal-income-tax refunds due to noncustodians who are at least $150 or three months in arrears in child-support payments. The money is sent directly to the state, which then disburses the funds according to a predetermined formula. Don't forget to ask about this interceptor program if it seems appropriate in your case.

- *Assistance from your state government.* Most states are fighting back against the alarming problem of child-support delinquencies. New Jersey, for example, provides for automatic attachment of the wages of a noncustodial parent who is twenty-five days or more in arrears. Other states, including New York, have passed laws requiring that all court orders of child support automatically be sent to an official collection agent when a specified number of payments are in arrears. Some states permit automatic withholding of all state and federal income-tax refunds, require that all child-support payments be made through a court so delinquencies can be monitored and pursued, and authorize the use of liens on property and other capital holdings.

- *Assistance from the federal government.* The Child-Support Enforcement Act of 1984 was passed to improve the child-support enforcement program, secure financial support from parents, and increase the effectiveness of state programs. This new federal law, enacted in August 1984 and generally effective as of October 1, 1985, made many new changes in the national child-support-enforcement system. Most of the services required by this new law are available only to those parents whose support is paid through their state.

  Table 8-1 provides a basic summary, furnished by the Organization for the Enforcement of Child Support, of changes and benefits contained in this new law. Speak to an attorney, your Legal Aid Society, or an appropriate state agency for more details.

9. *Seek assistance from an appropriate agency if you have difficulty locating your spouse.* There are a number of ways to locate nonpaying absent spouses, either by yourself or through your state's absent parent locator service. Some effective techniques are:

- Ascertain your spouse's address (if he or she is still living in your state) by contacting the motor vehicles bureau.
- If the telephone number is unpublished, obtain the absent parent's address from your local police department's crisscross telephone directory.
- Contact nationwide credit bureaus, labor unions, and financial institutions to uncover this information.

In addition, your state may have a parent locator service. Contact your local department of social services for further details.

10. *Sue your spouse for breach of contract or specific performance if you have a properly executed separation agreement.* An agreement, if properly written and exe-

Table 8-1
Summary of Provisions of the Child-Support Enforcement Act of 1984

Income withholding	All states must implement income-withholding procedures to begin when arrears reach an amount equal to one month's support payments or when an absent parent requests it. Withholding for child-support payments takes priority over any legal process against the same wage. Withholding may include other forms of income besides wages. States must agree to reciprocity with other states. All child-support orders issued or modified after 10/1/85 must include provision for withholding of wages if arrears occur.
State income tax refund offsets	States must implement programs to intercept state income tax refunds for past-due support owed by an absent parent. Provision must be made for withholding in interstate cases.
Liens against property	Procedures for imposing liens against real and personal property for amounts of past-due support may be imposed at the state's option.
Paternity Statute of Limitations	State paternity laws must permit establishment of paternity until a child's 18th birthday.
Security or bond in certain cases	Procedures to require an individual to post bond or give security or some other type of guarantee (if individual shows a pattern of past-due support) may be implemented at the state's option.

Table 8-1 (Continued)

Providing information on overdue support to credit agencies	States must make available to consumer credit bureau organizations, at the request of such agencies, the amount of past-due support owed by absent parents totaling $1,000 or more. States may make available information on smaller arrears.
Tracking and monitoring of support payments by public agency	At the state's option, child-support payments may be made through the agency that administers the state's income withholding system; annual fee of $25.
Notification of support collected	States must notify each AFDC recipient, at least once each year, of the amount of child support collected on behalf of that recipient.
Medical support required as part of child-support orders	State agencies must petition to include medical support as part of any child-support order whenever health-care coverage is available to absent parent at reasonable cost.
Increased availability of federal parent locator service	States need not exhaust all state child-support locator resources before they request assistance of federal Parent Locator Service.
Collection of past-due support from federal tax refunds	Present system for withholding past-due support from federal tax refunds is extended to absent parents of non-AFDC *minor* children, but is limited to cases where there are arrears of $500 or more. States may limit arrears which they submit to the IRS to amounts that have accrued since the state undertook to collect sup-

(continued)

Table 8-1 (*Continued*)

	port for the non-AFDC family. Program is effective for refunds payable after 12/31/85 and before 1/1/91. Some states do not certify arrears which preexisted 1975, and there is no provision for collecting arrears originally ordered to be paid directly to the custodial parent. Support orders may be modified to make money payable through state agency, but arrears existing prior to modification will not be collected through this program.
Limitations on bankruptcy provision	There is no change in present law; the Bankruptcy Act does not allow discharge of support in bankruptcy.
Guidelines for child-support awards	States must establish guidelines for child-support awards by law or administrative action; they must be made available to all judges and others who determine child-support awards but need not be binding on them.
Availability of social-security numbers	Absent parent's social-security number must be made available to child-support agencies.
Special grants to promote improvements in interstate enforcement	Appropriations will be made to fund special projects developed by states for innovative techniques or procedures improving child-support collections in interstate cases.
Periodic review of effectiveness of state programs, modification of penalty	Audit plan is decreased to every three years where states have been in substantial compliance with federal law. Annual audits are required otherwise. Penalty may be suspended, but only if state is actively pursuing a corrective action plan

Table 8-1 (*Continued*)

	to bring the state into substantial compliance.
Child-support enforcement for children in foster care	States must undertake child-support collections on behalf of children in foster care.
Enforcement of both child and spousal support	At the state's option, services may include enforcement of spousal support, but only if support obligation has been established with respect to the spouse, if child and spouse are living in same household, and if child support is being collected along with spousal support.
Publicizing availability of child-support services	States must frequently publicize availability of child-support-enforcement services, indicating application fees and phone number or address for additional information.
State commissions on child support	Governor of each state is required to appoint a commission to study establishment of appropriate standards for support, enforcement of interstate obligations, and additional legislation needed.

cuted, is a contract. Failure to pay child support, including medical support where specified, is a breach of contract, and a court may enter a money judgment for the unpaid arrears and may order that payments be made in the future. In addition, you may ask the court to enforce the agreement to pay support in *equity*. This is most effective where no court order for support exists. In both of these actions, it is best to proceed with the assistance of a lawyer.

11. *Seek to hold your nonpaying spouse in contempt.* A petition to cite for contempt is the most commonly used method of civil enforcement of child or spousal support. It may be filed by anyone having direct knowledge that the

support order is not being obeyed. In most states, judges hearing such complaints have the power to punish the offender by fine or by imprisonment for an indefinite time, or to order payment of the arrears either within a set time or by an addition to the regular payment. Usually judges are reluctant to impose a jail sentence upon a first offender (although some people believe that a short-term jail sentence is an effective tool in collecting arrears).

To be found in contempt, the noncustodian must have had the ability to pay when she or he defaulted. Quitting a job without a new one or voluntarily changing jobs to one which pays less is generally no excuse. However, closing a business in order to retire is not contempt, if the noncustodian is of normal retirement age.

Note: If there is no previous court order or decree, contempt of court is not available as a remedy. Therefore, you must obtain a court order of support before you commence contempt proceedings.

The following is a brief outline of the advantages and disadvantages of pressing contempt charges.

Advantages of Instituting Contempt Proceedings:

- A finding of contempt may result in jailing for an indefinite period; this may force the offending person to pay all or part of his or her arrears to avoid incarceration.
- The standard of proof for civil contempt proceedings only requires a preponderance of the evidence (a lower standard than in criminal proceedings).
- The contempt order becomes permanent and does not have to be renewed.

Disadvantages of Instituting Contempt Proceedings:

- Court costs and lawyer fees can make proceedings costly unless the court orders the noncustodian to pay a portion of the costs.
- It may take a long time before a hearing is scheduled and the matter is disposed of.

- Service of process upon defaulting individuals may be difficult, especially when you don't know where the defaulting party lives.

12. **Bring criminal charges against your nonpaying spouse.** In addition to civil remedies, the nonpaying spouse may be exposing himself or herself to criminal remedies as well. Many states have laws which make willful failure to support a spouse or child a crime. The state of Maryland, for example, makes this a misdemeanor punishable by a fine of up to $100 and/or a jail term of up to three years.

To file criminal nonsupport charges, you will have to appear in court and swear out a formal complaint. Some states require screening by the state district attorney's office before charges can be brought. Criminal prosecution of nonpayment is advantageous for many reasons.

Advantages of Filing Criminal Charges:

- When the action is handled by your state district attorney's office, there is no cost to you.
- Criminal cases normally proceed faster than civil cases.
- No prior order is needed to file a criminal action; it can be put on the FBI interstate computer through your local police department.
- If a warrant is issued, authorities in other jurisdictions may be alerted so that locating and arresting an offender can be substantially speeded up.
- The stigma of a criminal conviction may prompt the offending parent to start support payments.

However, there are distinct disadvantages to this course of action as well.

Disadvantages of Filing Criminal Charges:

- If the noncustodian pays a fine or serves time in jail for nonpayment of a criminal support order, the conviction may result in wiping out arrears which have accumulated under the criminal order.

- Judges may reduce, change, or modify your prior support order after time in jail has been served.
- Imprisonment usually eliminates or reduces a person's income; therefore, your main purpose may be frustrated.
- Criminal conviction may affect employment in some occupations.
- The standard of evidence required for conviction is proof beyond a reasonable doubt (a higher standard than used in civil proceedings).

Thus you need to speak to an experienced attorney before deciding what course of action to take. In most situations, resort to criminal prosecution for nonpayment of child and spousal support should be done only after all other methods, both private and governmental, fail.

Final Tips on Recovering Support Arrears

Despite this growing problem, there are many strategies that will minimize the chances you will be victimized by child-support delinquency. The following suggestions have met with varying degrees of success.

1. *Plan ahead.* Proper planning may save you aggravation and expense in the long run. For example, I recommend that you make arrangements for child support while the divorce action is proceeding and *put it in writing*. Child support should be spelled out carefully and completely in the separation agreement or other document. This will allow you to proceed quickly in court if your ex-spouse fails to pay the specified amount; it will also prove that there was an agreement and what the agreement was.

2. *Negotiate the support provisions of your separation agreement carefully.* Many clients fail to express all the current and anticipated needs of their children in such agreements; later this comes back to haunt them. I strongly recommend that you carefully consider some specific items in drafting your agreement:

- Be sure child support is listed separately from alimony and other obligations.
- Be sure that a separate amount for each child is listed in the agreement rather than a lump sum for all the children.

Both of these points are included for obvious reasons. Alimony is taxable income, child support is not. In addition, where alimony and child support are not divided, the IRS views the entire payment as alimony. Finally, alimony ceases upon remarriage, child support does not. *Remember this.*

Other items you should specify in the agreement include:

- Provisions for the medical, dental, and other special needs of the children, including insurance coverage of these items
- Provisions for child-support payments from the noncustodian's estate in the event of his or her death
- Where possible, provisions for the child's education needs, *including college*
- Provision for a salary lien in case the noncustodian ceases payment in the future
- An escalation clause providing for an automatic or cost-of-living increase in the amount of payments when either the noncustodian's income or the child's need increases
- The amount of payment and the intervals of payment (for example, weekly on Saturday)

Specifying these items in your agreement will anticipate problems before they occur and make it easier for you to enforce arrears in the event the support clauses are not observed.

3. *Take appropriate action immediately in the event of the first default.* Your ex-spouse must know that you intend to take all necessary steps to collect what is due you and your children. Thus you should contact an attorney immediately before the problem gets out of hand. Your lawyer

will properly advise you on how to deal with your spouse in the event of a default.

If you cannot afford a lawyer, contact a legal clinic, the Legal Aid Society, or an appropriate state agency for immediate assistance. Remember, the goal is to nip the problem before the arrears accumulate. And if you show your spouse that you mean business, he or she will probably think twice before defaulting on payments in the future.

4. *Assert yourself.* Educate yourself about what services are available and what new laws are being passed. Check your phone book to find referral services and information groups in your area. Contact your local child-support-enforcement agency; it has programs to aid you. In addition, contact your state attorney general, district attorney, or county attorney for information and assistance.

Learn the local procedures for filing your own court papers if you cannot afford a lawyer. Contact the clerk of your local family court for further information (including forms and instructions for representing yourself in court).

5. *Don't be intimidated if your ex-spouse has moved to another state.* The law allows each state to honor another state's orders and decrees regarding child support. Even federal laws allow a child-support case to move into the federal courts when state court efforts have been exhausted. Many people do not realize that a state order filed in one state can be carried out in another.

A real-life example will illustrate this: A client recently came to me seeking support arrears accumulated since 1975. It seems that her husband had moved from New York to California that year, remarried, and stopped paying support. Through the use of a competent domestic-relations lawyer I contacted in California, we were able to collect $46,000 in support arrears after we subpoenaed the husband's tax returns and other private business information and tried the case in California.

6. *Be prepared when you go to court.*

7. *Obtain a court order as soon as possible.* A petition for a court order for support can and should be filed the day the noncustodial parent leaves. This will enable you to

proceed with other enforcement mechanisms in the event of nonpayment. Remember, a separation agreement is *not* a court order; it is simply a contract between two parties that must be reduced to a court order as soon as possible.

8. *Review your legal papers.* Always be sure that the court order or decree specifies the amount of support to be paid and the payment intervals. Otherwise it is nearly impossible to enforce it when payments are skipped or lowered. *Do not depend on a lawyer to take care of this for you.* Check your papers carefully upon receipt. Remember, verbal agreements are unenforceable, even if stipulated in court, unless they are specified in the written order or decree.

9. *Locate your ex-spouse as soon as possible.* This must be done to enforce your decree. If it can be shown that the absent parent is preparing to leave the state and is in arrears on child-support payments, you may be able to petition the court to order him or her to remain in state. Usually the absent parent will be required to post a bond in the amount of the arrears. If he or she then leaves the state without paying, the bond may be forfeited and the money turned over to you or an appropriate child-support agency.

Speak to a lawyer or other trained professional for further details about this if it seems appropriate in your case.

9 | Working It Out: Mediation, Arbitration, and the Law

Introduction

The attitude of most Americans toward the institution of divorce has changed dramatically during the recent past. As the number of divorces has increased, the stigma of divorce has decreased. Domestic-relations cases now dominate court calendars. As a result of an overload in their dockets, courts and the parties involved have turned to alternative methods of resolving disputes.

The most popular form of resolution has become mediation. One lawyer, acting as mediator, defines the conflicting interests of the parties, explains the legal implications, and helps to prepare a fair settlement.

In some situations, a couple will recognize that their marriage has ended. The spouses may prefer to work out their problems by themselves, negotiating the terms of a separation agreement based upon their best interests and the best interests of their children. When a mediator is retained to assist in the process, he or she will not make decisions for the parties but will assist them in reaching an agreement within the realistic limits of their budget.

Thus mediation is a commitment by the parties involved to reach a settlement cooperatively instead of competitively. The agreement reached usually requires much less future court action and is likely far cheaper because the parties will not be paying for separate lawyers to "fight it out." In addition, the privacy afforded by mediation avoids the psychologically traumatic experiences of court confrontation.

Despite the usefulness of mediation, however, many people are unaware of its existence. This chapter will tell you what you should know about mediation. You will learn how it is obtained and conducted and its advantages and disadvantages. You will also become familiar with an alternative legal proceeding called "arbitration." All of this information will assist you to better manage your family controversies and help you select the most favorable legal forum for your particular problem.

All about Mediation

When Can Mediation Be Used?

Many family-related disputes are appropriate for mediation. These include:

1. *Divorce negotiations.* Many issues arising in a divorce action can be mediated. The following is a brief list of these issues:

- Custody of the children and visitation rights for the noncustodial parent
- The amount and duration of child-support payments, with particular attention to future education, camp, and other special costs
- The amount and duration of alimony payments
- The division and transfer of marital assets and other property acquired during the marriage

2. *Disputes between unmarried adults.* According to the Census Bureau, there are more than 4 million people living together as unmarried couples in the mid-'80s. In such households, disputes often arise over who is responsible for paying rent, who has the right to stay in the apartment, house, or co-op after the couple decides to split, and how to distribute property acquired during the relationship when it ends.

3. *Negotiating premarital agreements.* Some couples prefer to protect their interests by negotiating a premarital agreement, especially when third parties may be affected (such as the case of children from a previous marriage). In helping to negotiate such an agreement, a mediator with expertise in financial planning or tax matters may be particularly helpful.

4. *Disagreements between homosexual partners.* A public court may not be an acceptable place to resolve issues when the individuals need help—for example, the distribution of a valuable art collection upon a breakup.

5. *Disputes over inheritance.* Mediation can eliminate the need for litigation in this area.

6. Disagreements over family businesses. Which member of the family will control the firm? How is income to be allocated? Many closely held corporations include in their bylaws the stipulation that disputes are to be resolved through arbitration or mediation. You can also use it with your own intrafamily business disputes.

How Does It Work?

The American Arbitration Association (AAA) is most often selected to assist parties in the mediation process. It is a public-service, nonprofit organization which offers dispute-settlement services to business executives, employers, trade associations, unions, consumers, farmers, communities, families, and all levels of government. Services are available through AAA's national office in New York City and through twenty-five regional offices in major cities throughout the United States.

American Arbitration Association
New York (10020)
140 West 51st Street
(212)/484-4000

Atlanta (30361)
1197 Peachtree Street, N.E.
(404)/872-3022

Boston (02110)
230 Congress Street
(617)/367-6800

Charlotte (28226)
7301 Carmel Executive Park
(704)/541-1367

Chicago (60606)
205 West Wacker Drive
(312)/346-2282

Cincinnati (45202)
2308 Carew Tower
(513)/241-8434

Cleveland (44115)
1127 Euclid Avenue
(216)/241-4741

Dallas (75201)
1607 Main Street
(214)/748-4979

Denver (80203)
789 Sherman Street
(303)/831-0823

Detroit (48226)
615 Griswold Street
(313)/964-2525

Garden City, NY (11530)
585 Stewart Avenue
(516)/222-1660

Hartford (06106)
2 Hartford Square West
(203)/278-5000

Kansas City (64106)
1101 Walnut Street
(816)/221-6401

Los Angeles (90020)
443 Shatto Place
(213)/383-6516

Miami (33129)
2250 S.W. 3rd Avenue
(305)/854-1616

Minneapolis (55402)
510 Foshay Tower
(612)/332-6545

New Jersey (Somerset 08873)
1 Executive Drive
(201)/560-9560

New York (10020)
140 West 51st Street
(212)/484-4000

Philadelphia (19102)
1520 Locust Street
(215)/732-5260

Phoenix (85012)
77 East Columbus
(602)/234-0950

Pittsburgh(15222)
221 Gateway Four
(412)/261-3617

San Diego (92101)
530 Broadway
(619)/239-3051

San Francisco (94108)
445 Bush Street
(415)/981-3901

Seattle (98104)
811 First Avenue
(206)/622-6435

Syracuse (13202)
720 State Tower Building
(315)/472-5483

Washington, DC (20036)
1730 Rhode Island Avenue,
   N.W.
(202)/296-8510

White Plains, NY (10601)
34 South Broadway
(914)/946-1119

Once both parties agree to try to solve their differences informally through mediation, a joint request for mediation is usually made through one of the regional offices. The request should identify the individuals who are involved in the dispute, giving their present addresses and phone numbers, and should briefly describe the controversy and the issues involved. The parties should include whatever information would be helpful to the AAA in appointing a mediator.

The AAA assigns a mediator from its master list. The parties are then given information about the mediator. In most cases, the mediator will have no past or present relationship with the parties. A mediator recommended by the AAA is free to refuse the appointment or to resign at any time. Likewise, the parties are free to stop the mediation or to ask for the services of a different mediator if they wish. If any mediator is unwilling or unable to serve, or if one of the parties requests that the mediator resign from the case, the parties may ask the AAA to recommend another mediator.

Before settling on a mediator, you should first find out whether the mediator's approach is suited to your needs. At the initial interview, feel free to ask the following questions:

- How does the mediator operate?
- How much experience and training does the mediator have?
- What is the mediator's background?
- How many sessions will be required?
- How much will mediation cost?

Since family mediation creates a close relationship, the parties should be certain that they have chosen the right individual.

After the initial interview takes place (usually at designated AAA conference rooms) and the mediator is found to be acceptable, he or she will arrange the time and place for each conference with the parties.

At the first conference, the parties will be expected to produce all information reasonably required for the mediator to understand the issues presented. The mediator may require either party to supplement such information. At that first meeting, the mediator explains exactly what the parties should expect. Good mediators explain that the process is entirely voluntary, that they are not judges and have no power to dictate solutions, and that the parties are free to terminate the mediation process at any time.

A mediator does not have authority to impose a settlement upon the parties but will attempt to help the parties reach a satisfactory resolution of their disputes. Although usually trained in law, the mediator is *not* supposed to give legal advice or psychological counseling. Although parties are not represented by counsel at the mediation sessions, they are encouraged to seek independent legal advice about the process or about any legal issues that may arise.

Conferences are private. The mediator may sometimes meet

with both parties, sometimes with one of them privately. Other persons may attend only with the permission of the parties, and at the invitation of the mediator. In a custody case, the mediator may want to interview the child privately, to determine the child's attitude toward custodial arrangements or visitation rights. Such an interview may be arranged if both parties agree. In conducting the interview, the mediator should not encourage the child to choose between the parents. With the approval of both parties, the mediator may obtain a professional opinion as to the best interests of a child. The opinion should be shared with the parties.

In a sense, the mediator is hired as a consultant, jointly retained (typically paid by the hour) to help the parties work their way through their problems to resolution. At some point the mediator may make a recommendation or proposal. Both parties can agree or disagree. In the event both parties agree (or come to a compromise of their own), the mediator will record the agreement. The mediator's report may then be submitted by the parties to their personal attorneys for incorporation in a formal document (for example, a separation agreement).

If the parties fail to agree, or do not agree with the mediator's recommendation, they can break off the mediation, consult another mediator, give up, settle their disputes without a mediator, or go to court.

The following is a typical mediation scenario from start to finish.

1. The mediator and parties meet at the initial conference. A relationship is established with the parties, the mediator's role is explained, and the responsibilities and rights of the parties are set forth.

2. The mediator designs a schedule for the sessions.

3. The parties sign a formal retainer agreement (see below).

4. A method is adopted for obtaining whatever information is required to understand the parties' problems.

5. The mediator identifies the various areas of agree-

ment, defines the issues that must be resolved, and assists the parties in their negotiations.

6. A final settlement is formulated.

7. The mediator arranges for the terms of the settlement to be transmitted to the attorneys of the parties for filing in court, if necessary.

Some Final Words on the Subject

The process of mediation does not work for everyone. There are several reasons why. Some critics have remarked that many mediators do not possess sufficient skills or training to be effective. Some mediators have been criticized for not ending the process when the interests of each party are not receiving balanced treatment.

If the mediator is a lawyer, he or she often has to make an adjustment in attitude toward the client. For unlike the lawyer, who tells the client what to do, a mediator must allow the parties enough freedom to structure their own unique solutions to such problems as child custody, child support, maintenance support (alimony), and distribution of assets. Mediation by attorneys has also raised the concern of whether one lawyer can adequately advise two parties with opposing interests and whether a mediator can invoke the attorney-client privilege in any future litigation.

Many people have experienced difficulties in finding qualified mediators. Unlike lawyers, most mediators do not advertise. State bar associations may have a list of qualified local mediators who have had specific academic and practical training in the art of conflict resolution. The National Legal Research Center for Child Advocacy and Protection in Washington, D.C., has published a list of mediation specialists on a state-by-state basis. In some communities, a family-service agency may have a list of lawyers who serve as mediators.

Remember that you should always interview the mediator first. Then, to avoid any misunderstandings as to the mediator's role and compensation, be sure to hire the mediator only on the basis of a written retainer agreement. The following retainer agreement is recommended by the American Arbitration Association.

Sample Mediator-Client Agreement

_____ and _____ (the parties) have jointly requested _____ to act as their mediator in accordance with the Family Mediation Rules of the American Arbitration Association. The controversy between the parties concerns the terms of a separation agreement. The parties agree to negotiate in good faith toward such a settlement and to provide the mediator with full and accurate information about the case.

The mediator has accepted the parties' request and will provide mediation services to them on an impartial basis. The time and place of mediation will be set at the convenience of the parties and will be held in accordance with the above Rules.

The mediator has advised the parties that conflicts are likely to arise between them during the course of negotiations. To protect their legal rights, each party is encouraged to seek advice from counsel. There is no limitation on the right to seek such advice at any time during the mediation. Each party should advise the mediator of the name and telephone number of counsel.

The mediator has also advised the parties that they may terminate the mediation at any point, paying the mediator only what has accrued to that time. The mediator in turn reserves the right to resign from the case at any time.

The mediator acknowledges that all information received by the mediator during this procedure will be confidential. The mediator will not divulge such information to any third person without the consent of both parties. The mediator urges the parties, on their part, to keep such information confidential so that there can be a full and candid exchange.

The parties agree not to hold either the mediator or the AAA liable or to include either in any judicial proceedings involving the mediation or the parties' relationship. The mediator agrees not to represent or give support to either party in any subsequent matter or proceeding. The mediator will not provide any legal opinion as to the law or any other aspect of the case.

It is up to the parties themselves to negotiate their own agreement. If the parties are able to reach an agreement, the mediator will prepare a memorandum recording that understanding which may then be submitted to the parties' personal attorneys for incorporation into a formal separation agreement.

Each party agrees, during the course of the mediation, to respect the privacy of the other and not to transfer disputed property or assume additional debts without mutual consent. All interim agreements will be discussed with the mediator before being entered into.

The mediator's fees are $____ an hour, plus any costs incurred. Both parties will be billed monthly for the entire outstanding amount for which they will be jointly liable.

_____   _____
Mediator   Party

____   _____
Date   Party

Finally, recognize that mediation will not work unless both parties are willing to cooperate. Some people have a great need to even the score; in that event, mediation will probably fail.

Studies have shown that a mediated divorce is less expensive, time-consuming, and emotionally draining than its traditional legal counterpart. In areas relating to child custody, mediation has been found to be most helpful in keeping the children out of court. In fact, studies have shown that most child-custody settlements arranged through mediation are still observed by the parties long after the arrangement is consummated.

All about Arbitration

Arbitration has for years been used as a method of resolving domestic-relation disputes, particularly with respect to child custody, support requests, and other details spelled out in separation agreements.

Many separation agreements contain an arbitration clause similar to the following:

Any claim or controversy arising among or between the parties hereto and any claim or controversy arising out of or respecting any matter contained in this Agreement, or the breach of any understanding arising out of or in connection with said Agreement, including, but not limited to the obligation to pay child support, or modify the obligation of child support, or any difference as to the interpretation of any of the provisions of this Agreement shall be settled by arbitration in (Name of city) by three (3) arbitrators under the then prevailing rules of the American Arbitration Association.

Without such a clause, parties cannot resort to arbitration to resolve their differences. This is because arbitration works differently than litigation. Arbitrators have broader powers than judges and are not limited by strict rules of evidence. They can hear all relevant testimony when making an award, including some forms of evidence—hearsay, questionable copies of documents, etc.—that would be excluded in a regular court. Arbitrators have the authority to hear witnesses out of order. Their decision is usually final and unappealable. Thus the law requires both parties to agree to the arbitration process *beforehand* in writing to avoid claims of unfairness by the losing party.

Arbitration has many distinct advantages and disadvantages in relation to litigation.

Advantages of Arbitration:

1. **Expense.** Substantial savings are achieved through arbitration. Attorney fees are reduced because the average hearing is shorter than the average trial. Time-consuming and expensive pretrial procedures are usually eliminated. And out-of-pocket expenses are reduced because stenographic fees, transcript costs, and other expenses are not incurred.

2. **Time.** Arbitration hearings and final awards regarding property settlements, support payments, and other domestic-relations matters are obtained quickly; cases are usually

decided in a matter of weeks, compared with months or years in formal litigation.

3. *Privacy.* The arbitration hearing is held in a private conference room rather than a courtroom. Unlike a trial, the hearing cannot be attended by the general public. Thus unwanted publicity is often avoided.

4. *Expertise of arbitrators.* Arbitrators usually have special training in the areas of divorce litigation and separation agreements; most of them are lawyers. Their knowledge helps them identify and understand a problem more quickly than a judge or jury.

Disadvantages of Arbitration:

1. *Finality.* Arbitrators, unlike judges, need not give formal reasons for their decisions. They are not required to maintain a formal record of the proceedings. The arbitrator's decision is binding. This means that an appeal cannot be made if you lose the case or disagree with the size of the award, except in a few extraordinary circumstances where arbitrator misconduct, dishonesty, or bias can be proved.

2. *Arbitrator selection.* The parties sometimes agree that each will select an arbitrator. Here it is assumed that the selected arbitrators are more sympathetic to one side than the other. However, arbitrators are usually selected from a list of neutral names supplied by the AAA. This method all but eliminates bias.

3. *Loss of discovery devices.* Some claimants must rely upon an adversary's documents and records to prove their case. Many wives, for example, must depend on their husbands' business records to assess how much they are worth in determining a fair, equitable share of said business. In a dispute over assets acquired during the marriage, wives may be disadvantaged by the arbitration process. In the trial process, lawyers have ample opportunity to view the private books and records of an adversary long before the day in court. This is accomplished by pretrial discovery devices designed to obtain documents for inspection, including old tax returns, bank rec-

ords, and other private financial documents. However, pretrial discovery is not as readily available to litigants in arbitration. In many instances, records are not viewed until the day of the arbitration hearing. This makes it difficult to detect whether they are accurate and complete. And it is often up to the arbitrator's discretion whether to grant an adjournment for the purposes of reviewing such records.

Consider all your particular needs when contemplating resolving your domestic-relations disputes through arbitration. In many cases, the process will work to your advantage. However, there may be problems with your particular matter; don't forget to discuss this with your lawyer *before* you agree to arbitration as the means of resolving your disputes.

10 | Figuring the Breaks: Family Matters and Tax Law

Introduction

Failure to know how taxes affect your overall finances in a divorce or separation can lead to devastating consequences. Counsel in matrimonial cases must realize that every major judgment automatically brings into operation the provisions of the IRS applicable to alimony, child support, division of property, and/or other matters. (*Note*: Variations exist throughout the country in statutory and case law regarding these matters; however, the Internal Revenue Code governs and standardizes taxation in family-related matters in all fifty states.)

The following information will serve as a good summary and enable you to discuss a variety of items intelligently with your lawyer. However, since tax laws are very complex and are constantly changing as a result of new legislation, treasury regulations, and court decisions, it is essential that you seek the advice of an attorney or other professional with detailed knowledge of tax matters.

Important: At the time this chapter was written, Congress had not yet passed the sweeping tax reform bill that will probably be implemented during the 1987 fiscal year. Some of the information in this chapter may be liable to modification if/when this bill becomes law. Therefore, it is essential that you consult with a professional advisor, accountant, or attorney before implementing any of the strategies I suggest here.

Alimony

Alimony (also referred to in many equitable-distribution states as "maintenance") has traditionally involved the payment of support by one spouse to another in satisfaction of the marital obligation. The Tax Reform Act of 1984 made significant changes in defining alimony payments in connection with tax treatment. If you and your attorney do not understand the new rules, you will run into unfortunate, and in many cases, costly surprises when filing your return after a divorce or separation.

The new rules apply to divorces and separation decrees and agreements signed beginning in 1985 as well as prior ones modified in 1985 and thereafter.

Generally, alimony and maintenance payments are taxable income for the receiving spouse and tax deductible for the paying spouse. Payments received or made for child support, however, are neither taxable nor deductible. Thus it is important to understand the distinction between the two.

Divorce and separation agreements executed before 1985 must meet four criteria to be taxable by the receiving spouse and deductible by the paying spouse:

1.   Payments must be under a judicial decree of divorce or legal separation, a written separation agreement, or a court-approved decree for support (for example, temporary support). *Note*: Your separation must be *legal*—that is, by judicial decree or written agreement—for payments to qualify as alimony. Merely living apart is not enough.

2.   Payments must be in discharge of a legal obligation for support as outlined in state laws dealing with marital or family relationships.

3.   Payments must be periodic, as opposed to a property settlement payable in a large lump sum during a short period of time. To be considered periodic, the payments must be contingent as to duration (for example, until your spouse remarries) or as to amount (that is, based on a percentage of your business income) or continuing for at least ten years. In the latter case, no more than 10 percent of the amount to be paid over the entire time is treated as alimony in any one year.

4.   Payments cannot have fixed portions specifically allocated to the receiving spouse *and* minor children, since any portion of the total alimony payment allocated for support of a minor child is neither taxable nor deductible. For example, if a written separation agreement specifies payment of $300 per week, with $200 designated as support for the wife and the remaining $100 for support of a minor child, only the $200 would qualify as alimony. That is why you must be careful what you define as support in a separation agreement.

For divorce and separation agreements executed after 1984, payments no longer must be "periodic" nor arise out of the marital obligation.

Now for payments to qualify as alimony the following conditions must be met:

1. Payments still must be made under a judicial decree of divorce or legal separation, a written separation agreement, or a decree for support. However, the decree or agreement can specify whether a payment will be treated as alimony for tax purposes. For example, you and your spouse can agree that otherwise-qualifying alimony payments are to be *excluded* from the receiving spouse's income and nondeductible by the paying spouse, or vice versa.

2. Payments must be made in the form of *money*. Under prior rules, alimony payments could be made in any item having or conferring an economic benefit upon the recipient; now all payments must be made in cash. However, this will not eliminate the ability of the parties to agree that the spouse paying alimony can pay certain expenses, including rent or mortgage payments, directly to a third party on behalf of the other spouse.

3. Payments cannot extend beyond the death of the receiving spouse; the liability for alimony ends upon the death of the payee spouse. Thus any arrangement to provide a post-death substitute for continuation of payments to a decedent or his/her estate will preclude deductible treatment.

4. Payments exceeding $10,000 in any calendar year must continue for at least six years unless either spouse dies or the payee spouse remarries. If, during the six-year period, payments decrease by more than $10,000 from payments in the previous year, the payer must recapture prior alimony deductions and report the amount as income. No recapture applies in any year in which payments terminate because of the death of either spouse or the remarriage of the payee.

The following example illustrates this:

Under a divorce decree entered in 1985, Mr. Green pays and deducts alimony payments of $25,000. In 1986, he pays only $12,000. In 1986, $3,000 of the deduction of the prior year is recaptured ($25,000 − $10,000 = $15,000 and $15,000 − $12,000 = $3,000), is included as income on his return and deductible from Mrs. Green's gross income in 1986.

Caution: This six-year provision is complex and conflicts with many standard settlement procedures devised by divorce lawyers in the past. Be sure its ramifications are clearly explained to you, particularly if you will pay or receive alimony exceeding $10,000 per year.

In addition, the new rules state that both spouses can no longer file a joint return nor live in the same household. When all these conditions are met, payments still qualify as alimony even if they are designated as:

- A return payment for property
- A discharge of a fixed-dollar obligation, or
- Are for less than ten years

Prior to 1985, the presence of any of these three factors would have disqualified the payments from being treated as alimony, and thereby deductible by the payer.

Note: If you are legally separated under a judicial decree of divorce or separation, be sure that you and your spouse or former spouse are not members of the same household at the time support payments are made. If so, such payments cannot qualify as alimony. However, you will not be treated as members of the same household if either of you is in the process of leaving shortly. This rule applies only to decrees of divorce or separation, not to payments arising out of a written separation agreement.

In addition to direct support payments, alimony can also include payments for certain living expenses made on behalf of your former spouse. These include medical expenses, life insurance premiums, utility bills, and payments for a residence. Care should be taken in structuring the whole package of alimony payments so the desired tax effect is realized and the combined package meets the tests of the 1984 tax act. Let's examine these items in greater detail.

1. Life insurance premiums. If you make premium payments on a life insurance policy covering you, and your former spouse is the sole and irrevocable beneficiary, you may deduct these payments as alimony and your spouse must include them as gross income. However, payment of the premiums will not be treated as alimony if your spouse is only a contingent beneficiary or can be taken off the policy at any time. (*Note*: Amounts payable under life insurance on the life of the payee will not affect the status of other payments by the payer under the previously discussed six-year rule.)

2. Residence expenses. Utility bills paid on behalf of a spouse can be part of total alimony payments and deductible by the payer. Where payment of mortgage principal, interest, insurance, and taxes is involved, the *form of ownership* of the residence is a major factor in characterizing the payments as alimony. In order to prevent unfavorable treatment in this area, remember the following:

- Where the paying spouse owns the residence, none of the payments constitute deductible or taxable alimony. The paying spouse may, however, deduct the interest and taxes if he or she itemizes.

- Where the former spouse owns the residence, the paying spouse can deduct all the payments as alimony, and they are taxable to the former spouse. The former spouse may deduct the interest and taxes if he or she itemizes.

- Where both spouses own the property as *tenants in common* (that is, each owns one-half of the residence with no right of survivorship for the other's half) and one pays all the expenses, only half can be deducted as alimony. Of the remaining half, the paying spouse can deduct only the interest and taxes if he or she itemizes. The payee spouse must include the half counted as alimony in gross income, but may take the interest and taxes as itemized deductions.

- Where both spouses own the property as *joint tenants* with the right of survivorship, the tax treatment depends on whether there is joint liability for the mortgage payment. If so, then the same rules apply as for tenants in common. If there is no joint liability, then the same rules apply as for sole ownership (first example).

- Where the paying spouse owns a co-op apartment on which he or she makes the lease payments on behalf of the former spouse, then the rental payments are deductible as alimony, provided the former spouse resides there and the decree or separation agreement labels the payments as rent with a portion allocable to mortgage, interest, principal, insurance, or taxes.

3. Medical expenses. If your divorce decree or separation agreement requires you to pay the medical expenses of your former spouse, those payments are deductible by you as alimony and are taxable for your former spouse.

4. Alimony trusts. You may also satisfy your alimony obligations by transferring property to a trust, the income from which would be paid to your spouse for support. An alimony trust is a useful settlement vehicle for divorcing couples with considerable marital assets. Use of a trust minimizes contact and friction between the parties, assures the recipient of timely support payments regardless of the payer's financial circumstances or willingness to pay, and protects the paying spouse by effectively protecting the assets used to fund the settlement.

The 1984 tax act made changes governing the treatment of trust payments. Now payments made by a trust to a divorced or separated spouse pursuant to a post-1984 divorce or separation will *not* be treated as alimony. However, only the income of the trust and not the principal will be taxable to your spouse.

Speak to your attorney, accountant and other professional advisor to learn more about an alimony trust if it seems applicable in your case.

Final point: Effective for alimony payments made after 1984, the new law authorizes the IRS to issue regulations requiring the paying spouse to include the receiving spouse's taxpayer identification number on his return for the year the payments begin. A $50 penalty is provided for failure to comply with this request unless it is shown that the failure was not the result of willful neglect.

Child Support

Payments made under a divorce or separation decree, written separation agreement, or decree for support specifically allocated for a minor child are not considered alimony. Hence, they are neither taxable to the receiving spouse nor deductible for the payer.

The Tax Reform Act of 1984 closed a major loophole which had allowed certain cases of combined alimony/child support payments to be treated entirely as alimony. Prior to the act, the Supreme Court ruled that if an agreement did not expressly fix the portion of payments allocated to child support, the payment could be treated as all alimony. This was true even if the payments were to be reduced to a stated amount upon the happening of a child-related contingency (for example, the child's reaching a certain age, leaving school, marrying, etc.).

The act overrides prior law by providing that where any payment is specified in the agreement to be reduced upon the occurrence of a child-related contingency, the amount of the specified reduction will be treated as child support. For example, if the separation agreement states that alimony payments of $200 per week will be reduced by $50 per week when a child reaches 18, only $150 of the weekly payment will qualify as alimony. The rest will be considered nondeductible child support.

In addition, if the agreement specifies one amount for alimony and another for child support, and the payment in any period is less than the total of the two amounts, that payment will be allocated first to child support in calculating the tax status of the payment. For example, if the agreement states that the wife will receive $150 per week as alimony and $50 per week as child support, and the husband only pays the wife a total of $100, the husband may only deduct $50 ($100 − $50) as alimony.

Note: The divorce process carries significant federal-income-tax consequences for both spouses, offering tax benefits to one while imposing tax burdens on the other. Negotiation can resolve differences by offering a better after-tax package for both parties, if one is smart enough to ascertain the tax impact on each party. Proper planning in this area should never be overlooked. For example, the husband is generally in a higher tax bracket than the wife. Thus it is better, tax-wise, for the husband to classify all payments as alimony. This is because such payments may shift his adjustable gross income into a lower tax bracket. In light of this, the wife might ask for a larger payment, taking into account her husband's tax savings. The following example illustrates this:

John Jones earns $100,000 per year and is in a 50 percent tax bracket. His wife Jane earns $25,000 per year and is in a 20 percent bracket. John agrees to pay his wife $20,000 a year in alimony:

John pays	$20,000
Tax saving because of his tax bracket	$10,000
Net cost of alimony to John after taxes each year	**$10,000**
Jane receives	$20,000
Taxes paid in her bracket	$ 4,000
Net cash left to Jane	**$16,000**

In effect, the difference between the $10,000 John saves in taxes and the $4,000 Jane pays in taxes results in a reduction of $6,000 in the total taxes paid. This $6,000 ends up as additional disposable income for Jane.

Thus it is best to carefully calculate the *after-tax* benefits of a properly structured settlement. It may pay, for example, for a husband in a high tax bracket to agree to pay a greater amount in alimony in order to obtain the deduction; on the other hand, a wife in a high income tax bracket may be reluctant to receive additional payments as alimony because such payments must be reported as income to her.

For further information, discuss this concept with your accountant, attorney, or professional advisor.

Dependency Exemptions

New rules for dependency exemptions in the case of children of divorced or separated parents became effective beginning with the 1985 taxable year no matter the year of the divorce or separation.

If one parent has custody of a child for the greater part of the calendar year, that parent can take the $1,000 exemption provided three conditions can be proved:

1. The parents are divorced or legally separated under a decree of divorce or separate maintenance; are separated under a written separation agreement; *or* have lived apart at all times during the last six months of the calendar year.

2. Both parents together provided more than half of the child's support during the year.

3. One or both parents had custody of the child for more than half the year.

Note: Once you remarry, any amount contributed by your new spouse for support is included in the above determination.

Notwithstanding the above rules, there are still two ways where the noncustodial parent (the one having custody for the shorter portion of the year) can receive the dependency exemption for the child. This can occur when:

1. The custodial parent signs a waiver authorizing the noncustodial parent to claim the dependency exemption, or

2. The noncustodial parent is entitled, under a pre-1985 decree or agreement to claim the exemption and that parent contributes at least $600 to the child's support during the year.

If either of these two conditions are met, the noncustodial parent will receive a $1,000 deduction per child off his or her income taxes. However, this will not affect the custodial parent's right to claim head-of-household status or to receive a child-care credit. Moreover, each parent can still treat the child as a dependent for purposes of claiming medical deductions.

Under the new act, the parent paying the medical bills is entitled to claim them on his or her separate return as long as the parents are divorced, legally separated, have a written separation agreement, or have lived apart for the last six months of the calendar year. That parent must also have had custody for more than half the year and must have provided more than half of the child's support. (Remember, in order to claim your child as a dependent, present rules state that the child must have a gross income of less than $1,000 during the year, unless the child is under 19 years of age at the end of the taxable year or is a full-time student.)

Final point: The noncustodial parent may claim the personal exemption, provided the custodial parent signs a written entitlement waiver, as prescribed by the IRS, and the noncustodial parent attaches it to his or her return.

Child-Care Expenses

Some parents are eligible for credits worth up to $720—if one qualifying child or dependent is involved—and up to $1440—if more than one is involved—*if* they incur expenses for the care of their child(ren) which enables them to work. A tax credit is significant because it is used to directly offset tax due to the IRS and not merely used as a deduction from taxable income.

You are eligible to receive the credit if your child is under 15 years of age and if you claim him or her as an exemption.

Expenses that can be counted in figuring the credit include home-care expenses (for example, cooking and cleaning) and outside expenses (for example, day care, nursery costs, and day-camp fees).

For taxable years beginning in 1985, if you have custody of your child, you may be able to take the child-care credit even though you do not claim your child as a dependent on your tax return. To do so, you will have to meet the following requirements:

1. You must be divorced or separated under a court decree, be separated under a written separation agreement, or have lived apart during the last six months of the calendar year.

2. The child's other parent must be claiming the child as a dependent either under a pre-1985 decree or under your express waiver. This requirement would not be met if, say, a grandparent were claiming your child as a dependent.

3. More than half your child's support must be provided by one or both parents, and the child must have been in the custody of one or both parents for more than half the year.

The tax credit is figured by multiplying eligible expenses of up to $2,400 for one child or of up to $4,800 for two or more children by a rate ranging from 20 to 30 percent, depending on your level of adjusted gross income. The credit is applicable only in connection with *earned income*—that is, income from wages, salary, and self-employment—as opposed to investment income. If your earned income is less than your eligible child-care expenses, then the percentage determined by your level of adjusted gross income will be applied to the lower earned-income amount.

For example, if your adjusted gross income is $20,000 and you incur child-care expenses of $4,800 during the year, the tax credit would be 20 percent of $4,800, or $960. However, the child-care credit cannot be used to the extent it would result in a cash refund to you. If it cannot be used to reduce your tax liability in the current year, it is lost forever.

Head-of-Household Status

If you maintain a home for yourself and your children and meet certain requirements, you may qualify as *unmarried* for tax purposes even though you are not yet legally separated or divorced. By qualifying for the head-of-household tax-filing status, your tax rate will be computed at 93 to 94 percent of the tax rate paid by single taxpayers.

To qualify as a head of household:

- You must file a separate tax return.
- You and your spouse will have to have lived apart for the last six months of the taxable year starting in 1985 and thereafter.
- Your home must be the principal place of residence for your child(ren) at least half the year.
- Either you or your child's noncustodial parent must claim your child as a dependent. A third party claiming your child as a dependent, for example, a grandparent, would fail this requirement.
- You must provide over half the cost of maintaining the household.

If you are living apart and contemplating a divorce or legal separation, be aware of this advantageous tax treatment for single parents. Plan ahead to meet the requirements listed above. For example, don't be careless in allowing your spouse to remain a member of your household during the last six months of the calendar year and keep track of where your child resides the majority of the year.

Lump-Sum or Installment Settlements

Prior to the 1984 Tax Act, lump-sum settlements to satisfy an alimony obligation did not qualify as alimony since they were not periodic. However, under the new law, payments up to $10,000 a year can be made with no minimum duration as long as they end upon the death of the receiving spouse. This would seem to indicate that small lump-sum or installment sum payments can be made. Speak to your lawyer, accountant, or other professional advisor on this matter if it seems appropriate in your case.

Transfers of Property

Some spouses transfer property as part of a marital settlement to satisfy a support obligation. Often this is accomplished through an outright transfer, transfer in trust, or a transfer of a life insurance or annuity contract.

The domestic-relations provisions of the Deficit Reduction Act of 1984 completely changed the tax rules governing property settlements incident to a divorce. Now all transfers during and after the marriage incident to a divorce are *tax-free*.

This change reflects Congress's rejection of the concept that tax liability should be triggered solely by a division of property between spouses in a divorce. The following is an example of how the new law works:

Charles and Bambi obtain a divorce. The marital home is held solely by Bambi—this is, the title is in her name. By settlement agreement, Bambi agrees to convey the home to Charles in return for all the other marital property. The home, which Bambi purchased five years ago for $100,000, is now worth $200,000.

Under the old law, Bambi would have paid a capital gain of $100,000 (the difference between the current value of the home and the price for which it was purchased five years ago). However, under the new law, Bambi pays no tax on the transfer and Charles takes as a basis $100,000, the original purchase price of the home.

Any gain on a subsequent sale by Charles will be taxed to him, and the taxable gain will be the difference between the original cost of the transferred property and what it is ultimately sold for.

It is important to remember this rule. Since more and more judges are awarding property settlements in divorce actions, especially in states which have enacted equitable-distribution laws, this tax-free treatment is becoming increasingly important.

The new rules apply to transfers made after July 18, 1984. What is significant is that the property transfers do not have to be pursuant to any type of agreement or court order and the property does not have to be owned during the marriage. The spouse who receives the property either during the marriage or incident to a divorce is generally treated as having acquired the property by gift. The recipient reports no income on receipt, and the dollar value of the property to the recipient is the same as the price the transferor originally paid.

The particular type of property you transfer to your spouse should be chosen carefully. If you transfer property with a low basis relative to current value (for example, highly appreciated but low-yielding stocks) and the property will have to be sold to provide liquid cash for your spouse's expenses, less net cash will be realized because of the capital-gains taxes involved. Thus it may be better for you to give relatively high-basis property so that the tax bite upon sale by the receiving spouse will be much less, especially if the spouse needs the money to live.

Conversely, it is always in the best interest of the person transferring the property to give low-basis property which has appreciated greatly; this is because you pass along the high tax liability to your former spouse rather than receiving it yourself. *Remember this.*

Attorney Fees

Many people fail to realize that if you are seeking or receiving alimony, you can deduct attorney fees paid to obtain taxable alimony payments incident to a separation or divorce and attorney fees paid to obtain tax advice incident to a separation or divorce. Attorney fees paid to obtain the divorce or separation itself or in connection with determining child support or child custody are *not* deductible.

Request that your lawyer itemize legal fees according to those charged for handling the nondeductible items, those charged for securing alimony, and those charged for giving tax advice. In addition, part of the legal costs allocable to a property settlement may be added to the basis (the value based on its original cost) of the property you obtain in that settlement. This is important because the amount of tax paid upon the sale of such property will be reduced. (*Note*: A higher property basis means that you will show less profit upon the sale.)

If you are incurring legal fees in the fight to resist your spouse's claims for alimony or to retain income-producing property for yourself, you *cannot* deduct these fees even though a successful claim by your spouse would reduce your income. Again, however, you *can* deduct legal fees incurred for tax advice.

Don't forget to ask your attorney to structure the fee arrangement to maximize your tax deductions. This is especially true for wives who will obtain alimony pursuant to a divorce or separation.

Ask for a written statement that justifies the bill on the basis of time spent on specific tasks. This will help support your claim. Keep the statement in a safe place until tax time and show it to your tax preparer. Accountants and other professionals often clip copies of the statement directly to the return so that the IRS won't question the deduction.

The following is an example of a statement showing the allocation of legal fees according to deductible and nondeductible items. (*Note*: The fees and the hourly arrangement cited on this sample statement are approximations used for illustrative purposes only.)

Sample Statement of Legal Fees

STEVEN MITCHELL SACK

ATTORNEY AT LAW

450 SEVENTH AVENUE, SUITE 1011

NEW YORK, N.Y. 10123

—

(212) 695-2535

(Date)

Barbara Jones
1000 Main Street
Centerville, N.Y. 12345

Statement for professional services rendered in the Jones v. Jones divorce matter computed at the rate of $100/hour per agreement:

2/10/87	1.	Initial consultation: 10:00–11:45	105 min.	*No charge*
2/11/87	2.	Telephone calls to Mrs. Jones regarding gathering of facts for settlement negotiations and alimony: 12:00–12:15; 1:05–1:30; 3:05–3:20	55 min.	
2/13/87	3.	Conference with Mrs. Jones regarding settlement negotiations including alimony payments: 9:30–11:30	120 min.	
2/17/87	4.	Conference with Stacey Smith, opposing counsel, regarding drafting of separation agreement and settlement negotiations including alimony: 2:30–4:45	135 min.	
2/17/87	5.	Telephone call with Mrs. Jones regarding settlement discussions: 4:50–5:25	35 min.	
2/18/87	6.	Telephone call with Stacey Smith regarding settlement negotiations and tax ramifications of alimony to both parties: 10:30–11:10	40 min.	

2/18/87	7.	Telephone calls with Stacey Smith regarding settlement discussions: 11:15–11:30; 2:15–2:20	20 min.
2/23/87	8.	Review of separation agreement and discussions with Stacey Smith concerning same: 10:30–1:15	165 min.

Flat fee received for commencing an uncontested divorce action in Supreme Court, New York County, and obtaining same: $600.00

Tax advice incident to the divorce and alimony settlement: $250.00

Total time spent on matter: 570 min. (9.5 hours) $950.00

TOTAL FEES RECEIVED: $1,800.00

    Thank you.

In the preceding example, Barbara Jones paid her lawyer $1,800 for legal services in connection with her divorce. Using this hypothetical example for illustration, she would probably be able to deduct the full $250 paid for tax advice incident to her divorce and a portion of the $950 paid for the lawyer's efforts in negotiating her alimony settlement, perhaps 50 percent or $475. She would not be able to deduct the $600 paid for actually obtaining the divorce. Thus her deductible attorney fees would total $725 and her nondeductible fees would total $1,075.

The "Innocent-Spouse" Rule

Often it is not until after a divorce forces the valuation of a family business or an audit of past tax returns that tax irregularities are discovered. In the past, the so-called innocent spouse, in most cases, the wife, was jointly and severally liable for the payment of all taxes due, including interest and penalties.

The new law will revise the rules relating to relief for the innocent spouse who files a joint return but is unaware that the return is inaccurate as to items generated by the other spouse. The act potentially provides that a spouse may be relieved of personal liability for a substantial understatement of tax (that is, an understatement exceeding $500) on a joint return that is attributable to grossly erroneous items cited by the other spouse.

Note: The innocent-spouse revisions will apply only when a joint return is filed. No relief will be afforded when spouses have filed separate returns or when no returns for the tax period in question have been filed. In addition, as under the earlier law, community-property laws will be disregarded in determining whether a grossly erroneous item is attributable to the other spouse. Thus, for example, compensation paid to the spouse responsible for the understatement of tax liability is treated as attributable to that spouse, even though one-half is considered to be the income of the innocent spouse under community-property law.

Speak to a lawyer, accountant, or other professional advisor for more information on this law if it seems applicable to your case.

The Marriage Tax Penalty

While Congress has taken steps to reduce the so-called marriage penalty, husbands and wives who earn about the same salary still pay a steeper tax bill than two single individuals with the same income. (That is why we sometimes read about taxpayers who get divorced before December 31 of a particular year, only to remarry right after the start of the next year.) Remember, the IRS discourages this type of conduct and often audits individuals who resort to it.

IRAs for Divorced Individuals

It is projected that, under the new law, if a divorced or legally separated individual does not receive compensation from employment or self-employment, he or she may be entitled to establish an IRA. This is because "compensation" is defined to include alimony. Thus a divorced individual may deduct contributions to an IRA to the extent that they do not exceed his or her compensation (including alimony), or $2,000, whichever is less. Currently, alimony can be taken into account only under highly restrictive conditions and a lower dollar limit ($1,125) applied.

Note: The rule applies only to alimony paid under a decree of divorce or legal separation, or a written agreement incident to such a decree.

Summary of Key Points

As you can see, tax laws relating to family matters have become quite complex. In addition, the impending enactment of the new tax bill makes it imperative for the lawyer and the layperson alike to understand these changes and incorporate them properly.

One thing is certain: Be sure that the lawyer handling your domestic matter is thoroughly knowledgeable with respect to provisions of the Internal Revenue Code applicable to alimony, child support, and the division of marital property. If your attorney is not familiar with this body of law nor prepared to learn it, he or she should not undertake to handle matters involving these questions because of the enormous tax consequences now involved.

The following is a summary of some of the key points that have been stressed in this chapter:

1. If you are contemplating a divorce or separation, be aware of the tax consequences in the negotiation process.

2. Try to have your lawyer structure a settlement that makes economic tax sense if possible; be sure you understand the tax decisions that are being made on your behalf.

3. Ask your lawyer to itemize his or her fees according to deductible and nondeductible items.

4. Be sure you understand the estate-planning factors incident to a divorce, particularly if you are a middle-aged individual.

5. Be sure you understand the difference between alimony and child-support payments so you can maximize your desired tax results.

Glossary

The terms below are commonly used in legal proceedings pertaining to family affairs. If you understand the meaning of these words, you will reduce your chances of being exploited in personal dealings and relationships; in addition, you will be better able to communicate with your lawyer and to use the legal system to your benefit.

Admissible   Capable of being introduced in court as evidence

Adoptee   The child or person who is adopted

Adoption   A legal process whereby one or more persons enter into a parental-child relationship with another

Affidavit   A written statement signed under oath

Alimony   The payment of support by one spouse to another in satisfaction of marital obligations; also referred to as "maintenance"

Alimony trust   A vehicle often used by divorcing couples to save taxes

Allegations   Charges one party expects to prove in a lawsuit

Annulment   An action whereby a void or voidable marriage is treated as if it never occurred

Answer   The defendant's reply to the plaintiff's charges in a lawsuit

Antenuptial agreement   A contract signed between two individuals before marriage that limits a spouse's rights to property, support, and inheritance in the event of a divorce; also referred to as a "prenuptial agreement"

Appeal   A proceeding whereby the losing party in a lawsuit applies to a higher court to determine the correctness of the decision

Arbitration A proceeding where both sides submit their dispute to the binding decision of arbitrators rather than judges

Assault and battery A harmful, offensive, unpermitted touching of one person by another

Assignment The transfer of a right or interest by one party to another

Award A decision made by a judicial body to compensate the winning party for losses or injuries caused by another

"Best interests of the child" The legal standard most often used by judges when making decisions regarding adoption, custody, and support for the child

Bill of particulars A document used in a lawsuit which adds information contained in the plaintiff's complaint

Breach of contract The unjustified failure of a party to perform a duty or obligation specified in an agreement

Brief A concise statement of the main contentions in a lawsuit

Burden of proof The responsibility of a party in a lawsuit to provide sufficient evidence to prove his or her claims

Business deduction A legitimate expense that can be used to decrease the amount of reportable income subject to tax

Calendar The list of cases to be heard each day in court

Cause of action Legal theories which the plaintiff alleges in a complaint to recover from an opponent

Cease-and-desist letter A letter, usually sent by a lawyer, notifying an individual to stop engaging in a particular type of behavior or conduct

Check A negotiable instrument; the depositor's written order requesting the bank to pay a definite sum of money to a named individual or business

Child custody Determination either by argument or judicial intervention giving an individual legal control over a minor

Child support A sum of money paid, usually periodically, by a divorcing parent for the continued medical, educational, and financial needs of the child

Civil court Generally any court that presides over noncriminal matters

Clerk of the court An official who determines whether court papers are properly filed and court procedures followed

Closely held business A business typically owned by family members

Cohabitants Persons residing together

Cohabitation agreement A contract signed between two individuals, typically lovers, that defines the rights, property, and interests of the parties

Common law Law evolving from reported case decisions that are relied upon for their precedential value

Community property Assets and property acquired during a marriage and owned equally by the parties

Common-law marriage A marriage legally recognized in some states even though the parties did not participate in a formal civil ceremony

Compensatory damages A sum of money awarded to a party by a court or jury that represents the actual harm or loss suffered

Complaint A legal document that starts a lawsuit, alleging facts and causes of action which the plaintiff relies upon to collect damages, obtain a divorce, seek an annulment, etc.

Conflict of interest The ethical inability of a lawyer to represent a client because of competing loyalties—e.g., representing both a husband and a wife in a divorce action

Consideration An essential element of an enforceable contract; something of value given or promised by one party in exchange for an act or promise of another

Constitutional Recognized as legal or valid

Contempt A legal sanction imposed when a rule or order of a judicial body is disobeyed

Contingency fee A type of fee arrangement whereby a lawyer is paid a percentage of the money recovered; frowned upon in divorce actions

Continuance The postponement of a legal proceeding to another date

Contract An enforceable agreement, either written, oral, or implied

Contract modification The alteration of contract terms

Counterclaim A claim asserted by the defendant in a lawsuit

Covenant A promise

Credibility The believability of a witness as perceived by a judge or jury

Creditor   The party to whom money is owed

Cross-examination   The questioning of a witness by the opposing lawyer

Custodial parent   The parent with whom a child typically resides

Custodian   The keeper or caretaker of another or another's property

Damages   An award, usually money, given to the winning party in a lawsuit as compensation for the wrongful acts of another

Debtor   The party who owes money

Decision   The determination of a case or matter by a judicial body

Deductible   The unrecoverable portion of insurance proceeds

Defamation   An oral or written statement communicated to a third party which impugns a person's reputation in the community

Default judgment   An award rendered after one party fails to appear in a lawsuit

Defendant   The person or entity who is sued in a lawsuit

Defense   The defendant's justification for relieving himself or herself of fault

Dependency exemption   A tax deduction

Deposition   A pretrial proceeding where one party is questioned, usually under oath, by the opposing party's lawyer

Discovery   A general term used to describe several pretrial devices (e.g., depositions and interrogatories) that enable lawyers to elicit information from the opposing side

Divorce   An action whereby a legal marriage relationship is terminated

Domicile   The place where a person lives and to which, whenever absent, he or she has the intention of returning

Due process   Constitutional protections which guarantee that a person's life, liberty, and property cannot be taken away without the opportunity to be heard in a judicial proceeding

Duress   Unlawful threats, pressure, or force that induce a person to act contrary to his or her intentions; if proved, allows a party to disavow a contract

Eligibility requirement   Criterion that must be met in order to receive approval for some act (as in adoption)

Emancipation   The status whereby a child is no longer legally eligible to receive financial support from a parent

Equitable distribution   Laws governing the distribution of property and assets upon divorce

Equity   Fairness; usually applied when a judicial body awards a suitable remedy other than money to a party (e.g., an injunction)

Escrow account   A separate fund where lawyers are obligated to deposit money received from or on behalf of a client

Evidence   Information in the form of oral testimony, exhibits, affidavits, etc., used to prove a party's claim

Examination before trial   A pretrial legal device; also called a "deposition"

Exhibit   Tangible evidence used to prove a party's claim

Express contract   An agreement whose terms are manifested by clear and definite language, as distinguished from those agreements inferred from conduct

False imprisonment   The unlawful detention of a person who is held against his or her will without authority or justification

Family court   Generally any court that presides over matters pertaining to the family

Filing fee   Money paid to start a lawsuit

Final decree   A court order or directive of a permanent nature

Financial statement   A document, usually prepared by an accountant, which reflects a business's (or individual's) assets, liabilities, and financial condition

Flat fee   A sum of money paid to a lawyer as compensation for services

Flat fee plus time   A form of payment where a lawyer receives one sum for services and then receives additional money calculated on an hourly basis

Fraud   A false statement that is relied upon and causes damages to the defrauded party

General denial   A reply contained in the defendant's answer

Ground   The basis for an action or an argument

Guaranty   A contract where one party agrees to answer for or satisfy the debt of another

Guardian   A person given the legal power to take care of another

Guardian ad litem   A court-appointed lawyer whose typical responsibility is to protect the legal interests of a child

Head of household   A tax-designated status

Hearsay evidence   Unsubstantiated evidence that is often excluded by a court

Home study   An investigation, usually conducted by social workers and/or adoption agencies, of an individual's home

Hourly fee   Money paid to a lawyer for services, computed on an hourly basis

Implied contract   An agreement that is tacit rather than expressed in clear and definite language; an agreement inferred from the conduct of the parties

Infliction of emotional distress   A legal cause of action where one party seeks to recover damages for mental pain and suffering caused by another

Injunction   A court order restraining one party from doing or refusing to do an act

Innocent-spouse rule   The IRS rule that states that the spouse (typically the wife) who innocently signs an erroneous joint tax return is not personally responsible for the underlying payment of tax due

Instrument of Surrender   Typically the document signed by the natural parent authorizing his or her child to be placed for adoption

Interrogatories   A pretrial device used to elicit information; written questions are sent to an opponent to be answered under oath

Intestate   Having made no valid will

Invasion of privacy   The violation of a person's constitutionally protected right to privacy

Joint custody   An arrangement where both divorced parents must mutually agree on all major decisions affecting their child

Joint property   Property or assets owned equally by husband and wife or other persons

Joint venture   An association of two or more persons to carry out a business enterprise for profit, for which they combine their property, efforts, money, skill, and knowledge

Judgment   A verdict rendered by a judicial body; if money is awarded, the winning party is the "judgment creditor" and the losing party is the "judgment debtor"

Jurisdiction   The authority of a court to hear a particular matter

Lease   An agreement typically regarding the renting of property from one person to another

Legal duty The responsibility of a party to perform a certain act

Letter agreement An enforceable contract in the form of a letter

Letter of protest A letter sent to document a party's dissatisfaction

Liable Legally in the wrong or legally responsible for

Lien A claim asserted against another party's property to satisfy a judgment

Liquidated damages An amount of money agreed upon in advance by parties to a contract to be paid in the event of a breach or dispute

Maintenance The payment of support from one spouse to another in satisfaction of marital obligations; also referred to as "alimony"

Malicious interference with contract rights A legal cause of action where one party seeks to recover damages against an individual who has induced or caused another party to terminate a valid contract

Malpractice The failure of a professional to render work, labor, services, or skill of suitable competence

Marital assets Property or assets produced or developed during the marriage that both spouses may claim upon divorce

Marriage tax penalty Current inequity in the tax law whereby two working spouses pay a combined tax greater than they would if they were not married

Matrimonial Having to do with marriage

Mediation A voluntary dispute-resolution process where both sides attempt to settle their differences without resorting to formal litigation

Misappropriation The unlawful taking of another party's personal property

Misrepresentation A legal cause of action which arises when one party makes untrue statements of fact that induce another party to act and be damaged as a result

Mixed adoption An adoption whereby the adoptive parents are of a different race, religion, or culture than the adoptee

Motion A written request made to a court by one party during a lawsuit

Natural parents The mother and father who physically produced the child

Nominal damages A small sum of money awarded by a court

Noncustodial parent   The parent with whom the child does not reside

Notary public   A person authorized under state law to administer an oath or verify a signature

Notice to show cause   A written document in a lawsuit asking a court to rule on a matter

Objection   A formal protest made by a lawyer in a lawsuit

Offer   The presentment of terms, which, if accepted, may lead to the formation of a contract

Open adoption   An arrangement whereby the adoptee is allowed to continue contact with certain relatives

Opinion letter   A written analysis of a client's case, prepared by a lawyer

Oral contract   An enforceable verbal agreement

"Pain and suffering"   A form of compensable injury

Palimony   The payment of money by one lover to another

Parol evidence   Oral evidence introduced at a trial to alter or explain the terms of a written agreement

Partnership   A voluntary association between two or more competent persons engaged in a business as coowners for profit

Party   A plaintiff or defendant in a lawsuit

Perjury   Commiting false testimony while under oath

Petition   A request filed in court by one party

Plaintiff   The party who commences a lawsuit

Pleading   A written document that states the facts or arguments put forth by a party in a lawsuit

Power of attorney   A document executed by one party authorizing another to act on his or her behalf in specified situations

Premenstrual stress   A defense used by some lawyers when their female clients have committed violent or illegal acts

Prenuptial agreement   A contract signed between two individuals before marriage that limits one of the spouse's rights to property, support, and inheritance in the event of a divorce; also referred to as an "antenuptial agreement"

Pretrial discovery   A legal procedure used to gather information from an opponent before the trial

Process server   An individual who delivers the summons and/or complaint to the defendant

Proof Evidence presented at a trial and used by a judge or jury to fashion an award

Protective order A court directive forbidding one party to visit, harass, or communicate with another

Punitive damages Money awarded as punishment for a party's wrongful acts

Quantum meruit A legal principle whereby a court awards reasonable compensation to a party who performs work, labor, or services at another party's request; also referred to as "unjust enrichment"

Rebuttal The opportunity for a lawyer at a trial to ask a client or witness additional questions to clarify points elicited by the opposing lawyer during cross-examination

Release A written document which, when signed, relinquishes a party's rights to enforce a claim against another

Remedy The means by which a right is enforced or protected

Replevin A type of lawsuit where one party attempts to recover personal property unlawfully held by another

Reply A written document in a lawsuit conveying the plaintiff's answer to the defendant's counterclaim

Residence The place where a person physically lives; also called a "domicile"

Restraining order A court directive forbidding one party to do something

Retainer A sum of money paid to a lawyer for services to be rendered

Revocation of consent The act or process whereby the natural parent (usually the mother) decides to modify her earlier consent to her child's adoption

Separate property Assets or property typically produced prior to or after the marriage and not subject to division upon divorce

Separation agreement A contract typically entered into between divorcing spouses that spells out their rights

Slander Oral defamation of a party's reputation

Small-claims court A particular court that presides over small disputes (e.g., those involving sums of less than $1,500)

Sole custody The condition whereunder the child of divorcing parents resides with one parent who has the legal authority to make all decisions regarding that child

Sole proprietorship   An unincorporated business

Statute   A law created by an administrative body

Statute of frauds   A legal principle requiring certain contracts to be in writing to be enforceable

Statute of limitations   A legal principle requiring a party to commence a lawsuit within a certain period of time

Stipulation   An agreement between lawyers

Submission agreement   A signed agreement whereby both parties agree to submit a present dispute to binding arbitration

Subpoena   A written order demanding a party or witness to appear at a legal proceeding; a *subpoena duces tecum* is a written order demanding a party to bring books and records to the legal proceeding

Summation   The last part of the trial wherein both lawyers recap the respective positions of their clients

Summons   A written document served upon the defendant giving notification of a lawsuit

Temporary decree   A court order or directive of a temporary nature, capable of being modified or changed

Tender-years doctrine   The rule or legal presumption that the mother is best suited for custody of a small child, particularly a young daughter

Testimony   Oral evidence presented by a witness under oath

Tort   A civil wrong

Trespass   A legal cause of action that arises when one party comes or remains on the property of another without permission

"Time is of the essence"   A legal expression often included in agreements to specify the requirement of timeliness

Verdict   The decision of a judge or jury

Verification   A written statement signed under oath

Void   Legally without merit

Waiver   A written document that, when signed, relinquishes a party's rights

Witness   A person who testifies at a judicial proceeding

Bibliography

Areen, Judith: *Cases and Materials on Family Law*, Foundation Press, Mineola, N.Y., 1978.

Benet, Mary K.: *The Politics of Adoption*, Free Press, New York, 1976.

Clair, Bernard E., and Anthony R. Daniele: *Love Pact*, Grove Press, New York, 1980.

Coulson, Robert: *Business Arbitration—What You Need to Know*, American Arbitration Association, New York, 1980.

Coulson, Robert: *Fighting Fair: Family Mediation Will Work for You*, Free Press, New York, 1983.

Deuthwaite, Graham: *Unmarried Couples and the Law*, Allen Smith Co., Ind., 1979.

Emerson, Debash R.: *Violence against Wives*, Free Press, New York, 1979.

Englebardt, Leland S.: *Living Together*, Crown, New York, 1981.

Fields, Marjory D., and Elyse Lehman: *Handbook for Beaten Women*, Brooklyn Legal Services Corporation B, Brooklyn, 1981.

Foster, Henry H., Jr., and Doris Jonas Freed: *Law and the Family*, Lawyer's Co-Operative Publishing Co., Rochester, N.Y., 1980.

Fromm, Elaine M.: *Child Support Enforcement in Maryland*, Maryland Commission for Women, Annapolis, 1984.

Gillers, Stephen: *The Rights of Lawyers and Clients*, Avon, New York, 1979.

Green, Samuel, and John V. Long: *Marriage and Family Agreements*, Shepard's/McGraw-Hill, Colorado Springs, Colo., 1985.

Helfer, A., and C. Kempe: *Helping the Battered Child and His Family*, Lippincott, Philadelphia, 1972

Ihara, Toni, and Ralph Weaver: *The Living Together Kit*, Fawcett Columbine, New York, 1980.

Katz, Sanford N.: *Child Snatching*, ABA Press, Chicago, 1981.

Katz, Sanford N., and Monroe L. Inker: *Fathers, Husbands and Lovers*, ABA Press, Chicago, 1979.

Krauskopf, Joan: *Marital and Non-Marital Contracts*, American Bar Association, Chicago, 1983.

Lasser, J. K.: *101 Plans to Pay Less Income Tax*, Simon and Schuster, New York, 1985.

Leavy, Morton L.: *Law of Adoption*, Oceana Publications, Dobbs Ferry, N.Y., 1968.

Lindey, Alexander: *Separation Agreements and Antenuptial Contracts*, Matthew Bender & Co., New York, 1984.

Marks, Burton, and Gerald Goldfarb: *Winning with Your Lawyer*, McGraw-Hill, New York, 1980.

Martin, J. P.: *Violence and the Family*, Wiley, New York, 1978.

Meezan, William, Sanford N. Katz and E. Russo: *Adoptions without Agencies*, Child Welfare League of America, New York, 1978.

Minton, Michael H., and Jean Libman Block: *What Is a Wife Worth?* Morrow, New York, 1983.

Mitchelson, Marvin: *Living Together,* Simon and Schuster, New York, 1980.

Pomroy, Martha: *What Every Woman Needs to Know about the Law*, Doubleday, Garden City, N.Y., 1980.

Rondell, Florence: *New Dimensions in Adoption*, Free Press, New York, 1976.

Ross, Martin J.: *Handbook of Everyday Law*, Fawcett, Greenwich, Ct., 1967.

Russell, Diana E. H.: *Rape in Marriage*, Macmillan, New York, 1982.

Sack, Steven Mitchell: *Don't Get Taken!: A Preventive Legal Guide to Protect Your Home, Family, Money and Job*, McGraw-Hill, New York, 1985.

Sack, Steven Mitchell, and Howard Jay Steinberg: *The Salesperson's Legal Guide*, Prentice-Hall, Englewood Cliffs, N.J., 1981.

Schaefer, Michael W.: *Child Snatching*, McGraw-Hill, New York, 1984.

Sloan, Irving J.: *Living Together: Unmarrieds and the Law*, Oceana Publications, Dobbs Ferry, N.Y., 1980.

Sonenblick, Jerry: *The Legality of Love*, Jove, New York, 1981.

Weitzman, Lonore J.: *The Divorce Revolution*, Free Press, New York, 1985.

Witmar, Helen: *Independent Adoptions*, Russell Sage Foundation, New York, 1963.

Wodarski, J.: *Comprehensive Treatment of Parents Who Abuse Their Children*, Libra Publishers, New York, 1981.

Index

About the Author

Steven Mitchell Sack is a practicing lawyer, author, lecturer, and disseminator of the law in a variety of media. He is a Phi Beta graduate of State University of New York at Stony Brook and Boston College Law School. He is a member of the New York County Lawyer's Association and the American Bar Association and is admitted to practice before the United States Tax Court.

In addition to conducting a private law practice in New York City devoted substantially to domestic relations matters, Mr. Sack serves as general counsel for many business associations, companies, and individuals and as a commercial arbitrator for the American Arbitration Association.

The author of *Don't Get Taken!* and co-author of *The Salesperson's Legal Guide*, Mr. Sack also creates legal training films and newsletters and conducts seminars throughout the United States with the American Management Association. His views on legal matters have been reported in such publications as *The Wall Street Journal* and *The New York Times*, and he has appeared on numerous television and radio programs nationwide.

Mr. Sack lives in Manhattan and enjoys boating in his spare time.